Common Law:
1. Unlawful (under the traditional rule husbands are exempted, not under modern statutes);
2. Sexual intercourse (slightest penetration is sufficient);
3. With a woman (gender specific);
4. Without consent (being incapable of giving consent due to unconsciousness, intoxication, or mental condition is sufficient);
5. By force;
6. Against her will.

EXCUSE DEFENSES

INSANITY DEFENSES

State v. Johnson, 399 A.2d 469 (R.I. 1979).

1. M'Naghten Test: The defendant may be found insane if at the time of the act, she was under a defect of reason, as:
   a. She did not know the nature and quality of the act she was doing; OR
   b. If she did know, then she did not know that what she was doing was wrong.
2. Irresistible Impulse Test: A defendant is insane if, as the result of a mental disease or defect, she "acted with an irresistible and uncontrollable impulse."
3. The "Product" Test: A person is excused if her unlawful act was the product of a mental disease or defect.
4. Model Penal Code Test: A person is not responsible for criminal conduct if at the time of the act as a result of mental disease or defect she lacked the substantial capacity to:
   a. Appreciate the criminality of her actions; OR
   b. Conform her conduct to the requirements of the law
   MPC § 4.01(1).
5. Federal Insanity Test: A person is excused if she proves by clear and convincing evidence that at the time of the crime, as the result of a "severe mental disease or defect," she was unable to appreciate the nature and quality or wrongfulness of her conduct.

Note: Since insanity is an affirmative defense, a majority of states and Congress place the burden of proving insanity on the defendant.

MISTAKE OF LAW

1. Generally, it is not a defense (ignorance of the law is NO excuse). *People v. Marrero*, 507 N.E.2d 1068 (N.Y. 1987).
2. Exemptions: (Authorized-Reliance Doctrine):
   a. Law not published. Reasonably relied on statute that was later invalidated.
   b. Reasonably relied on court decision.
   c. Reasonably relied on official in position to interpret statute (i.e., must be someone like the U.S. Attorney General, NOT one's personal attorney).
   d. Statute specifically requires defendant to know that the activity is illegal. MPC § 2.04.

INFANCY

1. If the accused is younger than the age of seven, she has an absolute defense to all crimes.
2. If older than the age of seven but younger than fourteen, then the accused's age is a rebuttable defense.
3. If older than fourteen, a rebuttable presumption that the accused will be treated as an adult.

Note: Modern statutes may modify the above.

4. Model Penal Code: Being under the age of 16 constitutes a defense. MPC § 4.10(1)(a).

VOLUNTARY INTOXICATION

1. Self-induced intoxication is not a true defense to a crime.
   a. Yet, voluntary intoxication may be used as a defense to specific intent crimes. MPC § 2.08(1).
   b. Voluntary intoxication may NOT be used as a "temporary insanity" defense.

Example: Sarah, the defendant, gets so inebriated that she starts to shoot aimlessly at blurry blobs, not knowing that they are humans. She kills Chenin, an innocent bystander, with a bullet. Voluntary intoxication may be used as a defense against the specific intent crime of first degree murder, but it will not be a defense against lesser degrees of murder that do not require specific intent (i.e., second degree "heat of passion," or common law murder).

2. Intoxication does not of itself constitute mental disease. MPC § 2.08(3).

MISTAKE OF FACT

1. Is only a defense if it negates the mens rea required by the crime.
2. Common Law (majority):
   a. General intent crimes need reasonable mistake of fact.
   b. For specific intent crimes, mistake of fact can be unreasonable (but must be sincere).

Example: Jacquie, the defendant, sees Bill's bicycle that is EXACTLY like hers in every way. Jacquie sincerely believes that this is her own and she pedals off on it. She is NOT guilty of the specific intent crime of larceny because she had a sincere mistake of fact as to its the ownership.

3. Model Penal Code: Under MPC § 2.04(1), ignorance or mistake as to a fact is a defense if it negates the knowledge, recklessness, or negligence required to establish the offense.
4. Mistake of fact cannot be used as a defense in strict liability crimes.

INVOLUNTARY INTOXICATION

Involuntary intoxication occurs when the defendant unknowingly ingests an intoxicant or is coerced through the use of force to ingest alcohol or a narcotic.

1. Involuntary intoxication may be used as a defense equivalent to that of insanity.
2. Thus, involuntary intoxication may be a defense to all crimes. MPC §2.08(4).

DIMINISHED CAPACITY (MINORITY)

1. As a result of a mental defect (which does not reach insanity), the defendant could not form the requisite mens rea to commit the crime.
2. This only applies to specific intent crimes.
3. Modernly, "partial responsibility" is recognized, if at all, in states adopting the MPC "extreme mental or emotional disturbance" manslaughter provision. MPC § 210.3(1).

...e met:

   b. Intent to inflict grievous bodily injury.
   c. Reckless indifference to human life ("depraved or malignant heart").
   d. Intent to commit a felony (felony murder).

2. **Voluntary Manslaughter** ("Heat of Passion")
A killing that would be murder if not for adequate provocation. Provocation is adequate only if:
   a. The provocation would arouse sudden and intense passion in a reasonable person.
   b. There were not enough time for a reasonable person to "cool off" between the provocation and the killing.

Note: Always carefully examine the adequacy of provocation.

Important: "Heat of passion" manslaughter is NOT a defense, it merely reduces the crime from common law murder to voluntary manslaughter.

Example: Eugene, the defendant, walks into his bedroom. He sees his wife in bed with the Marc, the neighbor. Eugene becomes enraged and immediately leaves the room. Eugene plots to kill Marc. Three weeks later he kills Marc. This is NOT voluntary manslaughter. There was too much time for premeditation and deliberation. If Eugene had killed Mark when he caught his wife in bed with him, it might have been voluntary manslaughter.

3. **Involuntary Manslaughter** (Unlawful Act Doctrine):
   a. If a killing occurred through the gross negligence of the defendant, OR
   b. During the commission of an unlawful act (misdemeanor or felony not included in the felony murder rule).
   c. Lack of causation is a defense.

4. **Felony Murder**:
   a. Any death caused in the commission of or in an attempt to commit a felony is murder.
   b. Malice is implied from the intent to commit the underlying felony.
   c. The felony being committed must be inherently dangerous (e.g., burglary, arson, rape, etc.)
   d. The defendant must be guilty of the underlying felony.
   e. The death must have been a foreseeable result of the felony.

Additional Considerations: The death of the victim must occur a "year and a day" from the day on which the felony occurred.

Note: Some jurisdictions classify homicides differently according to statute. Most murders would be classified as second degree murder unless the defendant killed in a manner that was deliberate and premeditated in which case, it would be first degree murder.

Criminal Homicide
continues on page 4 ▶

MODEL PENAL CODE

A person is guilty of criminal homicide if she takes the life of another human being purposely, knowingly, recklessly, or negligently. MPC § 210.1(1).

There are three types of homicide under the MPC:

1. Murder;
2. Manslaughter;
3. Negligent Homicide; and
4. Causing or Assisting Suicide

MURDER

(As with Common Law, the MPC makes no distinction between first degree murder and second degree murder.) MPC § 210.2.

1. **Intent to Kill:** A criminal homicide is murder if the killing is committed purposely or knowingly.
2. **Extreme Recklessness:** A killing will also be an MPC murder if committed "recklessly under circumstances manifesting extreme indifference to the value of human life." MPC § 210.2(1)(b).
3. **Model Penal Code:** The MPC does not have the common law felony murder rule. However, The MPC may use the "extreme recklessness" standard in regard to the murder during the commission of an enumerated felony. The burden of proof, however, rests with the prosecution.

MANSLAUGHTER

MPC § 210.3.

1. **Recklessness:** This is different from the above standard of "extreme recklessness," where there is no extreme indifference to the value of human life.
2. **Awareness:** The defendant must be aware of the risk that she is creating to human life (contrast this to common law involuntary manslaughter where such awareness is not necessary).
3. **Extreme mental or emotional disturbance:** A person may bring up the affirmative defense of "extreme mental or emotional disturbance" in order to lessen the offense from murder to manslaughter. MPC § 210.3(1)(b).

NEGLIGENT HOMICIDE

MPC § 210.4.

A criminally negligent killing is the lesser offense.

CAUSING OR ASSISTING SUICIDE

MPC § 210.5.

Criminal homicide only if the assistor purposely causes said suicide by force, duress, or deception.

CAUSATION

ACTUAL AND PROXIMATE

1. **Actual Causation (Cause-in-Fact):** A person charged with a crime must have been the actual cause of the crime.
2. **Proximate Causation (Legal Cause):** A person who is an actual cause of resulting crime is not responsible for it unless he is also the proximate cause of the harm.

(*Remember:* Proximate causation is always the actual cause of the crime, but actual causation may not be the proximate cause.) See Venn diagram below.

Note: MPC § 2.03 uses "fresh approach" theory that "but for" causation is the sole strictly causal requirement to be imposed, and the remaining issue is the proper scope of liability in view of the actor's culpability.

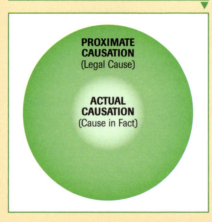

PROXIMATE CAUSATION (Legal Cause)

ACTUAL CAUSATION (Cause in Fact)

DURESS DEFENSES

DURESS: MIDDLE GROUND BETWEEN JUSTIFICATION AND EXCUSE DEFENSES

1. If one reasonably believes that another will imminently harm one or one's family member (with death or serious bodily injury) if one did not commit the crime and there is no reasonable opportunity to escape, duress is a defense. *United States v. Contento-Pachon*, 723 F.2d 691 (9th Cir. 1984).
2. NEVER a defense to homicide under common law.
3. **Model Penal Code:** Duress may be a defense to any crime, even homicide. MPC § 2.09.

ACCOMPLICE LIABILITY

COMMON LAW

Parties to a crime at common law include:

1. **Principal in the First Degree:** Defendant who actually engaged in the criminal act.
2. **Principal in the Second Degree:** Defendant who aided or encouraged the principal and was present at the crime.
3. **Accessory Before the Fact:** Defendant who assisted or encouraged by was NOT present.
4. **Accessory After the Fact:** Defendance who, with knowledge that the other committed the felony, assisted her to escape punishment.

Note: Under common law, the conviction of the principal is required for the conviction of the accessory.

MODERN STATUTES

1. Most modern statutes have abrogated the criminal law distinctions between principals in the first degree and principals in the second degree or even accessories before the fact. All are "parties to the crime" and may be liable for the principle crime. Those who are principals in the second degree or accessories before the fact are labeled as "accomplices."
2. **Accessory After the Fact:** Treated more leniently under modern statutes. Usually liable for the less serious crime.
3. There needs to be criminal intent. *People v. Lauria*, 251 Cal. App. 2d 471 (Cal. App. 1967).

SCOPE OF LIABILITY

An accomplice is responsible for the crime she did or counseled and for any other crimes committed in the course of committing the crime contemplated, to the same extent as the principal, as long at the other crimes were probably or foreseeable.

STRICT LIABILITY CRIMES

1. No mens rea required.
2. Reasonable mistake of fact is NOT a defense. *People v. Cash*, 351 N.W.2d 822 (Mich. 1984).

ACCOMPLICE LIABILITY DEFENSES

DEFENSES

1. **Withdrawal:** A person who effectively withdraws from a crime before it is committed cannot be held guilty as an accomplice. Withdrawal must occur before the crime becomes unstoppable. MPC § 2.06(6)(c).
2. If defendant offers mere encouragement, repudiation is sufficient.
3. If defendant offered more than encouragement, there must be an attempt to neutralize one's assistance in order to effectively withdraw.
   Example: Calling the police.

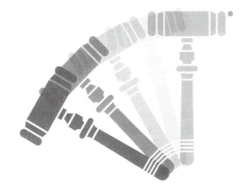

Casenote® Legal Briefs

CRIMINAL LAW

Keyed to Courses Using

Kadish, Schulhofer, Steiker, and Barkow's
Criminal Law and Its Processes
Ninth Edition

Wolters Kluwer
Law & Business

This publication is designed to provide accurate and authoritative information in regard to the subject matter covered. It is sold with the understanding that the publisher is not engaged in rendering legal, accounting, or other professional services. If legal advice or other expert assistance is required, the services of a competent professional person should be sought.

> — From a Declaration of Principles adopted jointly by a Committee of the American Bar Association and a Committee of Publishers and Associates

Printed in the United States of America.

1 2 3 4 5 6 7 8 9 0

ISBN 978-1-4548-1985-1

About Wolters Kluwer Law & Business

Wolters Kluwer Law & Business is a leading global provider of intelligent information and digital solutions for legal and business professionals in key specialty areas, and respected educational resources for professors and law students. Wolters Kluwer Law & Business connects legal and business professionals as well as those in the education market with timely, specialized authoritative content and information-enabled solutions to support success through productivity, accuracy and mobility.

Serving customers worldwide, Wolters Kluwer Law & Business products include those under the Aspen Publishers, CCH, Kluwer Law International, Loislaw, Best Case, ftwilliam.com and MediRegs family of products.

CCH products have been a trusted resource since 1913, and are highly regarded resources for legal, securities, antitrust and trade regulation, government contracting, banking, pension, payroll, employment and labor, and healthcare reimbursement and compliance professionals.

Aspen Publishers products provide essential information to attorneys, business professionals and law students. Written by preeminent authorities, the product line offers analytical and practical information in a range of specialty practice areas from securities law and intellectual property to mergers and acquisitions and pension/benefits. Aspen's trusted legal education resources provide professors and students with high-quality, up-to-date and effective resources for successful instruction and study in all areas of the law.

Kluwer Law International products provide the global business community with reliable international legal information in English. Legal practitioners, corporate counsel and business executives around the world rely on Kluwer Law journals, looseleafs, books, and electronic products for comprehensive information in many areas of international legal practice.

Loislaw is a comprehensive online legal research product providing legal content to law firm practitioners of various specializations. Loislaw provides attorneys with the ability to quickly and efficiently find the necessary legal information they need, when and where they need it, by facilitating access to primary law as well as state-specific law, records, forms and treatises.

Best Case Solutions is the leading bankruptcy software product to the bankruptcy industry. It provides software and workflow tools to flawlessly streamline petition preparation and the electronic filing process, while timely incorporating ever-changing court requirements.

ftwilliam.com offers employee benefits professionals the highest quality plan documents (retirement, welfare and non-qualified) and government forms (5500/PBGC, 1099 and IRS) software at highly competitive prices.

MediRegs products provide integrated health care compliance content and software solutions for professionals in healthcare, higher education and life sciences, including professionals in accounting, law and consulting.

Wolters Kluwer Law & Business, a division of Wolters Kluwer, is headquartered in New York. Wolters Kluwer is a market-leading global information services company focused on professionals.

Format for the Casenote® Legal Brief

Nature of Case: This section identifies the form of action (e.g., breach of contract, negligence, battery), the type of proceeding (e.g., demurrer, appeal from trial court's jury instructions), or the relief sought (e.g., damages, injunction, criminal sanctions).

Fact Summary: This is included to refresh your memory and can be used as a quick reminder of the facts.

Rule of Law: Summarizes the general principle of law that the case illustrates. It may be used for instant recall of the court's holding and for classroom discussion or home review.

Facts: This section contains all relevant facts of the case, including the contentions of the parties and the lower court holdings. It is written in a logical order to give the student a clear understanding of the case. The plaintiff and defendant are identified by their proper names throughout and are always labeled with a (P) or (D).

Palsgraf v. Long Island R.R. Co.

Injured bystander (P) v. Railroad company (D)

N.Y. Ct. App., 248 N.Y. 339, 162 N.E. 99 (1928).

NATURE OF CASE: Appeal from judgment affirming verdict for plaintiff seeking damages for personal injury.

FACT SUMMARY: Helen Palsgraf (P) was injured on R.R.'s (D) train platform when R.R.'s (D) guard helped a passenger aboard a moving train, causing his package to fall on the tracks. The package contained fireworks which exploded, creating a shock that tipped a scale onto Palsgraf (P).

🏛 RULE OF LAW
The risk reasonably to be perceived defines the duty to be obeyed.

FACTS: Helen Palsgraf (P) purchased a ticket to Rockaway Beach from R.R. (D) and was waiting on the train platform. As she waited, two men ran to catch a train that was pulling out from the platform. The first man jumped aboard, but the second man, who appeared as if he might fall, was helped aboard by the guard on the train who had kept the door open so they could jump aboard. A guard on the platform also helped by pushing him onto the train. The man was carrying a package wrapped in newspaper. In the process, the man dropped his package, which fell on the tracks. The package contained fireworks and exploded. The shock of the explosion was apparently of great enough strength to tip over some scales at the other end of the platform, which fell on Palsgraf (P) and injured her. A jury awarded her damages, and R.R. (D) appealed.

ISSUE: Does the risk reasonably to be perceived define the duty to be obeyed?

HOLDING AND DECISION: (Cardozo, C.J.) Yes. The risk reasonably to be perceived defines the duty to be obeyed. If there is no foreseeable hazard to the injured party as the result of a seemingly innocent act, the act does not become a tort because it happened to be a wrong as to another. If the wrong was not willful, the plaintiff must show that the act as to her had such great and apparent possibilities of danger as to entitle her to protection. Negligence in the abstract is not enough upon which to base liability. Negligence is a relative concept, evolving out of the common law doctrine of trespass on the case. To establish liability, the defendant must owe a legal duty of reasonable care to the injured party. A cause of action in tort will lie where harm,

though unintended, could have been averted or avoided by observance of such a duty. The scope of the duty is limited by the range of danger that a reasonable person could foresee. In this case, there was nothing to suggest from the appearance of the parcel or otherwise that the parcel contained fireworks. The guard could not reasonably have had any warning of a threat to Palsgraf (P), and R.R. (D) therefore cannot be held liable. Judgment is reversed in favor of R.R. (D).

DISSENT: (Andrews, J.) The concept that there is no negligence unless R.R. (D) owes a legal duty to take care as to Palsgraf (P) herself is too narrow. Everyone owes to the world at large the duty of refraining from those acts that may unreasonably threaten the safety of others. If the guard's action was negligent as to those nearby, it was also negligent as to those outside what might be termed the "danger zone." For Palsgraf (P) to recover, R.R.'s (D) negligence must have been the proximate cause of her injury, a question of fact for the jury.

▶ ANALYSIS

The majority defined the limit of the defendant's liability in terms of the danger that a reasonable person in defendant's situation would have perceived. The dissent argued that the limitation should not be placed on liability, but rather on damages. Judge Andrews suggested that only injuries that would not have happened but for R.R.'s (D) negligence should be compensable. Both the majority and dissent recognized the policy-driven need to limit liability for negligent acts, seeking, in the words of Judge Andrews, to define a framework "that will be practical and in keeping with the general understanding of mankind." The Restatement (Second) of Torts has accepted Judge Cardozo's view.

Quicknotes

FORESEEABILITY A reasonable expectation that change is the probable result of certain acts or omissions.

NEGLIGENCE Conduct falling below the standard of care that a reasonable person would demonstrate under similar conditions.

PROXIMATE CAUSE The natural sequence of events without which an injury would not have been sustained.

Party ID: Quick identification of the relationship between the parties.

Concurrence/Dissent: All concurrences and dissents are briefed whenever they are included by the casebook editor.

Analysis: This last paragraph gives you a broad understanding of where the case "fits in" with other cases in the section of the book and with the entire course. It is a hornbook-style discussion indicating whether the case is a majority or minority opinion and comparing the principal case with other cases in the casebook. It may also provide analysis from restatements, uniform codes, and law review articles. The analysis will prove to be invaluable to classroom discussion.

Issue: The issue is a concise question that brings out the essence of the opinion as it relates to the section of the casebook in which the case appears. Both substantive and procedural issues are included if relevant to the decision.

Holding and Decision: This section offers a clear and in-depth discussion of the rule of the case and the court's rationale. It is written in easy-to-understand language and answers the issue presented by applying the law to the facts of the case. When relevant, it includes a thorough discussion of the exceptions to the case as listed by the court, any major cites to the other cases on point, and the names of the judges who wrote the decisions.

Quicknotes: Conveniently defines legal terms found in the case and summarizes the nature of any statutes, codes, or rules referred to in the text.

Note to Students

Wolters Kluwer Law & Business is proud to offer *Casenote® Legal Briefs*—continuing thirty years of publishing America's best-selling legal briefs.

Casenote® Legal Briefs are designed to help you save time when briefing assigned cases. Organized under convenient headings, they show you how to abstract the basic facts and holdings from the text of the actual opinions handed down by the courts. Used as part of a rigorous study regimen, they can help you spend more time analyzing and critiquing points of law than on copying bits and pieces of judicial opinions into your notebook or outline.

Casenote® Legal Briefs should never be used as a substitute for assigned casebook readings. They work best when read as a follow-up to reviewing the underlying opinions themselves. Students who try to avoid reading and digesting the judicial opinions in their casebooks or online sources will end up shortchanging themselves in the long run. The ability to absorb, critique, and restate the dynamic and complex elements of case law decisions is crucial to your success in law school and beyond. It cannot be developed vicariously.

Casenote® Legal Briefs represents but one of the many offerings in Legal Education's Study Aid Timeline, which includes:

- *Casenote® Legal Briefs*
- *Emanuel® Law Outlines*
- Emanuel® *Law in a Flash* Flash Cards
- Emanuel® *CrunchTime®* Series
- *Siegel's Essay and Multiple-Choice Questions and Answers Series*

Each of these series is designed to provide you with easy-to-understand explanations of complex points of law. Each volume offers guidance on the principles of legal analysis and, consulted regularly, will hone your ability to spot relevant issues. We have titles that will help you prepare for class, prepare for your exams, and enhance your general comprehension of the law along the way.

To find out more about Wolters Kluwer Law & Business' study aid publications, visit us online at *www.wolterskluwerlb.com* or email us at *legaledu@wolterskluwer.com*. We'll be happy to assist you.

How to Brief a Case

A. Decide on a Format and Stick to It

Structure is essential to a good brief. It enables you to arrange systematically the related parts that are scattered throughout most cases, thus making manageable and understandable what might otherwise seem to be an endless and unfathomable sea of information. There are, of course, an unlimited number of formats that can be utilized. However, it is best to find one that suits your needs and stick to it. Consistency breeds both efficiency and the security that when called upon you will know where to look in your brief for the information you are asked to give.

Any format, as long as it presents the essential elements of a case in an organized fashion, can be used. Experience, however, has led *Casenote® Legal Briefs* to develop and utilize the following format because of its logical flow and universal applicability.

NATURE OF CASE: This is a brief statement of the legal character and procedural status of the case (e.g., "Appeal of a burglary conviction").

There are many different alternatives open to a litigant dissatisfied with a court ruling. The key to determining which one has been used is to discover *who is asking this court for what.*

This first entry in the brief should be kept as *short as possible.* Use the court's terminology if you understand it. But since jurisdictions vary as to the titles of pleadings, the best entry is the one that addresses who wants what in this proceeding, not the one that sounds most like the court's language.

RULE OF LAW: A statement of the general principle of law that the case illustrates (e.g., "An acceptance that varies any term of the offer is considered a rejection and counteroffer").

Determining the rule of law of a case is a procedure similar to determining the issue of the case. Avoid being fooled by red herrings; there may be a few rules of law mentioned in the case excerpt, but usually only one is *the* rule with which the casebook editor is concerned. The techniques used to locate the issue, described below, may also be utilized to find the rule of law. Generally, your best guide is simply the chapter heading. It is a clue to the point the casebook editor seeks to make and should be kept in mind when reading every case in the respective section.

FACTS: A synopsis of only the essential facts of the case, i.e., those bearing upon or leading up to the issue.

The facts entry should be a short statement of the events and transactions that led one party to initiate legal proceedings against another in the first place. While some cases conveniently state the salient facts at the beginning of the decision, in other instances they will have to be culled from hiding places throughout the text, even from concurring and dissenting opinions. Some of the "facts" will often be in dispute and should be so noted. Conflicting evidence may be briefly pointed up. "Hard" facts must be included. Both must be *relevant* in order to be listed in the facts entry. It is impossible to tell what is relevant until the entire case is read, as the ultimate determination of the rights and liabilities of the parties may turn on something buried deep in the opinion.

Generally, the facts entry should not be longer than three to five *short* sentences.

It is often helpful to identify the role played by a party in a given context. For example, in a construction contract case the identification of a party as the "contractor" or "builder" alleviates the need to tell that that party was the one who was supposed to have built the house.

It is always helpful, and a good general practice, to identify the "plaintiff" and the "defendant." This may seem elementary and uncomplicated, but, especially in view of the creative editing practiced by some casebook editors, it is sometimes a difficult or even impossible task. Bear in mind that the *party presently* seeking something from this court may not be the plaintiff, and that sometimes only the cross-claim of a defendant is treated in the excerpt. Confusing or misaligning the parties can ruin your analysis and understanding of the case.

ISSUE: A statement of the general legal question answered by or illustrated in the case. For clarity, the issue is best put in the form of a question capable of a "yes" or "no" answer. In reality, the issue is simply the Rule of Law put in the form of a question (e.g., "May an offer be accepted by performance?").

The major problem presented in discerning what is *the* issue in the case is that an opinion usually purports to raise and answer several questions. However, except for rare cases, only one such question is really the issue in the case. Collateral issues not necessary to the resolution of the matter in controversy are handled by the court by language known as *"obiter dictum"* or merely *"dictum."* While dicta may be included later in the brief, they have no place under the issue heading.

To find the issue, ask *who wants what* and then go on to ask *why did that party succeed or fail in getting it.* Once this is determined, the "why" should be turned into a question.

The complexity of the issues in the cases will vary, but in all cases a single-sentence question should sum up the issue. *In a few cases,* there will be two, or even more rarely, three issues of equal importance to the resolution of the case. Each should be expressed in a single-sentence question.

Since many issues are resolved by a court in coming to a final disposition of a case, the casebook editor will reproduce the portion of the opinion containing the issue or issues most relevant to the area of law under scrutiny. A noted law professor gave this advice: "Close the book; look at the title on the cover." Chances are, if it is Property, you need not concern yourself with whether, for example, the federal government's treatment of the plaintiff's land really raises a federal question sufficient to support jurisdiction on this ground in federal court.

The same rule applies to chapter headings designating sub-areas within the subjects. They tip you off as to what the text is designed to teach. The cases are arranged in a casebook to show a progression or development of the law, so that the preceding cases may also help.

It is also most important to remember to *read the notes and questions* at the end of a case to determine what the editors wanted you to have gleaned from it.

HOLDING AND DECISION: This section should succinctly explain the rationale of the court in arriving at its decision. In capsulizing the "reasoning" of the court, it should always include an application of the general rule or rules of law to the specific facts of the case. Hidden justifications come to light in this entry: the reasons for the state of the law, the public policies, the biases and prejudices, those considerations that influence the justices' thinking and, ultimately, the outcome of the case. At the end, there should be a short indication of the disposition or procedural resolution of the case (e.g., "Decision of the trial court for Mr. Smith (P) reversed").

The foregoing format is designed to help you "digest" the reams of case material with which you will be faced in your law school career. Once mastered by practice, it will place at your fingertips the information the authors of your casebooks have sought to impart to you in case-by-case illustration and analysis.

B. Be as Economical as Possible in Briefing Cases

Once armed with a format that encourages succinctness, it is as important to be economical with regard to the time spent on the actual reading of the case as it is to be economical in the writing of the brief itself. This does not mean "skimming" a case. Rather, it means reading the case with an "eye" trained to recognize into which "section" of your brief a particular passage or line fits and having a system for quickly and precisely marking the case so that the passages fitting any one particular part of the brief can be easily identified and brought together in a concise and accurate manner when the brief is actually written.

It is of no use to simply repeat everything in the opinion of the court; record only enough information to trigger your recollection of what the court said. Nevertheless, an accurate statement of the "law of the case," i.e., the legal principle applied to the facts, is absolutely essential to class preparation and to learning the law under the case method.

To that end, it is important to develop a "shorthand" that you can use to make marginal notations. These notations will tell you at a glance in which section of the brief you will be placing that particular passage or portion of the opinion.

Some students prefer to underline all the salient portions of the opinion (with a pencil or colored underliner marker), making marginal notations as they go along. Others prefer the color-coded method of underlining, utilizing different colors of markers to underline the salient portions of the case, each separate color being used to represent a different section of the brief. For example, blue underlining could be used for passages relating to the rule of law, yellow for those relating to the issue, and green for those relating to the holding and decision, etc. While it has its advocates, the color-coded method can be confusing and time-consuming (all that time spent on changing colored markers). Furthermore, it can interfere with the continuity and concentration many students deem essential to the reading of a case for maximum comprehension. In the end, however, it is a matter of personal preference and style. Just remember, whatever method you use, underlining must be used sparingly or its value is lost.

If you take the marginal notation route, an efficient and easy method is to go along underlining the key portions of the case and placing in the margin alongside them the following "markers" to indicate where a particular passage or line "belongs" in the brief you will write:

N   (NATURE OF CASE)
RL   (RULE OF LAW)
I   (ISSUE)
HL   (HOLDING AND DECISION, relates to the RULE OF LAW behind the decision)
HR   (HOLDING AND DECISION, gives the RATIONALE or reasoning behind the decision)
HA   (HOLDING AND DECISION, APPLIES the general principle(s) of law to the facts of the case to arrive at the decision)

Remember that a particular passage may well contain information necessary to more than one part of your brief, in which case you simply note that in the margin. If you are using the color-coded underlining method instead of marginal notation, simply make asterisks or checks in the margin next to the passage in question in the colors that indicate the additional sections of the brief where it might be utilized.

The economy of utilizing "shorthand" in marking cases for briefing can be maintained in the actual brief writing process itself by utilizing "law student shorthand" within the brief. There are many commonly used words and phrases for which abbreviations can be substituted in your briefs (and in your class notes also). You can develop abbreviations that are personal to you and which will save you a lot of time. A reference list of briefing abbreviations can be found on page xii of this book.

C. Use Both the Briefing Process and the Brief as a Learning Tool

Now that you have a format and the tools for briefing cases efficiently, the most important thing is to make the time spent in briefing profitable to you and to make the most advantageous use of the briefs you create. Of course, the briefs are invaluable for classroom reference when you are called upon to explain or analyze a particular case. However, they are also useful in reviewing for exams. A quick glance at the fact summary should bring the case to mind, and a rereading of the rule of law should enable you to go over the underlying legal concept in your mind, how it was applied in that particular case, and how it might apply in other factual settings.

As to the value to be derived from engaging in the briefing process itself, there is an immediate benefit that arises from being forced to sift through the essential facts and reasoning from the court's opinion and to succinctly express them in your own words in your brief. The process ensures that you understand the case and the point that it illustrates, and that means you will be ready to absorb further analysis and information brought forth in class. It also ensures you will have something to say when called upon in class. The briefing process helps develop a mental agility for getting to the *gist* of a case and for identifying, expounding on, and applying the legal concepts and issues found there. The briefing process is the mental process on which you must rely in taking law school examinations; it is also the mental process upon which a lawyer relies in serving his clients and in making his living.

Abbreviations for Briefs

acceptance	acp	offer	O
affirmed	aff	offeree	OE
answer	ans	offeror	OR
assumption of risk	a/r	ordinance	ord
attorney	atty	pain and suffering	p/s
beyond a reasonable doubt	b/r/d	parol evidence	p/e
bona fide purchaser	BFP	plaintiff	P
breach of contract	br/k	prima facie	p/f
cause of action	c/a	probable cause	p/c
common law	c/l	proximate cause	px/c
Constitution	Con	real property	r/p
constitutional	con	reasonable doubt	r/d
contract	K	reasonable man	r/m
contributory negligence	c/n	rebuttable presumption	rb/p
cross	x	remanded	rem
cross-complaint	x/c	res ipsa loquitur	RIL
cross-examination	x/ex	respondeat superior	r/s
cruel and unusual punishment	c/u/p	Restatement	RS
defendant	D	reversed	rev
dismissed	dis	Rule Against Perpetuities	RAP
double jeopardy	d/j	search and seizure	s/s
due process	d/p	search warrant	s/w
equal protection	e/p	self-defense	s/d
equity	eq	specific performance	s/p
evidence	ev	statute	S
exclude	exc	statute of frauds	S/F
exclusionary rule	exc/r	statute of limitations	S/L
felony	f/n	summary judgment	s/j
freedom of speech	f/s	tenancy at will	t/w
good faith	g/f	tenancy in common	t/c
habeas corpus	h/c	tenant	t
hearsay	hr	third party	TP
husband	H	third party beneficiary	TPB
injunction	inj	transferred intent	TI
in loco parentis	ILP	unconscionable	uncon
inter vivos	I/v	unconstitutional	unconst
joint tenancy	j/t	undue influence	u/e
judgment	judgt	Uniform Commercial Code	UCC
jurisdiction	jur	unilateral	uni
last clear chance	LCC	vendee	VE
long-arm statute	LAS	vendor	VR
majority view	maj	versus	v
meeting of minds	MOM	void for vagueness	VFV
minority view	min	weight of authority	w/a
Miranda rule	Mir/r	weight of the evidence	w/e
Miranda warnings	Mir/w	wife	W
negligence	neg	with	w/
notice	ntc	within	w/i
nuisance	nus	without	w/o
obligation	ob	without prejudice	w/o/p
obscene	obs	wrongful death	wr/d

Table of Cases

CHAPTER 1

Institutions and Processes

Quick Reference Rules of Law

People v. Zackowitz

State (P) v. Criminal defendant (D)

N.Y. Ct. App., 254 N.Y. 192, 172 N.E. 466 (1930).

NATURE OF CASE: Appeal from first-degree murder conviction.

FACT SUMMARY: Zackowitz (D) claimed that evidence relating to his possession of other weapons at home should not have been admitted at his murder trial because its sole purpose was to give the impression he had a general criminal disposition.

🏛 RULE OF LAW
Unless the defendant has made his general character an issue in a criminal prosecution, evidence thereon is inadmissible (unless admissible for some other purpose).

FACTS: After engaging in a verbal confrontation with Coppola, who made insulting remarks to his wife on a Brooklyn street, Zackowitz (D) returned home. There, his wife informed him that Coppola had specifically offered her two dollars to sleep with him. Zackowitz (D) then returned to the street where Coppola was repairing a car. A fight ensued, and Zackowitz (D) shot and killed Coppola with a .25-calibre pistol. Zackowitz (D) told the police he had obtained the pistol at home, before he went back to confront Coppola. At trial, however, he insisted that he had had the pistol on his person the entire evening. The People (P) were permitted to put into evidence the fact that Zackowitz (D) had a radio box, three pistols, and a teargas gun at his apartment. In appealing his first-degree murder conviction, Zackowitz (D) maintained this evidence was inadmissible because it was designed to show he had a general criminal disposition.

ISSUE: Unless a criminal defendant has put his general character at issue, is evidence thereon admissible at a criminal trial?

HOLDING AND DECISION: (Cardozo, C.J.) No. The character of a criminal defendant is never an issue in criminal prosecution unless the defendant makes it one, which Zackowitz (D) did not do. Nonetheless, the court permitted introduction of evidence designed to show that he was a man of evil life—a man of murderous heart, of criminal disposition, and therefore more likely to commit the crime charged. There could have been no other purpose because these other weapons Zackowitz (D) had at home had no connection with the crime with which he was charged. Thus, the evidence was not admissible. Judgment reversed; new trial ordered.

▶ ANALYSIS

The exclusion of evidence as to the "bad character" of the defendant (including evidence of his other crimes) is relevant but is kept out because, as McCormick puts it, "in the setting of jury trial the danger of prejudice outweighs the probative value." Some courts have recognized that a judge trying a case is less likely to give undue weight to such evidence.

■═■

Quicknotes

CHARACTER EVIDENCE Evidence of someone's moral standing in a community based on reputation.

FIRST DEGREE MURDER The willful killing of another person with deliberation and premeditation; first-degree murder also encompasses those situations in which a person is killed within the perpetration of, or attempt to perpetrate, specified felonies.

RELEVANCE The admissibility of evidence based on whether it has any tendency to prove or disprove a matter at issue to the case.

■═■

In re Winship

State (P) v. Juvenile (D)

397 U.S. 358 (1970).

NATURE OF CASE: Appeal from affirmance of juvenile delinquency charge.

FACT SUMMARY: Winship (D), a 12-year-old boy, was found by a preponderance of the evidence to have committed an act that if committed by an adult would have been a crime, thus supporting his being charged with juvenile delinquency. Winship (D) claimed that such a finding had to be based on proof beyond a reasonable doubt.

RULE OF LAW

Proof beyond a reasonable doubt is among the essentials of due process and fair treatment required during the adjudicatory stage when a juvenile is charged with an act that would constitute a crime if committed by an adult.

FACTS: Relying on a preponderance of the evidence, the standard of proof required by § 744(b) of the New York Family Court Act, a New York Family Court judge found that Winship (D), then a 12-year-old boy, had committed an act (stealing money from a pocketbook in a locker) that "if done by an adult, would constitute the crime or crimes of Larceny." The judge acknowledged that the proof might not establish guilt beyond a reasonable doubt. That finding supported Winship's (D) being charged with juvenile delinquency. The New York Court of Appeals affirmed, sustaining the constitutionality of § 744(b). The United States Supreme Court granted review.

ISSUE: Is proof beyond a reasonable doubt among the essentials of due process and fair treatment required during the adjudicatory stage when a juvenile is charged with an act that would constitute a crime if committed by an adult?

HOLDING AND DECISION: (Brennan, J.) Yes. Proof beyond a reasonable doubt is among the essentials of due process and fair treatment required during the adjudicatory stage when a juvenile is charged with an act that would constitute a crime if committed by an adult. Constitutional questions concerning the juvenile process have centered on the adjudicatory stage at which a determination is made as to whether a juvenile is a "delinquent" as a result of alleged misconduct. Although the Fourteenth Amendment does not require that the hearing at this stage conform to all the requirements of a criminal trial or even of the usual administrative proceeding, the Due Process Clause does require application during the adjudicatory hearing of "the essentials of due process and fair treatment." The requirement that guilt of a criminal charge

be established by proof beyond a reasonable doubt has a long history and has been constitutionally required in most of this Court's opinions. It plays a vital role in the American scheme of criminal procedure and is a prime instrument for reducing the risk of convictions resting on factual error. The issue then is whether juveniles are constitutionally entitled to this degree of proof when they are charged with violation of a criminal law. The same considerations that demand extreme caution in factfinding to protect the innocent adult apply as well to the innocent child. The state's highest court sought to distinguish a delinquency adjudication from a criminal prosecution, but such a distinction is unconvincing. Regardless of whether a juvenile proceeding is labeled as a civil proceeding, and regardless of its purpose, such a proceeding can result in the child's losing his or her liberty for years and is comparable in seriousness to a felony prosecution. Moreover, to afford juveniles the protection of proof beyond a reasonable doubt will not negatively impact the beneficial aspects of the juvenile process, nor will it force the State to abandon the substantive benefits of such proceedings. Accordingly, the constitutional safeguard of proof beyond a reasonable doubt is as much required during the adjudicatory stage of a delinquency proceeding as it is in adult criminal prosecutions. Reversed.

CONCURRENCE: (Harlan, J.) Even though the labels used for alternative standards of proof are vague and not a very sure guide to decision making, the choice of the standard for a particular variety of adjudication does reflect a very fundamental assessment of the comparative social costs of erroneous factual determinations. This is so because in a judicial proceeding in which there is a dispute about the facts of some earlier event, the factfinder cannot acquire unassailably accurate knowledge of what happened. Instead, all the factfinder can acquire is a belief of what probably happened. The different standards of proof communicate to the factfinder how intense such a belief should be. Also, the factfinder will sometimes, despite his best efforts, be wrong in his factual conclusions. The two erroneous outcomes in a criminal case are either that a guilty person is set free or an innocent person is wrongly convicted. The standard of proof influences the relative frequency of these two types of erroneous outcomes. In a criminal case, the social disutility of convicting an innocent person is not viewed by society as equivalent to the disutility of acquitting someone who is guilty. When one assesses the consequences of an erroneous factual determination in a juvenile delinquency proceeding in which a youth is

Continued on next page.

accused of a crime, I think it must be concluded that, while the consequences are not identical to those in a criminal case, the differences will not support a distinction in the standard of proof. First, and of paramount importance, a factual error here, as in a criminal case, exposes the accused to a complete loss of his personal liberty through a state-imposed confinement away from his home, family, and friends. And, second, a delinquency determination, to some extent at least, stigmatizes a youth in that it is by definition bottomed on a finding that the accused committed a crime. As in a criminal case, it is far worse to declare an innocent youth a delinquent than to let a guilty youth go free. Therefore, a judge in a juvenile proceeding should be no less convinced of the factual conclusion that the accused committed the criminal act with which he is charged than would be required in a criminal trial. Imposing such a standard of proof, however, should not interfere with the worthy goals of the juvenile justice system.

▶ *ANALYSIS*

Seemingly in response to Justice Black's dissent, where he says, "The Court has never clearly held, however, that proof beyond a reasonable doubt is either expressly or impliedly commanded by any provision of the Constitution," the majority responded by saying, "Lest there remain any doubt about the constitutional stature of the reasonable-doubt standard, we explicitly hold that the Due Process Clause protects the accused against conviction except upon proof beyond a reasonable doubt of every fact necessary to constitute the crime with which he is charged."

■═■

Quicknotes

DUE PROCESS RIGHTS The constitutional mandate requiring the courts to protect and enforce individuals' rights and liberties consistent with prevailing principles of fairness and justice and prohibiting the federal and state governments from such activities that deprive its citizens of a life, liberty or property interest.

PROOF BEYOND A REASONABLE DOUBT Standard of proof necessary to convict a defendant, requiring the absence of evidence that would cause a reasonable person to hesitate in making an important decision in his personal affairs.

■═■

Patterson v. New York

Convicted murderer (D) v. State (P)

432 U.S. 197 (1977).

NATURE OF CASE: Appeal from a conviction of second-degree murder.

FACT SUMMARY: Patterson (D) alleged as an affirmative defense that he was emotionally disturbed at the time of the killing.

🏛 RULE OF LAW
So long as the state proves every element of the charge beyond a reasonable doubt, the defendant may be required to prove an affirmative defense.

FACTS: Patterson (D), after separating from his wife, killed her new boyfriend. Patterson (D) was charged with second-degree murder. Patterson (D) raised a statutorily authorized affirmative defense that he had been emotionally disturbed at the time. If proved, this would have reduced the offense to manslaughter. The jury convicted Patterson (D) of second-degree murder and he appealed on the grounds that the State (P) had failed to prove, beyond a reasonable doubt, that he was not emotionally disturbed at the time. The State (P) alleged that the burden of proving an affirmative defense was on Patterson (D). Since it had proved every element of its case beyond a reasonable doubt, the burden was on Patterson (D) to show, by a preponderance of the evidence, that mitigating circumstances warranted a lesser charge.

ISSUE: Where an affirmative defense does not include an element of the crime is the defendant required to bear the burden of proof?

HOLDING AND DECISION: (White, J.) Yes. Due process considerations only require the state to prove each element of the charge beyond a reasonable doubt. They do not require the state to prove the nonexistence of all affirmative defenses or mitigating factors. Here, emotional distress is not an element of the charge of second-degree murder. The State (P) proved every element of its case. It was up to Patterson (D) to prove that he was entitled to a lesser charge. Merely because a state makes a defense available does not require it to negate the existence of the defense. Affirmed.

DISSENT: (Powell, J.) The Court is focusing on the wording of a statute that just as easily could have required a showing that no mitigating factors such as emotional distress be present. If this were the case, the burden would fall on the state to negate the existence of the defense. Constitutional protections should not be left to the whim and caprice of chance as to how a statute is drawn. Such a formalistic approach is indefensible.

▶ ANALYSIS

In *Mullaney v. Wilbur*, 421 U.S. 684 (1975), the Court held that Maine's murder law could not shift the burden to the defendant of showing that heat of passion or sudden provocation existed. This was included within the state's definition of mens rea. However, in *Rivera v. Delaware*, 429 U.S. 877 (1976), the Court held that the burden of proof was on the defendant to establish his affirmative defense of insanity. The rationale was substantially the same as herein.

Quicknotes

AFFIRMATIVE DEFENSE A manner of defending oneself against a claim not by denying the truth of the charge but by the introduction of some evidence challenging the plaintiff's right to bring the claim.

DUE PROCESS The constitutional mandate requiring the courts to protect and enforce individuals' rights and liberties consistent with prevailing principals of fairness and justice and prohibiting the federal and state governments from such activities that deprive its citizens of a life, liberty or property interest.

MANSLAUGHTER The killing of another person without premeditation, deliberation or with the intent to kill or to commit a felony, which may be reasonably expected to result in death or serious bodily injury; manslaughter is characterized by reckless conduct or by some adequate provocation on the part of the actor, as determined by a subjective standard.

PREPONDERANCE OF THE EVIDENCE A standard of proof requiring the trier of fact to determine whether the fact sought to be established is more probable than not.

REASONABLE DOUBT Standard of proof necessary to convict a defendant, requiring the absence of evidence that would cause a reasonable person to hesitate in making an important decision in his personal affairs.

SECOND-DEGREE MURDER The unlawful killing of another person, without premeditation, and characterized by either an intent to kill or by a reckless disregard for human life.

Duncan v. Louisiana

Convicted batterer (D) v. State (P)

391 U.S. 145 (1968).

NATURE OF CASE: Appeal from conviction for simple battery.

FACT SUMMARY: Duncan (D), a black youth, was convicted on disputed evidence, without a jury, of simple battery on a white youth.

RULE OF LAW
Because trial by jury in criminal cases is fundamental to the American scheme of justice, the Fourteenth Amendment guarantees a right of jury trial in all criminal cases which, were they to be tried in federal court, could come within the Sixth Amendment's guarantee.

FACTS: Upon disputed evidence, Duncan (D), a black youth, was convicted of simple battery upon a white youth. It was agreed that he at least touched the other boy on the elbow, but unclear whether he slapped him. Duncan's (D) request for a jury trial was denied. Under Louisiana law, a jury trial is guaranteed in cases where capital punishment or imprisonment at hard labor may be imposed. Simple battery is punishable as a misdemeanor with up to two years' imprisonment and a $300 fine. Duncan (D) appealed, claiming denial of a jury trial was a denial of due process in violation of the Sixth and Fourteenth Amendments.

ISSUE: Is the right to a jury trial so fundamental a principle of liberty and justice as to be guaranteed in state courts by the Fourteenth Amendment?

HOLDING AND DECISION: (White, J.) Yes. The test for determining whether rights found in the Fifth and Sixth Amendments should apply to the states by the Fourteenth Amendment is to determine whether that right is basic in our system of jurisprudence; a fundamental right essential to a fair trial. The right to a jury trial is such a right. The right to a jury trial has historically received protection in English and American law. It protects against unfounded criminal charges brought to eliminate enemies, judges too responsive to higher authority, and overzealous prosecutors. This does not mean that an accused cannot choose to waive a jury trial. Also, crimes carrying possible penalties up to six months do not require a jury trial if otherwise a petty offense. The possible penalty for a particular crime is of major importance in determining whether it is serious or not. The possible penalty may, in itself, if so severe, require a jury trial upon request. It was error to deny a jury trial here. Reversed and remanded.

DISSENT: (Harlan, J.) When the criminally accused argues that his state conviction lacked due process of law, the question is actually whether he was denied an element of fundamental procedural fairness. A criminal trial can be fundamentally fair without a jury.

▶ ANALYSIS

Few justices have gone as far as Justices Black and Douglas in arguing that the Fourteenth Amendment was designed to extend the Bill of Rights to the states. Even so, the historical support for that view is strong, particularly in the statements of the senator who introduced the Amendment. The prevailing view, however, is that of selective incorporation. Only those rights found in the Bill of Rights deemed to be "fundamental," "basic," or "essential" have been held to apply to the states. Over the years, the vast majority of rights found in the first eight amendments have been extended by the court to the states. Yet it is strange to think that for the good part of a century after adoption of the Fourteenth Amendment and 150 years after adoption of the Bill of Rights, rights guaranteed for trials in federal court were not usually guaranteed in the same type of case in state courts, unless the constitution of the state in question also guaranteed those rights.

■■■

Quicknotes

BATTERY Unlawful contact with the body of another person.

DUE PROCESS The constitutional mandate requiring the courts to protect and enforce individuals' rights and liberties consistent with prevailing principals of fairness and justice and prohibiting the federal and state governments from such activities that deprive its citizens of a life, liberty or property interest.

MISDEMEANOR Any offense that does not constitute a felony, which is generally less severe and for which a lesser punishment is imposed.

RIGHT TO JURY TRIAL The right guaranteed by the Sixth Amendment to the federal constitution that in all criminal prosecutions the accused has a right to a trial by an impartial jury of the state and district in which the crime was allegedly committed.

SELECTIVE INCORPORATION Doctrine providing that the Bill of Rights is incorporated by the Due Process Clause only to the extent that the Supreme Court decides that the privileges and immunities therein are so essential to fundamental principles of due process to be preserved against both state and federal action.

■■■

United States v. Dougherty

Federal government (P) v. Criminal defendant (D)

473 F.2d 1113 (D.C. Cir. 1972).

NATURE OF CASE: Appeals from conviction for unlawful entry and malicious destruction of property.

FACT SUMMARY: Dougherty (D) contends that the trial judge erred in refusing to instruct the jury of its right to acquit without regard to the law and the evidence.

🏛 RULE OF LAW
While the jury's prerogative to disregard the court's instructions even as to matters of law does exist and is approved of, the jury should not be formally informed of that power by the judge.

FACTS: Dougherty (D) and eight others broke into Dow Chemical Company offices and destroyed property as part of an attack on Dow's role in supporting U.S. military action in Vietnam. The trial judge refused to instruct the jury of its right to acquit Dougherty (D) without regard to the law and the evidence.

ISSUE: Should the jury be instructed of its power to nullify the law in a particular case?

HOLDING AND DECISION: (Leventhal, J.) No. An undoubted jury prerogative to disregard the law has evolved. It is derived from the jury's power to bring in a verdict of not guilty in a criminal case that is not reversible by the court. However, the fact that this power exists and is approved of as a necessary counter to hardened judges and arbitrary prosecutors does not mean that the jury must be informed by the judge of its power. The prerogative is reserved for the exceptional case and the judge's instruction acts as a generally effective constraint. To hold otherwise would unnecessarily burden the jury system, since the jury, that must be unanimous, would not merely have to come to a united determination of the facts, but also of the law. It would also burden the individual jurors.

CONCURRENCE AND DISSENT: (Bazelon, C.J.) Nullification serves the important function of permitting the jury to bring to bear on the criminal process a sense of fairness and particularized justice. Pretending the jury does not have this power may allow it to avoid its responsibility. Further, the use of the nullification power provides important feedback on the standards of the criminal laws. For example, the reluctance of juries to hold defendants responsible for unmistakable violation of the prohibition laws told us much about the morality of those laws.

▶ ANALYSIS

The ability of the jury system to render a fair verdict for militant, radical, and minority defendants has been strongly questioned. Some of the criticism has been dissipated by the refusal of juries to convict in cases such as Huey Newton's, Bobby Seale's, and Angela Davis's. William Kunstler, defense attorney for many militants, commented, "For many, the inability of prosecutors in recent trials of radicals to convince any—or even most—of their respective panels that the defendants were guilty has been regarded as a stunning vindication of our legal system. For others, including myself, these results only indicate that just verdicts are, under certain conditions, attainable."

Quicknotes

ACQUITTAL The discharge of an accused individual from suspicion of guilt for a particular crime and from further prosecution for that offense.

CHAPTER 2

The Justification of Punishment

Quick Reference Rules of Law

Regina v. Dudley and Stephens

Government (P) v. Crew members (D)

Queen's Bench Division, 14 Q.B.D. 273 (1884).

NATURE OF CASE: Appeal of jury's special verdict finding Dudley (D) and Stephens (D) guilty of murder.

FACT SUMMARY: Dudley (D) and Stephens (D) killed Parker, with whom they were stranded on the high seas in a lifeboat, in order to survive off Parker's remains after having run out of food and water.

🏛 RULE OF LAW
Homicide may not be excused when the person killed is an innocent and unoffending victim.

FACTS: Dudley (D), Stephens (D), Brooks, and Parker, crew members of an English yacht, were cast adrift on the high seas 1,600 miles from land in an open lifeboat. They had no water and two one-pound tins of turnips. After 12 days adrift, they were without food. Dudley (D) and Stephens (D) suggested to Brooks that one of the four may be sacrificed so that the others might survive. Brooks dissented, and Parker, a 17-year-old boy, was never consulted. On the twentieth day, Dudley (D) and Stephens (D) killed Parker, who was too weak either to resist or assent. Four days after Parker's death, the surviving three were rescued. They would not have survived had they not fed off Parker's remains.

ISSUE: Was the homicide excusable by the necessity of saving some of the crewmen?

HOLDING AND DECISION: (Lord Coleridge, C.J.) No. An innocent person may not be killed in order to save the life of another. Where the victim has not assaulted or otherwise endangered the killer, the killer has not, by necessity, been placed in a position which permits him to kill the innocent victim. The extreme necessity of hunger does not justify larceny, nor can it justify murder. While, generally, the preservation of one's own life is a duty; in some cases, the highest duty may be to sacrifice it. Neither can the temptation caused by hunger be called an excuse. Affirmed.

▶ ANALYSIS

While this case actually discusses a defense to murder, necessity (which here did not excuse the murder), the case appears here in the casebook more for its moral discussion of why the defendants, unwillingly placed in a tragic situation, must be punished for their act. The court notes that "Law and morality are not the same, and many things may be immoral which are not necessarily illegal," but that law would be divorced from morality if the temptation to kill, which arose, could be an excuse for the actual killing. Even if the temptation were a valid excuse, who is to determine who must die so that the others might live? Note that the death sentence was later commuted by the crown to six months' imprisonment.

■━■

Quicknotes

EXCUSE A reason that releases a person or party from the performance of a legal duty.

HOMICIDE The killing of another individual.

LARCENY The illegal taking of another's property with the intent to deprive the owner thereof.

NECESSITY DEFENSE A defense to liability for unlawful activity where the conduct is unavoidable and is justified by preventing the occurrence of a more serious harm.

■━■

United States v. Bernard L. Madoff

Federal government (P) v. Individual (D)

United States District Court, S.D.N.Y. (June 29, 2009).

NATURE OF CASE: Federal district court's consideration of proper sentence for criminal defendant.

FACT SUMMARY: Madoff (D) plead guilty to 11 counts of fraud, money laundering, perjury and theft relating to his orchestration of a Ponzi scheme allegedly resulting in the loss of $65 billion dollars of client funds.

RULE OF LAW
When choosing a proper criminal sentence, symbolism plays an important role in both the retribution and deterrence contexts.

FACTS: Madoff (D) plead guilty to 11 counts of fraud, money laundering, perjury and theft relating to his orchestration of a Ponzi scheme allegedly resulting in the loss of $65 billion dollars of client funds. At the sentencing hearing, Madoff (D), 71 years old, argued for a maximum sentence of 12 years, based upon his life expectancy of thirteen years and the fact that he turned himself in to the FBI. The Government (P) sought the maximum sentence: 150 years under the federal sentencing guidelines.

ISSUE: When choosing a proper criminal sentence, does symbolism play an important role in both the retribution and deterrence contexts?

HOLDING AND DECISION: (Chin, J.) Yes. When choosing a proper criminal sentence, symbolism plays an important role in both the retribution and deterrence contexts. Regarding retribution, the court must send the message that Madoff's (D) irresponsible and intentional actions have real consequences to families, institutions, charities and pension funds. Accordingly, symbolism is important because society will see that Madoff (D) is getting the type of punishment he deserves based upon his admitted culpability. Regarding deterrence, symbolism is important because the strongest message must be sent that those who would engage in this type of conduct will be caught, prosecuted, and punished to the fullest extent of the law. Lastly, symbolism is important in the context of giving the victims of Madoff's (P) Ponzi scheme some level of comfort that the person responsible for their predicament has been punished. Based upon such factors, the court sentences Madoff (D) to a term of imprisonment of 150 years.

▶ ANALYSIS

Many courts will not often expressly refer to the concept of symbolism in their sentencing decisions, but clearly symbolism plays a central role when courts sentence defendants in larger and more high profile cases.

■■■

Quicknotes

RETRIBUTION One of the purposes of punishment, it refers to punishment in return for the crime committed.

■■■

United States v. Jackson

Federal government (P) v. Convicted armed robber (D)

835 F.2d 1195 (7th Cir. 1987).

NATURE OF CASE: Appeal from life sentence without possibility of parole for weapons possession.

FACT SUMMARY: Under a statute forbidding possession of weapons by career criminals, Jackson (D) was sentenced to life in prison without possibility of parole.

🏛 RULE OF LAW
The imposition of life in prison is permissible under a statute that forbids parole.

FACTS: Jackson (D), who had been convicted of four armed bank robberies and one armed robbery, robbed another bank 30 minutes after being released from prison on a work release program. Under a statute forbidding possession of weapons by career criminals, he was sentenced to life in prison without possibility of parole. Jackson (D) argued that the statute did not authorize a life sentence but only allowed the imposition of a determinate number of years.

ISSUE: Is an imposition of life in prison permissible under a statute that forbids parole?

HOLDING AND DECISION: (Easterbrook, J.) Yes. The imposition of life in prison is permissible under a statute that forbids parole. When parole is forbidden, a judge may impose a long term of imprisonment or, alternatively, a life sentence in order to reach the same result. It would be silly to read the statute as authorizing one but not the other. Jackson's (D) convictions mark him as a career criminal, and the statute reflects a judgment that career criminals who persist in possessing weapons should be dealt with most severely. Affirmed.

CONCURRENCE: (Posner, J.) The sentence Jackson (D) received is too harsh, but he presents no ground on which to set aside an excessively severe sentence. The fact that he has never inflicted a physical injury should be relevant in deciding whether his conduct warrants imprisonment for the rest of his life as a matter of retributive justice. People who would rob banks in the face of a more appropriate 20-year sentence would probably not be deterred by a life sentence either. A civilized society would lock them up until age made them harmless but not keep them in prison until they die.

▶ ANALYSIS

In a subsequent proceeding, the sentencing judge stated that Judge Posner's concerns did not persuade him to reduce Jackson's (D) sentence. He cited, as aggravating circumstances, Jackson's (D) lack of remorse and prior record, which revealed accusations of attempted murder and assault dating from his stint in Vietnam. See *United States v. Jackson*, 780 F. Supp. 1508 (N.D. Ill. 1991). The judge also cited the distinct possibility that an "incorrigible and hostile recidivist" like Jackson (D) would be likely to inflict severe injury or death if permitted to go free.

■■■

Quicknotes

PAROLE The release of a prisoner from jail for the remainder of his sentence if he complies with certain conditions.

■■■

United States v. Gementera

Federal government (P) v. Repeat offender (D)

379 F.3d 596 (9th Cir. 2004).

NATURE OF CASE: Appeal from a sentencing order requiring the defendant to stand with a sandwich board in front of a postal facility.

FACT SUMMARY: A young man whose criminal history was getting progressively more serious stole letters from mailboxes in San Francisco.

RULE OF LAW
Shaming conditions in a sentence can be reasonably related to the legitimate purpose of rehabilitation under the Sentencing Reform Act.

FACTS: Shawn Gementera (D) pled guilty to mail theft. He was 24 at the time of the offense, but his criminal history was already relatively long and contained increasingly serious crimes. At sentencing, the trial judge expressed concern that Gementera (D) did not appreciate the gravity of his offense or understand that his mail theft had truly harmed his victims' lives. The judge sentenced Gementera (D) to the minimum possible time served under the federal Sentencing Guidelines (two months), but the sentence also included a condition that required Gementera (D) to stand for eight hours in front of a local postal facility with a sandwich board that stated, "I stole mail; this is my punishment." Gementera appealed that condition of his sentence.

ISSUE: Can shaming conditions in a sentence be reasonably related to the legitimate purpose of rehabilitation under the Sentencing Reform Act?

HOLDING AND DECISION: (O'Scannlain, J.) Yes. Shaming conditions in a sentence can be reasonably related to the legitimate purpose of rehabilitation under the Sentencing Reform Act (SRA). The SRA grants a trial court the broad discretionary authority to impose sentences that contain "any . . . condition it considers to be appropriate." The only limitations on that authority are that such discretionary conditions must be reasonably related to one of the legitimate purposes identified by the SRA: deterrence, protecting the public, and rehabilitation. Here, although the judge expressly sought to humiliate Gementera (D) with the sandwich-board "shaming" condition, the judge also unambiguously intended any resulting humiliation to serve all three legitimate statutory purposes. Moreover, the shaming condition here was also reasonably related to the legitimate purpose of rehabilitation. The trial court voiced concern that Gementera's (D) rehabilitation depended on his acceptance of the important consequences of his crime; the shaming condition clearly promotes that purpose. Although the trial court did not base its shaming condition on scientific evidence, such evidence was not necessary. The sentencing condition at issue here was valid because it not only subjected Gementera (D) to social disapproval but also then gave him a way to reenter society by speaking to students at a school in the community. The shaming condition, then, was reasonably related to a legitimate purpose under the statute. Affirmed.

DISSENT: (Hawkins, J.) The shaming condition violates the SRA, but it should be reversed simply because it is also bad policy. Our society trusts that public institutions will not do all that they have the power to do. The shaming condition here violates that trust.

⏵ ANALYSIS

The *Gementera* court candidly addresses the broadly discretionary aspect of the shaming condition ordered by the trial judge. As the Ninth Circuit did here, appellate courts generally review sentencing orders with a great degree of deference to the trial judge's decision. In a case like *Gementera*, with the trial judge imposing the shaming condition under the SRA's catch-all discretionary provision, an appellate court will most likely affirm the sentence if the trial judge articulates a rationale that joins statutory standards with specific facts in the case.

■■■■

The Elements of a Just Punishment

Quick Reference Rules of Law

CHAPTER 3

Commonwealth v. Mochan
State (P) v. Morals convict (D)

Pa. Super. Ct., 177 Pa. Super. 454, 110 A.2d 788 (1955).

NATURE OF CASE: Appeal from a conviction for the common-law crime of intending to debauch, corrupt, and vilify another person.

FACT SUMMARY: Mochan (D) argued that since his acts did not constitute a statutory crime, he could not legally be indicted and convicted for those acts simply because they constituted a crime at common law.

RULE OF LAW
A person may be prosecuted for committing a common-law crime even if such crime has not specifically been enacted into legislation.

FACTS: Mochan (D) made a series of highly obscene phone calls to Louise Zivkovich, a stranger, for which he was indicted, tried, and found guilty. The crime for which he was indicted was for intending to debauch, corrupt, embarrass and vilify the person called. The conduct alleged in the indictments was not prohibited by statute. The prosecutor, however, successfully contended that the conduct did constitute a common-law crime and was punishable under the common law of Pennsylvania. Mochan (D) appealed the conviction, arguing that he could not legally be indicted for acts which did not constitute a statutory crime.

ISSUE: May a person be prosecuted for committing a common-law crime even if such crime has not specifically been enacted into legislation?

HOLDING AND DECISION: (Hirt, J.) Yes. A person may be prosecuted for committing a common-law crime even if such crime has not specifically been enacted into legislation. Although the conduct alleged in the indictments was not prohibited by statute, the state's Penal Code provides that every offense punishable by the statutes "or common law of this Commonwealth" and not specifically provided for by statute, shall continue to be an offense punishable as heretofore. Here, the testimony establishes that Mochan (D) on numerous occasions telephoned Louise Zivkovich, a stranger to him, and used language which was obscene, lewd, and filthy. He not only suggested intercourse with her but talked of sodomy as well, in loathsome language. The test is not whether precedents for prosecution of such conduct can be found in the books, but whether the alleged crimes could have been prosecuted and the offenders punished under the state's common law. The answer is that the common law is sufficiently broad to punish as a misdemeanor, although there may be no exact precedent or statute, any act which directly injures or tends to injure the public to such an extent as to require the state to interfere and punish the wrongdoer, as in the case of acts which injuriously affect public morality, or obstruct, or pervert public justice, or the administration of government. In sum, whatever openly outrages decency and is injurious to public morals is a misdemeanor at common law. Affirmed.

DISSENT: (Woodside, J.) Under the division of powers in our constitution it is for the legislature to determine what injures or tends to injure the public. One of the most important functions of a legislature is to determine what acts require the state to interfere and punish the wrongdoer. Notwithstanding the reprehensible conduct of Mochan (D), until the legislature says that what Mochan (D) did is a crime, the courts should not declare it to be such.

ANALYSIS

Nearly all jurisdictions have statutorily abolished common-law offenses, including now Pennsylvania. Some states, however, such as Rhode Island, still do authorize the prosecution of common-law offenses.

Quicknotes

COMMON-LAW CRIME An activity that has been defined as a crime not by legislative enactment but by the courts through case law.

McBoyle v. United States

Airplane transporter (D) v. Federal government (P)

283 U.S. 25 (1931).

NATURE OF CASE: Appeal from a conviction for transporting a stolen airplane from Illinois to Oklahoma.

FACT SUMMARY: The defendant knowingly transported a stolen airplane from Illinois to Oklahoma, and he was convicted of violating the National Motor Vehicle Theft Act.

🏛 RULE OF LAW
An airplane is not a "vehicle" within the meaning of the National Motor Vehicle Theft Act.

FACTS: McBoyle (D) transported an airplane from Illinois to Oklahoma, and he knew at the time that the airplane was stolen. The National Motor Vehicle Theft Act, which prohibited the interstate transportation of stolen motor vehicles, defined "motor vehicle" as "an automobile, automobile truck, automobile wagon, motor cycle, or any other self-propelled vehicle not designed for running on rails. . . ." McBoyle (D) was charged with and convicted of violating the Act, and he appealed.

ISSUE: Is an airplane a "vehicle" within the meaning of the National Motor Vehicle Theft Act?

HOLDING AND DECISION: (Holmes, J.) No. An airplane is not a "vehicle" within the meaning of the National Motor Vehicle Theft Act. It is possible to read "self-propelled vehicle not designed for running on rails" to include any conveyance that works on land, water, or air. In common usage, however, "vehicle" connotes a machine that runs on land. In this case, the terms in the statutory definition that precede "vehicle" confirm that reading by denoting conveyances that run only on land. Accordingly, the statute did not fairly warn McBoyle (D) that his conduct would violate the National Motor Vehicle Theft Act. Reversed.

▶ ANALYSIS

Justice Holmes's primer in statutory construction shows that a government needs to have a clear law in place before it can convict a person of violating the law. As Justice Holmes concedes, the notice requirement often amounts to little more than a legal fiction: criminals seldom consult current statutes before they violate the law. At the same time, the notice requirement promotes the salutary purpose of forcing governments to govern through clear enactments that the executive branch then can enforce.

■▬■

United States v. Dauray

Federal government (P) v. Possessor of child pornography (D)

215 F.3d 257 (2nd Cir. 2000).

NATURE OF CASE: Appeal from a conviction for possession of child pornography.

FACT SUMMARY: A man was arrested in a state park for possession of individual, unbound depictions of minors engaging in sexually explicit conduct.

RULE OF LAW
Individual pictures are not "other matter which contain any visual depiction" within the meaning of the federal Protection of Children Against Sexual Exploitation Act.

FACTS: Charles Dauray (D) was arrested for possessing thirteen individual, unbound pictures of minors engaging in sexually explicit conduct. None of the pictures was in a bound volume; all were either separate pieces of magazine pages or photocopies of such pages. Dauray (D) was charged with possession of child pornography in violation of the federal statute prohibiting the possession of "three or more books, magazines, periodicals, films, video tapes [sic], or other matter" if such materials had passed through interstate commerce and "contain any visual depiction" of minors engaging in sexually explicit conduct. Dauray (D) moved to dismiss, arguing that each item he possessed was a "visual depiction," which disqualified each item, he argued, from being "other matter" that "contain[s] any visual depiction." The trial court refused to apply the rule of lenity in reading the statute and denied Dauray's (D) motion. A jury convicted Dauray (D), and he appealed.

ISSUE: Are individual pictures "other matter which contain any visual depiction" within the meaning of the federal Protection of Children Against Sexual Exploitation Act?

HOLDING AND DECISION: (Jacobs, J.) No. Individual pictures are not "other matter which contain any visual depiction" within the meaning of the federal Protection of Children Against Sexual Exploitation Act. Plain meaning is the first step in interpreting statutes, but that step yields no clear answers in this case. Congress did not define "other matter" or "contain," the dictionary definitions of the terms reasonably support both parties' readings of the statute, and no prior case in the country has answered the precise question presented by this case. Courts next use canons of construction to interpret statutes. One canon requires that terms be read to fit the characteristics of other items specifically enumerated in a statute; in this case, "other matter" thus should be interpreted as completing the class of items including "books, magazines, periodicals, films, [or] video tapes [sic]." That

conclusion, though, also can reasonably support both parties' interpretations of the statute. Further, neither the structure of the statutory scheme surrounding the statute nor the amendments to the statute lead to a clear reading; both parties' interpretations are reasonable, but both also lead to absurd results. As a last resort, courts consult legislative history, but here that history also sheds no light on the meaning of "other matter" or "contain." The court therefore can only conclude that the statute violates Dauray's (D) due-process right to be prosecuted under a statute that gave him fair warning of the proscribed conduct. The rule of lenity requires that the ambiguities in this statute must be resolved in Dauray's (D) favor. Reversed.

DISSENT: (Katzmann, J.) The rule of lenity requires "a grievous ambiguity or uncertainty in the statute." That standard is not present here.

ANALYSIS

The majority on this panel of the Second Circuit resolved this difficult case by resorting to the rule of lenity. When a court can only guess at the legislature's meaning in a criminal statute, the statute cannot be enforced consistent with due process.

■=■

Quicknotes

DUE PROCESS RIGHTS The constitutional mandate requiring the courts to protect and enforce individuals' rights and liberties consistent with prevailing principles of fairness and justice, and prohibiting the federal and state governments from such activities that deprive its citizens of a life, liberty or property interest.

RULE OF LENITY The doctrine that where a statute is ambiguous as to the term of punishment imposed, it will be construed in favor of the less severe punishment.

STATUTORY CONSTRUCTION The examination and interpretation of statutes.

■=■

Keeler v. Superior Court

Ex-husband (D) v. State (P)

Cal. Sup. Ct., 2 Cal. 3d 619, 470 P.2d 617 (1970).

NATURE OF CASE: Petition for a writ of prohibition in murder prosecution.

FACT SUMMARY: Keeler (D) was charged with murder after causing the death of an unborn viable fetus by kicking the mother in her abdomen.

> **RULE OF LAW**
> Causing the death of a viable fetus is not a homicide.

FACTS: Keeler (D), upon learning that his ex-wife was pregnant with another man's child, kicked her in the abdomen. The fetus was delivered stillborn via a caesarian section. Medical evidence proved that Keeler's (D) assault had killed the fetus. He was charged with murder. He moved to dismiss, contending that a fetus was not a "human being" within the meaning of the statute defining murder. The motion was denied. A petition for writ of prohibition was granted by the California Supreme Court.

ISSUE: Is causing the death of a viable fetus a homicide?

HOLDING AND DECISION: (Mosk, J.) No. Causing the death of a viable fetus is not a homicide. California's murder statute, Penal Code § 187, defines murder as "the unlawful killing of a human being, with malice aforethought." This law, adopted in 1872, has never been modified. The original codification of California law was meant to be based on common-law principles. Under common law existing since at least 1797, an unborn child was not considered a person for purposes of supporting a murder charge. Under rules of statutory construction, it is to be assumed that the legislature was aware of the common-law meanings of the terms it incorporated into the law it enacted. This being so, § 187's term "human being" does not include a viable fetus. Writ granted.

DISSENT: (Burke, J.) Penal statutes do not have to be strictly construed. Common-law changes with public mores. The holding here defies reason, logic, and common sense.

▶ ANALYSIS

The present decision was very unpopular. Within months, the California legislature amended § 187 to include "fetus" within the statute. The law now reads as follows: "(a) Murder is the unlawful killing of a human being, or a fetus, with malice aforethought. (b) This section shall not apply [if] (1) The act complied with Therapeutic Abortion Act. (2) . . . T]he result of childbirth would be death to the mother. . . . (3) The act was . . . consented to by the mother." Note that the amendment to § 187 does not mention viability of the fetus as a criterion.

Quicknotes

VIABLE FETUS The point at which a child is capable of living outside of its mother's womb.

City of Chicago v. Morales

Municipality (P) v. Accused gang member (D)

527 U.S. 41 (1999).

NATURE OF CASE: Appeal from the dismissal of a prosecution for loitering under a city ordinance.

FACT SUMMARY: Morales (D) challenged an anti-gang ordinance passed by the City of Chicago (P) on the basis that the wording of the statute defining "loitering" was so vague as to make the statute unconstitutional.

RULE OF LAW
A statute providing penalties for criminal conduct is unconstitutionally vague if it fails to give sufficient notice regarding the type of conduct prohibited and grants the police absolute discretion in deciding when to enforce the statute.

FACTS: Morales (D) and others were accused as "criminal street gang members" under a new ordinance passed by the City of Chicago (P) prohibiting persons from "loitering" with one another in public places. A City of Chicago (P) commission solicited witness testimony and made a series of findings suggesting that an increase in street activity was a primary cause of the escalation in violent and drug-related crimes, and that a common function of loitering was to enable a street gang to establish control over particular areas. In addition, the commission discovered that loitering by street gang members in public places intimidated law-abiding citizens and thus limited access to these areas where loitering took place. In response, the City of Chicago (P) passed the Gang Congregation Ordinance, which created a criminal offense punishable by a fine of up to $500, as well as imprisonment and community service, for "loitering" by suspected street gang members in public places. The statute defined four elements of the crime of "loitering:" first, a police officer must reasonably believe that at least one of the two or more persons present in a public place is a gang member; second, these persons must be "loitering" by remaining in one place with no apparent purpose; third, the officer must order these persons to disperse; and finally, the order to disperse is disobeyed by the suspected gang members. Morales (D) challenged the ordinance as unconstitutionally vague. The state supreme court agreed because the ordinance failed to provide notice of the proscribed conduct and did not provide specific limits on the discretion of police officers to determine what conduct constituted "loitering." The City of Chicago (P) filed for review of that determination.

ISSUE: Is a statute that provides penalties for criminal conduct unconstitutionally vague if it fails to give sufficient notice regarding the type of conduct prohibited and grants the police absolute discretion in deciding when to enforce the statute?

HOLDING AND DECISION: (Stevens, J.) Yes. A statute providing penalties for criminal conduct is unconstitutionally vague if it fails to give sufficient notice regarding the type of conduct prohibited and grants the police absolute discretion in deciding when to enforce the statute. Clearly, a law directly prohibiting intimidating conduct similar to that described by the City of Chicago (P) commission is constitutional on its face. However, such a law may still be found unconstitutionally vague for two reasons: first, the law fails to provide the type of notice that permits ordinary persons to understand the conduct prohibited; and second, the wording of the law encourages arbitrary and discriminatory enforcement. Citizens should not have to speculate as to the meaning of a criminal law. The requirement of notice is not met here because the order to disperse takes place before an officer knows whether the prohibited conduct has occurred, and the ordinance therefore unjustifiably impairs liberty if the loiterer is harmless and innocent. In addition, the statute establishes only minimal guidelines for law enforcement to follow. Police officers may exercise absolute discretion when assessing a group of bystanders for dispersal. The City of Chicago (P) asserts that the statute provides limitations on a police officer's discretion because it does not permit a dispersal order to issue if a person has an apparent purpose or until the officer reasonably believes that "loitering" is taking place. However, these limitations are insufficient because they do not directly address the degree of discretion an officer may exercise. The ability to assess a "loitering" situation is only subjectively limited by the officer's own evaluation of the circumstances. The Illinois Supreme Court's ruling that the statute in question is unconstitutional was correctly concluded and is therefore affirmed.

CONCURRENCE: (O'Connor, J.) Chicago's (P) gang ordinance is unconstitutionally vague because it lacks sufficient minimal standards to guide law enforcement officers. There remain open to Chicago (P) reasonable alternatives to combat the very real threat posed by gang intimidation and violence. For example, the Court properly and expressly distinguishes the ordinance from laws that require loiterers to have a "harmful purpose," from laws that target only gang members, and from laws that incorporate limits on the area and manner in which the law may be enforced.

Continued on next page.

DISSENT: (Thomas, J.) The ordinance is constitutional because it merely enables police officers to discharge their traditional responsibilities as preservers of the public peace. Those responsibilities necessarily require discretion that in turn requires guidelines, but not guidelines so precise that they restrict the officer's every move. That discretion requires the public's trust, the same trust that informs the enforcement of other imprecise legal standards. Any improper uses of that discretion can be left to case-by-case determinations. In this facial challenge, Respondents also have failed to meet their heavy burden of showing that no standard at all for "loitering" notifies the public of what conduct is being prohibited. The Court has exalted the "rights" of gang members over the so-called "freedom of movement" of the law-abiding majority of Chicago's (P) citizens.

ANALYSIS

Justice Stevens's opinion suggests that the Gang Congregation Ordinance could have been worded optimally to include conduct that was apparent, such as the effort by gang members to publicize the gang's dominance over a certain area. Use of this phrasing explicitly would have satisfied constitutional concerns of specificity. However, the Court noted further that the absence of this descriptive language not only expanded the statute's inclusion of harmless behavior but also excluded those exact circumstances where the statute would have played a critical role in addressing the intended problem.

Quicknotes

FOURTEENTH AMENDMENT Declares that no state shall make or enforce any law which shall abridge the privileges and immunities of citizens of the United States.

VAGUENESS AND OVERBREADTH Characteristics of a statute that make it difficult to identify the limits of the conduct being regulated.

Ewing v. California

Theft convict (D) v. State (P)

538 U.S. 11 (2003).

NATURE OF CASE: Appeal from sentencing under California's "Three Strikes" law.

FACT SUMMARY: When Gary Ewing (D), after shoplifting three golf clubs, was sentenced to a prison term of 25 years to life under California's (P) "Three Strikes" law, he argued that the sentence was so grossly disproportionate to the crime that it violated the Eighth Amendment's ban against cruel and unusual punishments.

🏛 RULE OF LAW
The Eighth Amendment does not prohibit a state from sentencing a repeat felon to a prison term of 25 years to life under the state's "Three Strikes" law.

FACTS: On parole from a nine-year prison term, Gary Ewing (D) shoplifted three golf clubs. He was charged and convicted of one count of felony grand theft in excess of $400. As required by California's (P) "Three Strikes" law, the prosecutor formally alleged, and the trial court later found, that Ewing (D) had been convicted previously of four serious or violent felonies and a robbery in an apartment complex. Ewing (D) was sentenced under California's (P) "Three Strikes" law to 25 years to life. Ewing (D) appealed his sentence to the United States Supreme Court, arguing that the Eighth Amendment's ban on cruel and unusual punishments prohibits sentences which are grossly disproportionate to the crime committed.

ISSUE: Does the Eighth Amendment prohibit a state from sentencing a repeat felon to a prison term of 25 years to life under the state's "Three Strikes" law?

HOLDING AND DECISION: (O'Connor, J.) No. The Eighth Amendment does not prohibit a state from sentencing a repeat felon to a prison term of 25 years to life under the state's (P) "Three Strikes" law. As to Ewing's (D) argument that his three strikes sentence of 25 years to life is unconstitutionally disproportionate to his offense of shoplifting three golf clubs, this Court notes that the gravity of his offense was not merely shoplifting the three clubs, but rather it was being convicted of felony grand theft for stealing nearly $1,200 worth of merchandise after previously having been convicted of at least two violent or serious felonies. In weighing the gravity of the offense, this Court must place on the scales not only his current felony, but also his long history of felony recidivism. Any other approach would fail to accord proper deference to the state legislature's choice of sanctions. In imposing a three strikes sentence, the state's (P) interest is not merely punishing the

offense of conviction, or the triggering offense. It is, in addition, the interest in dealing in a harsher manner with those who by repeated criminal acts have shown that they are simply incapable of conforming to the norms of society as established by its criminal law. Here, Ewing's (D) sentence is justified by the state's (P) public-safety interest in incapacitating and deterring recidivist felons, and amply supported by his own long, serious criminal record. Affirmed.

CONCURRENCE: (Scalia, J.) It is difficult to speak intelligently of proportionality once deterrence and rehabilitation are given significant weight. The plurality is not applying constitutional law but evaluating policy.

CONCURRENCE: (Thomas, J.) The cruel and unusual punishment clause of the Eighth Amendment contains no proportionality principle.

DISSENT: (Breyer, J.) In the instant case, the punishment is grossly disproportionate to the crime. Ewing's (D) sentence on its face imposes one of the most severe punishments available upon a recidivist who subsequently engaged in one of the less serious forms of criminal conduct. In any ordinary case, such as one under the Federal Sentencing Guidelines, Ewing's (D) sentence would not exceed 18 months in prison. Ewing's (D) 25-year term amounts to overkill.

▶ ANALYSIS

In *Ewing*, the Supreme Court noted that four years after passage of California's three strikes law, the recidivism rate of parolees returned to prison for the commission of a new crime dropped by nearly 25 percent. While the three strikes law has sparked controversy and some critics have doubted the law's wisdom and effectiveness in reaching its goals, the Supreme Court explained that such criticism is appropriately directed at the legislature, which has the primary responsibility for making the difficult policy choices that underlie any criminal sentencing scheme and that the Court does not sit as a "super legislature" to second-guess these policy choices.

■■■

Quicknotes

CRUEL AND UNUSUAL PUNISHMENT Punishment that is excessive or disproportionate to the offense committed

Continued on next page.

and which is prohibited by the Eighth Amendment to the U.S. Constitution.

EIGHTH AMENDMENT The Eighth Amendment to the federal constitution prohibits the imposition of excessive bail, fines, and cruel and unusual punishment.

■━■

Graham v. Florida

Individual (D) v. State (P)

130 S. Ct. 2011 (2010).

NATURE OF CASE: United States Supreme Court's review of criminal defendant's petition for habeas corpus.

FACT SUMMARY: While on probation for attempted robbery, Graham (D), 17 years old, was arrested for a home invasion and attempted robbery. After being found guilty, the state court sentenced him to life imprisonment without the possibility of parole.

🏛 RULE OF LAW
A sentence of life without parole imposed upon a juvenile for a nonhomicide offense is unconstitutional.

FACTS: While on parole for attempted robbery, Graham (D), age 17, was arrested for a home invasion robbery with two accomplices. The two accomplices held two other men at gunpoint while they all ransacked the house looking for money. Graham (D) was eventually arrested after dropping off one of the accomplices at the hospital with a gunshot wound. The state of Florida (P) charged Graham (D) with, among other counts, home invasion robbery. He received the maximum sentence of life imprisonment. Florida (P) had previously abolished its parole system, so Graham's (D) sentence constituted a life sentence without the possibility of parole. Graham (D) filed a petition for habeas corpus for review of his sentence in federal court and his case eventually came before the United States Supreme Court.

ISSUE: Is a sentence of life without parole imposed upon a juvenile for a nonhomicide offense unconstitutional?

HOLDING AND DECISION: (Kennedy, J.) Yes. A sentence of life without parole imposed upon a juvenile for a nonhomicide offense is unconstitutional. When adopting a new categorical rule for an entire class of criminal defendants, the Court first considers the objective indicia of society's standards, expressed in legislative enactments and state practice, to determine whether there is a national consensus against the current sentencing practice. The Court then makes its own determination based upon its precedents and its understanding of the Eighth Amendment's text, history and meaning. Here, life without the possibility of parole for juveniles in nonhomicide cases is a disproportionate sentence and accordingly, unconstitutional. Life sentences without parole are similar to death sentences. There is a forfeiture that is irrevocable. Moreover, none of the usual justifications for strong sentences apply for juveniles. Retribution and deterrence do not apply because juveniles are less likely to take potential punishments into account. Incapacitation, the removal of an individual from society, also does not justify the life sentence because juveniles have the potential of becoming functioning individuals in society as they get older. In addition, a categorical rule banning all such sentences is necessary because of the difficulties of the case by case approach. That approach would likely not be able to distinguish those incorrigible juveniles from those who have the capacity to change. In addition, juveniles often do not work well with the attorneys because of their natural mistrust of adults. This may prohibit a complete and sound legal defense. Accordingly, a categorical ban on life sentences without the possibility of paroles for juveniles committing nonhomicide offences is hereby unconstitutional.

CONCURRENCE: (Roberts, C.J.) In this particular case, Graham's (D) sentence violates the Eighth Amendment. However, a blanket rule prohibiting all such sentences in every case is unnecessary. The criminal justice system depends upon sentencing judges to apply their reasoned analysis to each case that comes before them, much in the same manner that they do with adult offenders. Clearly, the lower courts must be mindful that juveniles are generally less culpable than adults that commit similar crimes. However, that does not justify the new categorical rule the Court adopts in this case.

DISSENT: (Thomas, J.) The central issue in this case is which branch of government should have the ability to decide such questions. There is overwhelming evidence that most states seek to retain the option of punishing juveniles with life without the possibility of parole. This Court should defer to such widespread legislative intent.

▶ ANALYSIS

In 2012, the Court, in *Miller v. Alabama*, 132 S. Ct. 1733 (2012), extended the *Graham* holding by banning life sentences without parole for juveniles convicted of murder.

■═■

Quicknotes

EIGHTH AMENDMENT The Eighth Amendment to the federal constitution prohibits the imposition of excessive bail, fines, and cruel and unusual punishment.

PAROLE The release of a prisoner from jail for the remainder of his sentence if he complies with certain conditions.

■═■

Martin v. State

Drunk (D) v. State (P)

Ala. Ct. App., 31 Ala. App. 334, 17 So. 2d 427 (1944).

NATURE OF CASE: Appeal of a conviction for drunkenness on a public highway.

FACT SUMMARY: Martin (D), after being arrested at his home, was taken by officers on to the highway, where he manifested a drunken condition.

🏛 RULE OF LAW
Criminal liability must be based on conduct which includes a voluntary act or omission from committing an act which it was physically possible to have performed.

FACTS: Martin (D), who was convicted of being drunk on a public highway, was arrested at his home by officers who then took him on to the highway, where he allegedly used loud and profane language and otherwise manifested a drunken condition. He was charged with violation of a statute which proscribed such acts in a public place where more than one person is present.

ISSUE: Is criminal liability based on conduct which includes a voluntary act or omission from committing an act which was physically possible to have performed?

HOLDING AND DECISION: (Simpson, J.) Yes. The statute presupposes that the violator voluntarily appears drunk in public. Being involuntarily and forcibly brought into a public place when drunk by an arresting officer, is not a voluntary breach of the law, and is not punishable. Reversed and rendered.

▶ ANALYSIS

This case introduces the concept of actus reus, wrongful conduct. For conduct to be wrongful, it must either be a voluntary act or omission to act. This in itself is not sufficient to establish liability, but is an essential element for liability to arise. The law rests on the supposition that only voluntary acts or omissions are punishable, and while involuntary acts may be threatening, they are not of such nature so as to require correction by the penal system.

■—■

Quicknotes

ACTUS REUS The unlawful act that gives rise to criminal liability, as distinguished from the required mental state.

OMISSION The failure to perform an act or obligation that one is required to perform by law.

VOLUNTARY ACT An act that is undertaken pursuant to an individual's free will and without the influence of another.

■—■

People v. Newton

State (P) v. Convicted murderer (D)

Cal. Ct. App., 8 Cal. App. 3d 359 (1970).

NATURE OF CASE: Appeal from a conviction for voluntary manslaughter.

FACT SUMMARY: Newton (D), involved in an altercation with a police officer following his arrest, was shot and possibly acted unconsciously in shooting the officer while in a state of shock resulting from his (Newton's [D]) gunshot wound.

🏛 RULE OF LAW
Criminal liability must be based on conduct which includes a voluntary act or omission from committing an act which it was physically possible to have performed.

FACTS: Huey P. Newton (D) was charged with murder and convicted of voluntary manslaughter in the death of Officer Frey. Newton (D), after being arrested by Frey, became involved in a struggle with him for the officer's gun. Newton (D) was shot in the midsection but managed to grab the gun and fire several point-blank shots into Frey, who was killed. Newton (D) testified that he basically remembered nothing that occurred after he was shot, except for some events at an emergency hospital where he sought treatment, until recovering full consciousness at a second hospital. Expert medical testimony established that a profound reflex shock reaction would very likely result from a gunshot wound to a body cavity and could last up to a half hour.

ISSUE: Was it error to fail to instruct the jury on the matter of unconsciousness as a defense to the charge of criminal homicide?

HOLDING AND DECISION: (Rattigan, J.) Yes. Where not self-induced, unconsciousness is a complete defense to a charge of criminal homicide. Unconsciousness need not be a state commonly associated with the term, i.e., coma, but can apply where the subject can act physically but is not, in fact, aware of this act at the time of acting. An instruction to that effect can arise upon an inference of unconsciousness arising out of only the actor's own testimony that he did not recall the events. As the failure to so instruct the jury did not result from invited error, i.e., a deliberate tactical purpose by Newton's (D) counsel not to have an instruction regarding unconsciousness, judgment must be reversed.

▌ANALYSIS

Actus reus, wrongful conduct, does not include an involuntary act. An act can be involuntary when either one is forced to do something against his will or is not consciously aware of his act. Thus, an act which is a reflex, spasm, or convulsion, or even sleepwalking, would not be conscious, and hence, not voluntary. But an involuntary act does not include such acts where the doer simply cannot remember it or because he could not control his impulse to do it.

■━■

Quicknotes

ACTUS REUS The unlawful act that gives rise to criminal liability, as distinguished from the required mental state.

OMISSION The failure to perform an act or obligation that one is required to perform by law.

VOLUNTARY ACT An act that is undertaken pursuant to an individual's free will and without the influence of another.

VOLUNTARY MANSLAUGHTER The killing of another person without premeditation, deliberation or malice aforethought, but committed while in the "heat of passion" or upon some adequate provocation, thereby reducing the charge from murder to manslaughter.

■━■

Jones v. United States

Convicted murderer (D) v. Federal government (P)

308 F.2d 307 (D.C. Cir. 1962).

NATURE OF CASE: Appeal from conviction for involuntary manslaughter.

FACT SUMMARY: Jones was found guilty of the involuntary manslaughter of Green, a 10-month-old baby belonging to Shirley Green, who placed her baby in Jones's (D) care.

🏛 RULE OF LAW
Under some circumstances, the omission of a legal duty owed by one individual to another, where such omission results in the death of the one to whom the duty is owed, will make the other chargeable with manslaughter.

FACTS: Anthony Green, the 10-month-old illegitimate child of Shirley Green, was placed in the care of Jones (D), a family friend. The baby died of neglect and malnutrition. Jones (D) was convicted of involuntary manslaughter. There was a conflict in the evidence over whether Jones (D) was paid to take care of the baby. Medical evidence clearly showed the baby to have been shockingly neglected. Jones (D) had ample means to provide food and medical care. Jones (D) took exception to the trial court's failure to instruct the jury that it must find beyond a reasonable doubt that, as an element of the case, she was under a legal duty to provide for the baby.

ISSUE: Will omission of a legal duty owed by one individual to another, where such omission results in the death of the one to whom the duty is owed, make the other chargeable with manslaughter?

HOLDING AND DECISION: (Wright, J.) Yes. The omission of a legal duty owed by one individual to another, where such omission results in the death of the one to whom the duty is owed, will make the other chargeable with manslaughter. The duty must be imposed by law or contract. The omission must be the immediate cause of death. Breach of a legal duty can arise in four situations: (1) where a statute imposes the duty; (2) where one is in a certain status relationship to another; (3) where one has assumed a contractual duty to care for another; and (4) where one has voluntarily assumed the care of another. Whether Jones (D) fits any of those four situations is a question for the jury. Evidence was in conflict particularly on the third and fourth situations. Failure to instruct the jury on a critical element of the crime requires a reversal of the conviction with the matter to be remanded for a new trial.

▶ ANALYSIS

A tentative draft of the Model Penal Code dealing with the issue confronted in the instant case states, "Liability for the commission of an offense may not be based on an omission unaccompanied by action unless: (a) the omission is expressly made sufficient by the law defining the offense; or (b) a duty to perform the omitted act is otherwise imposed by law." M.P.C., Tent. Draft No. 4 (1955), § 2.01(3). Here, whether there was a duty was an element of the crime. Failure to find beyond a reasonable doubt on any element of a crime prohibits a conviction. Note that the duty must be legal, not merely moral.

Quicknotes

INVOLUNTARY MANSLAUGHTER The killing of another person without premeditation or deliberation or with the intent to kill or to commit a felony, which may be reasonably expected to result in death or serious bodily injury; involuntary manslaughter is characterized by reckless conduct in the commission of a lawful act, or by the commission of an unlawful act that is not a felony, but which leads to the killing of another.

LEGAL DUTY TO ACT The duty to take some action to assist another in danger; such a duty is only imposed under certain circumstances, such as in accordance with a statute, contract, or relationship between the parties; when the defendant voluntarily assumes responsibility for care of the victim; or if the defendant creates the circumstances placing the victim in danger.

OMISSION The failure to perform an act or obligation that one is required to perform by law.

REASONABLE DOUBT Standard of proof necessary to convict a defendant, requiring the absence of evidence that would cause a reasonable person to hesitate in making an important decision in his personal affairs.

Pope v. State

Bystander (D) v. State (P)

Md. Ct. App., 284 Md. 309, 396 A.2d. 1054 (1979).

NATURE OF CASE: Appeal of conviction for child abuse and misprision of felony.

FACT SUMMARY: Pope (D), who had let a woman and her child stay with her, did not intervene when the woman savagely attacked the child, or report it to authorities.

🏛 **RULE OF LAW**
One is not criminally liable for failing to intervene when a person staying in one's dwelling abuses her child.

FACTS: Norris was a young mother with a three-month-old child, Demiko. One day, Pope (D) allowed Norris and her child to stay with her, as they had apparently become homeless. (They knew each other from attending the same church.) Norris suffered from religious delusions. At one point, apparently believing that Satan had entered Demiko, Norris savagely attacked him, a course of action that apparently lasted several hours. Pope (D) did not intervene. Demiko died of injuries suffered in Norris's attack. Norris was held incompetent to stand trial. Pope (D) was charged with and convicted of child abuse and misprision of felony. She (D) appealed.

ISSUE: Is one criminally liable for failing to intervene when a person staying in one's dwelling abuses her child?

HOLDING AND DECISION: (Orth, J.) No. One is not criminally liable for failing to intervene when a person staying in one's dwelling abuses her child. Article 27, § 35A of the Maryland Code makes it a felony for one who is the parent of or is otherwise responsible for a minor to cause or allow injury or inhumane treatment to occur to the minor. There is no doubt that Demiko was subjected to such treatment. The question is whether Pope (D) was responsible therefor. In this court's view, those who permit a parent and child to reside with them do not, without more, make one responsible for the child. The child's responsibility remains with the parent. Such was the case here. Pope (D) had allowed Norris and Demiko into her house as guests, and this alone did not make her responsible for Demiko. Consequently, the conviction under § 35A was contrary to law. [The court then discussed the misprision of a felony conviction. This common-law offense involved not informing authorities of a felony committed in the presence of the defendant. The court noted that no one had been convicted of the crime in over a century in the state and concluded that the offense no longer existed.] Reversed.

▌ *ANALYSIS*

The duty of bystanders to a crime has long been a matter of both moral and legal debate. Most states have "Good Samaritan" laws which limit the civil liability of persons who aid crime or accident victims. Few states have elected to enact laws actually compelling bystanders to provide aid. Minnesota was the first state to enact such a law. Vermont and Rhode Island have also adopted forms of such a law.

■≡■

Quicknotes

GOOD SAMARITAN LAW A statute relieving a bystander from tort liability for the attempted rescue of another.

MISPRISION The concealment of a felony.

■≡■

Barber v. Superior Court

Court physician (D) v. Court (P)

Cal. Ct. App., 147 Cal. App. 3d 1006, 195 Cal. Rptr. 484 (1983).

NATURE OF CASE: Appeal from reinstatement of dismissal of murder charges.

FACT SUMMARY: When Clarence Herbert, permanently comatose following surgery, was taken off of artificial respiration and nutrition, leading to death, Barber (D), his physician, was charged with murder.

🏛 RULE OF LAW
There is no criminal liability for failure to act unless there is a legal duty to act.

FACTS: Clarence Herbert underwent surgery following a heart attack and lapsed into a coma from which medical authorities gave virtually no chance of his recovering. He was not completely brain-dead. His family expressed a desire that he be taken off all life support equipment, including nutrition. This was done, and Herbert died. The Government (P) then charged Barber (D), the attending physician, with murder. The complaint was dismissed, and then reinstated. Barber (D) appealed.

ISSUE: Is there criminal liability for failure to act if there is no legal duty to act?

HOLDING AND DECISION: (Compton, J.) No. There is no criminal liability for failure to act unless there is a legal duty to act. Absent objection from the spouse of one permanently comatose, a doctor is under no legal duty to keep the patient alive through forced respiration and nutrition. As Herbert was not clinically dead at the time support was withdrawn, the court must decide whether such withdrawal was unlawful. The best way to analyze this is in terms of a benefits-versus-burdens analysis. Where there is a reasonable chance of recovery, the benefits outweigh the burdens. Where, as here, there is no such chance, extraordinary measures confer no such benefit. Both respiration and nutrition are medical procedures that can be classified as extraordinary support. Thus, a doctor may, without objection from the patient's survivor, cease such support. A physician has no duty to continue treatment, once treatment has proved to be ineffective. Reversed.

▍ANALYSIS

The issue here has been grappled with by courts for some time, and they have understandably had difficulty with it. Criminal law was developed in times when such situations were unthinkable. This area is appropriate for legislative action, but as yet there has been little.

Quicknotes

LEGAL DUTY TO ACT The duty to take some action to assist another in danger; such a duty is only imposed under certain circumstances, such as in accordance with a statute, contract, or relationship between the parties; when the defendant voluntarily assumes responsibility for care of the victim; or if the defendant creates the circumstances placing the victim in danger.

MURDER Unlawful killing of another person either with deliberation and premeditation or by conduct demonstrating a reckless disregard for human life.

■=■

Regina v. Cunningham

Government (P) v. Thief (D)

Ct. of Crim. App., 2 Q.B 396 (1957).

NATURE OF CASE: Appeal from conviction for unlawfully and maliciously injuring another person.

FACT SUMMARY: Cunningham (D) intentionally stole a gas meter out of a house. A woman in the house was made ill by the escaping gas.

🏛 RULE OF LAW
"Malice" in a statutory crime means foresight of the consequences and requires either an actual intention to do the particular kind of harm that in fact was done or recklessness as to whether such harm should occur or not.

FACTS: Cunningham (D) wrenched a gas meter from the pipes and stole it. He had not turned off the gas, and escaping gas seeped into Wade's bedroom, injuring her and endangering her life.

ISSUE: Can a defendant be said to have maliciously done some harm where he did not intend to do the particular kind of harm done or did not foresee that the particular harm might be done?

HOLDING AND DECISION: (Byrne, J.) No. The word "maliciously" in a statutory crime postulates foresight of the consequences. It requires either an actual intention to do the particular kind of harm that, in fact, was done or recklessness as to whether such harm should occur or not, as where the accused foresees that the particular kind of harm might be done and yet goes on to take the risk of it. Malice is neither limited to, nor does it require, any ill will toward the person injured. Nor does the word mean wicked. In this case, the fact that Cunningham (D) acted unlawfully or wickedly in stealing the gas meter does not mean that he acted maliciously in causing Wade's injury. It should have been left to the jury to decide whether Cunningham (D) foresaw that the removal of the meter might cause injury to someone. His conviction is quashed.

▶ ANALYSIS

An intention to cause one type of crime cannot serve as a substitute for the required intention in another type of crime. Hence, where a defendant throws a rock with an intent to hit another and misses, unintentionally breaking a window, he is not guilty of malicious destruction of property. Likewise, where a defendant, intending to steal rum from a ship, lights a match in order to see, thereby causing a fire which destroys the ship, he is not guilty of intent-to-burn arson. However, such defendants might be convicted on the basis of having acted recklessly or negligently. As these cases demonstrate, the transferred intent doctrine is applicable only within the limits of the same crime.

■═■

Quicknotes

MALICE The intention to commit an unlawful act without justification or excuse.

NEGLIGENCE Conduct falling below the standard of care that a reasonable person would demonstrate under similar conditions.

RECKLESSNESS The conscious disregard of substantial and justifiable risk.

TRANSFERRED INTENT When a perpetrator acts with the intent to commit a crime against one person, and instead commits that crime against another person, the perpetrator's intent is transferred to the actual victim for the purposes of liability.

■═■

United States v. Jewell

Federal government (P) v. Driver (D)

532 F.2d 697 (9th Cir. 1976).

NATURE OF CASE: Appeal after conviction of violation of the federal drug abuse law.

FACT SUMMARY: Jewell (D) entered the United States driving a car in which marijuana had been concealed in a secret compartment. He claimed he did not have positive knowledge that the marijuana was present.

🏛 RULE OF LAW
Where a defendant is aware of facts indicating a high probability of illegality but purposely fails to investigate because he desires to stay ignorant, he has knowledge of the illegality, and positive knowledge is not required.

FACTS: Jewell (D) testified that while he was in Mexico, he was approached by a man who offered him $100 if he would drive a car back to the United States. The car contained a secret compartment in which marijuana was concealed. Jewell (D) was arrested and charged with knowingly or intentionally importing a controlled substance and knowingly or intentionally possessing, with intent to distribute, a controlled substance. But Jewell (D) also testified that although he knew of the compartment, he did not know that the marijuana was present. There was circumstantial evidence from which a jury could either infer that Jewell (D) did have such knowledge or that, although he knew of the compartment and had knowledge of facts indicating that it contained marijuana, he deliberately avoided investigating and thereby gaining positive knowledge of the marijuana's presence. The court instructed the jury that it could find Jewell (D) guilty even if it found that he was not actually aware of the presence of the marijuana if it found that his lack of knowledge resulted from a conscious effort by him to remain ignorant.

ISSUE: Is willful ignorance equivalent to knowledge in criminal law?

HOLDING AND DECISION: (Browning, J.) Yes. Where a defendant is aware of facts indicating a high probability of illegality but purposely failed to investigate because he desires to stay ignorant, he has knowledge of the illegality, and positive knowledge is not required. The substantive justification for this rule is that deliberate ignorance and positive knowledge are equally culpable. The textual justification is that in common understanding one "knows" facts of which he is less than absolutely certain. To act "knowingly," therefore, is not necessarily to act only with positive knowledge but also to act with awareness of the high probability of the existence of the fact in question. Hence, the jury instruction was proper, and Jewell's (D) conviction must be affirmed.

DISSENT: (Kennedy, J.) The instruction was defective in that it did not mention that Jewell (D) must have been aware of a high probability that a controlled substance was in the car. Secondly, it did not inform the jury that Jewell (D) would not be convicted if he "actually believed" there was no controlled substance in the car. This lack could allow a jury to convict on the objective theory of knowledge—that a reasonable person would have known that marijuana was concealed in the car.

▶ ANALYSIS

If the word "knowing" required absolute certainty, there would be few convictions, for as the *Jewell* court points out, one seldom knows anything to a certainty, and, secondly, often persons involved are careful not to learn all of the facts. Hence, positive knowledge is not required in any jurisdiction. In most, a belief on the part of the accused is all that is necessary. Obviously, usually there is no direct testimony of the defendant's actual belief, and so it must be inferred from the surrounding circumstances. It is proper for a jury to infer a defendant's belief from the surrounding circumstances.

Quicknotes

CIRCUMSTANTIAL EVIDENCE Evidence that, though not directly observed, supports the inference of principal facts.

KNOWINGLY Intentionally; willfully; an act that is committed with knowledge as to its probable consequences.

OBJECTIVE A standard that is not personal to an individual but is dependent on some external source.

REASONABLE PERSON STANDARD The standard of care exercised by a hypothetical person who possesses the intelligence, education, knowledge, attention, and judgment required by society of its members when governing behavior; the standard applies to a person's judgment when determining breach of a duty under the theory of negligence.

Regina v. Prince

Government (P) v. Misdemeanant (D)

Ct. of Cr. Cas. Res., L.R. 2 Cr. Cas. Res. 154 (1875).

NATURE OF CASE: Appeal from a misdemeanor conviction.

FACT SUMMARY: Prince (D), who was under the reasonable belief that Annie Phillips was 18, was convicted of violating a law making it a misdemeanor for anyone to lawfully take or cause to be taken an unmarried girl under the age 16 out of the possession and against the will of her father.

> ## 🏛 RULE OF LAW
> A reasonable but mistaken belief that the girl was 16 or older is not a defense against a charge that one violated the law which makes it a misdemeanor to unlawfully take any unmarried girl under age 16 out of the possession and against the will of her father.

FACTS: At the time Prince (D) took young Annie Phillips away, he was under the reasonable belief that she was 18 years old—which is what she had told him. Actually, she was only 14. Prince (D) was convicted of violating the law which made it a misdemeanor for anyone to "unlawfully take or cause to be taken any unmarried girl, being under the age of 16 years, out of the possession and against the will of her father or mother, or of any person having the lawful care or charge of her."

ISSUE: Is the reasonable but mistaken belief that the girl was 16 or older a defense against the charge that one violated a law making it a misdemeanor to unlawfully take any unmarried girl under 16 out of the possession and against the will of her father?

HOLDING AND DECISION: (Bramwell, J.) No. The fact that one was under the reasonable but mistaken belief that the girl was at least 16, is not a defense against the charge that one violated the law making it a misdemeanor to unlawfully take any unmarried girl under 16 out of the possession and against the will of her father. What the defendant would have us do is read into the statute in question language requiring that a person not believe the girl he takes is over 16 years of age when he takes her. These words are not there, and the question is, whether we are bound to construe the statute as though they were, on account of the rule that the mens rea is necessary to make an act a crime. It is my opinion that we are not. The legislature has enacted that if anyone does a particular wrongful act, i.e., takes a female of such tender years that she is properly called a girl, can be said to be in another's possession, and in the other's care or charge—he does it at the risk of her turning out to be under 16. This position gives full scope to the doctrine of mens rea. The defendant

can be convicted of violating this law despite the fact that he was under the reasonable belief the girl he took was over 16; the doctrine of mens rea is not threatened or controverted, because the defendant has done the act forbidden—an act wrong in itself. If the taker believed he had the father's consent, though wrongly, he would have no mens rea; so if he did not know she was in anyone's possession, nor in the charge or care of anyone. In those cases, unlike the one at bar, he would not know he was doing the act forbidden by that statute—an act which, if he knew she was in the possession and in the care or charge of anyone, he would know was a crime or not, according as she was under 16 or not. He would not know he was doing an act wrong in itself, whatever was his intention, if done without lawful cause. It seems to me impossible to say that where a person takes a girl out of her father's possession, not knowing whether she is or is not under 16, that he is not guilty; and equally impossible when he believes, but erroneously, that she is old enough for him to do a wrong act with safety. Affirmed.

DISSENT: (Brett, J.) There can be no conviction for crime in England in the absence of a criminal mind or mens rea. The maxim as to mens rea applies whenever the facts which are present in the prisoner's mind, and which he has reasonable ground to believe, and does believe to be the facts, would, if true, make his act no criminal offence at all. I come to the conclusion that a mistake of facts on reasonable grounds, to the extent that if the facts were as believed the acts of the prisoner would make him guilty of no criminal offence at all, is an excuse, and that such excuse is implied in every criminal charge and every criminal enactment in England.

▶ ANALYSIS

Many defendants have attempted to defeat statutory rape charges by claiming as a defense their erroneous belief that the "victim" was over the designated age of consent. The still predominant view is that such a mistake is no defense (even if reasonable)—that one simply runs a risk of engaging in sexual activity with a young person, that that person will turn out to be below the age of consent. This is much the same attitude expressed in the *Prince* case. Some courts have, however, recognized such a defense to statutory rape charges—if the mistake as to the "victim's" age was reasonable. Under the provisions of the Model Penal Code, such reasonable belief is not an affirmative defense where, as Professor Kadish explains,

Continued on next page.

criminality turns on the child's being below the age of 10, but where the critical age is higher. Some jurisdictions have adopted this approach in their codes.

■══■

Quicknotes

MENS REA Criminal intent.

MISDEMEANOR Any offense that does not constitute a felony, which is generally less severe and for which a lesser punishment is imposed.

MISTAKE OF FACT An unintentional mistake in knowing or recalling a fact without the will to deceive.

■══■

People v. Olsen

State (P) v. Convicted child molester (D)

Cal. Sup. Ct., 36 Cal.3d 638, 685 P.2d 52 (1984).

NATURE OF CASE: Appeal from conviction for committing a lewd act on a child under 14.

FACT SUMMARY: Olsen (D) was convicted of committing a lewd act on a child under 14 years of age whom he believed to be, and who looked, older.

> 🏛 **RULE OF LAW**
> A reasonable mistake as to the victim's age is not a defense to a charge of committing a lewd act on a child who is under 14 years of age.

FACTS: While exactly what happened was in dispute, Olsen (D) at some point had sexual intercourse with a girl just under 14. She had told Olsen (D) she was over 16, and she looked it. Olsen (D) was charged with a violation of Penal Code § 288(a), committing a lewd act on a child under 14, which carried a greater penalty than statutory rape. The court rejected his defense of reasonable mistake as to age, and the court of appeals affirmed.

ISSUE: Is a reasonable mistake as to the victim's age a defense to a charge of committing a lewd act on a child who is under 14 years of age?

HOLDING AND DECISION: (Bird, C.J.) No. A reasonable mistake as to the victim's age is not a defense to the charge of committing a lewd act on a child who is under 14 years of age. While statutory rape is not a strict liability offense in California, the law has always recognized a special need to protect its younger children. The fact that this offense carries a greater maximum penalty than statutory rape demonstrates this. Also, the fact that the code provides that reasonable mistake as to age can be a basis for probation rather than incarceration demonstrates that the legislature did not want reasonable mistake to be a defense. Affirmed.

CONCURRENCE AND DISSENT: (Grodin, J.) Strict liability offenses in all traditional crimes should be abolished.

▶ **ANALYSIS**

California is one of a handful of jurisdictions that make statutory rape a nonstrict liability offense. A reasonable belief as to the minor's majority is a viable defense. Most jurisdictions, in imposing strict liability, have made the policy judgment that the protection of its children is so grave a matter as to justify this harsh rule.

Quicknotes

LEWD Obscene or lustful.

STATUTORY RAPE Unlawful sexual intercourse by a man with a woman, either consensual or nonconsensual, under an age specified by statute.

STRICT LIABILITY Liability for all injuries proximately caused by a party's conducting of certain inherently dangerous activities without regard to negligence or fault.

■▬■

B (A Minor) v. Director of Public Prosecutions

Inciter of child indecency (D) v. State (P)

House of Lords, 1 All. Eng. Rep. 833 (2000).

NATURE OF CASE: Appeal from a conviction for inciting a child under the age of 14 to commit gross indecency.

FACT SUMMARY: A 15-year-old boy badgered a 13-year-old girl to perform oral sex, and she refused.

RULE OF LAW
Where Parliament fails to specify a mens rea requirement, a common-law presumption of an objective standard no longer governs the mental-state requirement for criminal statutes.

FACTS: B (D), who was 15 years old, repeatedly sought oral sex from a 13-year-old girl. After the girl refused, B (D) was charged with inciting a child under the age of 14 to commit gross indecency. The statute under which he was prosecuted did not expressly include an intention to commit the act with a child under the age of 14 as an element of the crime. At trial, B's (D) defense was that he honestly believed that the girl was older than 14. The trial justices rejected that defense, and B (D) pled guilty while also preserving his right to appeal. He then appealed the rejection of his "honest belief" defense to the House of Lords.

ISSUE: Where Parliament fails to specify a mens rea requirement, does a common-law presumption of an objective standard still govern the mental-state requirement for criminal statutes?

HOLDING AND DECISION: (Nicholls, L.) No. Where Parliament fails to specify a mens rea requirement, a common-law presumption of an objective standard no longer governs the mental-state requirement for criminal statutes. In this case, Parliament has not defined the requisite mental state in the statute at issue. Traditionally, this situation would have required application of the common-law presumption that the defendant's mistaken belief must be objectively reasonable. That traditional presumption has eroded, however, during the past 25 years. The applicable common-law standard today is whether the defendant holds an honest belief of the pertinent facts in his defense. Although a common-law presumption on mens rea should apply in this case, the appropriate presumption is the "honest belief" standard. [Reversed.]

CONCURRENCE: (Steyn, L.) The old rule no longer applies. Defendants today should be tried based on their honest belief of the facts.

▶ ANALYSIS

Note that the ruling by the House of Lords in *B (A Minor)* has not supplanted the traditional rule in the United States. This case reflects a recent trend in English law, not in U.S. law.

■=■

Quicknotes

MENS REA Criminal intent.

■=■

Morissette v. United States

Converter (D) v. Federal government (P)

342 U.S. 246 (1952).

NATURE OF CASE: Appeal of conviction for unlawful conversion of government property.

FACT SUMMARY: Morissette (D) converted spent air force shell casings, found on a military target range, into scrap metal which he sold.

🏛 RULE OF LAW
Crimes that are mala in se (bad in themselves) necessarily include the element of mens rea and no statutory strict liability version of them is permissible.

FACTS: Morissette (D) discovered a number of spent military shell casings while deer hunting in an area marked "Danger—Keep Out—Bombing Range." Seeing them merely dumped in heaps, he thought they had been abandoned. He thereupon loaded three tons of them on a truck, took them to a farm where he flattened them with a tractor, and then finally took them to a nearby town where he sold them for scrap for $84. He was charged under a federal statute that makes knowing conversion of government property a crime. Previous decisions had pointed out the right of the government to regulate its property on a strict liability basis. As a result when Morissette (D) attempted to prove that he had no intent to convert the scrap unlawfully because he felt it had been abandoned, his offer was refused by the trial court stating "The question in intent is whether or not he intended to take the property." In other words, no mens rea scienter need be shown to establish felonious intent. His conviction was affirmed subsequently. He appealed to the United States Supreme Court.

ISSUE: May a person be held criminally responsible on a strict liability basis for a crime that is mala in se?

HOLDING AND DECISION: (Jackson, J.) No. Crimes that are mala in se (bad in themselves) necessarily include an element of mens rea and no strict liability version of them is permissible. In short, felonious intent may not be presumed from the intentional doing of the act plus the proscribed result. At common law, where all crimes were mala in se, the mens rea requirement of scienter was always necessary. This rule has been followed even where modern statutory definitions of the common-law crimes have omitted mention of it. Here, conversion, as a common-law crime, always included scienter as a necessary element and mere omission from the statutory definition of it does not justify its abandonment. The underlying rationale here is that the purpose of exempting regulatory crimes from the requirements of mens rea (that no evil purpose can exist to do an act which is not evil in itself) is not served when crimes are mala in se, such as conversion.

The Court also points out that the previous decisions permitting strict liability involved regulatory (mala prohibita) statutes, where such is properly applied. Reversed.

▶ ANALYSIS

This case points up the general technical rationale for excluding malum in se crimes from strict liability. At common law, all such crimes had a mens rea requirement. The point here is that the statute is really a version of a common-law crime. Allowing the omission of an element of the definition of a crime alters the nature of the crime and creates a new one.

■=■

Quicknotes

CONVERSION The act of depriving an owner of his property without permission or justification.

MALUM IN SE An act that is wrong in accordance with natural law, without respect to whether it is prohibited by statute.

MENS REA Criminal intent.

SCIENTER Knowledge of certain facts; often refers to "guilty knowledge," which implicates liability.

STRICT LIABILITY Liability for all injuries proximately caused by a party's conducting of certain inherently dangerous activities without regard to negligence or fault.

■=■

Staples v. United States

Gun owner (D) v. Federal government (P)

511 U.S. 600 (1994).

NATURE OF CASE: Appeal from a criminal conviction for violating the National Firearms Act.

FACT SUMMARY: When Staples (D) was convicted because he had not registered in the National Firearms Registration and Transfer Record a rifle that had been modified to be capable of fully automatic fire, he claimed he did not know of the rifle's automatic firing capability.

RULE OF LAW
Some indication of congressional intent, express or implied, is required to dispense with the mens rea requirement.

FACTS: Upon executing a search warrant at Staples's (D) home, local police and agents of the Bureau of Alcohol, Tobacco and Firearms (BATF) recovered an AR-15 rifle. Staples (D), subsequently, was indicted for unlawful possession of an unregistered machine gun in violation of § 5861(d) of the National Firearms Act. The district court rejected Staples's (D) request for a jury instruction that the government must prove beyond a reasonable doubt that he knew that the gun would fire fully automatically. When found guilty and sentenced to five years' probation and a fine, Staples (D) appealed, claiming that his alleged ignorance of the gun's automatic firing capability should have shielded him from criminal liability for his failure to register the weapon.

ISSUE: Is some indication of congressional intent necessary to dispense with the mens rea requirement?

HOLDING AND DECISION: (Thomas, J.) Yes. Some indication of congressional intent, express or implied, is required to dispense with the mens rea requirement. In such a case, the usual presumption that a defendant must know the facts that make his conduct illegal should apply. Determining the mental state required for commission of a federal crime requires construction of the statute and inference of the intent of Congress. Offenses that require no mens rea generally are disfavored and some indication of congressional intent, express or implied, is required to dispense with mens rea as an element of a crime. Generally, offenses punishable by imprisonment cannot be understood to be public welfare offenses, but must require mens rea. If Congress had intended to make outlaws of ignorant gun owners, and subject them to lengthy prison terms, it would have spoken more clearly to that effect. Reversed and remanded.

CONCURRENCE: (Ginsburg, J.) The issue is not whether knowledge of possession is required, but what level of knowledge suffices. Conviction here requires proof that the defendant know he possessed not just a gun, but a machine gun.

ANALYSIS

There is no allowance made for a mistake of fact or of law if an offense is strict liability in nature. The common-law rule requiring mens rea can be dispensed with only when a statute expressly says so. Only public welfare or regulatory offenses are generally understood to impose a form of strict criminal liability.

Quicknotes

MENS REA Criminal intent.

STRICT LIABILITY Liability for all injuries proximately caused by a party's conducting of certain inherently dangerous activities without regard to negligence or fault.

State v. Guminga

State (P) v. Tavern owner (D)

Minn. Sup. Ct., 395 N.W.2d 344 (1986).

NATURE OF CASE: Certified question of law related to a prosecution for violation of a state liquor control statute.

FACT SUMMARY: Guminga (D), a tavern owner, was prosecuted under a statute providing vicarious criminal liability for the acts of one's employees.

🏛 RULE OF LAW
A person may not be vicariously liable for the acts of his employees that he did not ratify.

FACTS: Guminga (D) was a tavern owner. As part of an undercover investigation, a minor ordered alcohol, and was served. The waitress was arrested for violation of a state statute making it a misdemeanor to serve liquor to minors. Guminga (D), although he did not ratify the waitress's actions, was also prosecuted. Guminga (D) contended this violated due process. The trial court certified this issue for answer by the state supreme court.

ISSUE: May a person be vicariously liable for the acts of his employees that he did not ratify?

HOLDING AND DECISION: (Yetka, J.) No. A person may not be vicariously liable for the acts of his employees that he did not ratify. Due process analysis of a statute involves a balancing of the public interest advanced and the intrusion on personal liberty. The public interest of preventing intoxication among minors is important. However, the private interests involve loss of liberty, damage to reputation, and possible future disabilities. This is too great a burden to place on one not ratifying the proscribed conduct, particularly since there are civil remedies, such as fines or license revocation, to compel compliance. For this reason, the statute is unconstitutional and the certified question is thus answered in the affirmative.

DISSENT: (Kelley, J.) The imposition of light criminal sanctions is a penalty reasonably related to achieving the strong social policy of avoiding intoxication of minors.

▶ ANALYSIS

Vicarious liability, called the doctrine of respondeat superior, is an accepted part of tort law. For the most part, it has also made its way into criminal jurisprudence. The analysis of the court in this instance is accepted in a minority of jurisdictions, however.

Quicknotes

DUE PROCESS The constitutional mandate requiring the courts to protect and enforce individuals' rights and liberties consistent with prevailing principals of fairness and justice and prohibiting the federal and state governments from such activities that deprive its citizens of a life, liberty or property interest.

VICARIOUS LIABILITY The imputed liability of one party for the unlawful acts of another.

Regina v. City of Sault Ste. Marie

[Parties not identified]

Canada Sup. Ct., 85 D.L.R.3d 161 (1978).

NATURE OF CASE: Absolute liability case.

FACT SUMMARY: [Facts not stated in casebook excerpt.]

🏛 RULE OF LAW
Where an offense does not require full mens rea, it is a good defense for the defense to prove that he was not negligent.

FACTS: [Facts not stated in casebook excerpt.]

ISSUE: Where an offense does not require full mens rea, is it a good defense for the defense to prove that he was not negligent?

HOLDING AND DECISION: (Dickson, J.) Yes. Where an offense does not require full mens rea, it is a good defense for the defense to prove that he was not negligent. This doctrine is based on the assumption that the defendant could have avoided the prima facie offense through the exercise of reasonable care and the defendant is given the opportunity of establishing that he did in fact exercise such care. This burden falls upon the defendant to establish that on the balance of probabilities he has the reasonable care defense.

▶ ANALYSIS

The Supreme Court of Canada here recognizes a third category of offence in addition to the two traditional offenses requiring the prosecution to prove mens rea and absolute liability.

■≡■

Quicknotes

MENS REA Criminal intent.

NEGLIGENCE Conduct falling below the standard of care that a reasonable person would demonstrate under similar conditions.

■≡■

People v. Marrero

State (P) v. Firearm owner (D)

N.Y. Ct. App., 69 N.Y.2d 382, 507 N.E.2d 1068 (1987).

NATURE OF CASE: Appeal of conviction for illegal firearms possession.

FACT SUMMARY: Marrero (D), charged with illegal firearms possession, argued that he mistakenly believed himself to be exempt from the ambit of the statute proscribing possession.

🏛 RULE OF LAW
A good-faith mistaken belief as to the meaning of a criminal statute is no defense to a violation of the statute.

FACTS: Marrero (D) was a corrections officer in a federal prison. He was found to be carrying a handgun in public and was charged with violating a statute criminalizing such possession. He argued that he mistakenly believed that a subdivision exempting state correctional officers also applied to him. He was convicted, and the appellate division affirmed. He appealed.

ISSUE: Is a good-faith mistaken belief as to the meaning of a criminal statute a defense to a violation of the statute?

HOLDING AND DECISION: (Bellacosa, J.) No. A good-faith mistaken belief as to the meaning of a criminal statute is no defense to a violation of the statute. To admit the excuse of ignorance of law would work to encourage ignorance when policy should favor knowledge. While this rule will no doubt result in occasional unfair outcomes, the larger societal interest in promoting knowledge of the law is more important. Here, Marrero (D) was ignorant of the law, and this will not excuse him. Affirmed.

DISSENT: (Hancock, J.) The ancient rule that "ignorance of the law is no excuse" may have been proper in times when almost all laws proscribed conduct malum in se. Today, however, a vast array of laws prohibits conduct only malum prohibitum, and an arbitrary rule disallowing a good-faith mistake defense is unfair.

▌ANALYSIS

"Ignorance of the law is no excuse" is something of a cliché and is generally true. It is not universal, however. The Model Penal Code rule, accepted in numerous jurisdictions, permits the defense when mistake negates the purpose or belief necessary to establish a material element.

Quicknotes

MALUM IN SE An act that is wrong in accordance with natural law, without respect to whether it is prohibited by statute.

MALUM PROHIBITUM An action that is not inherently wrong, but which is prohibited by law.

MISTAKE OF LAW An error involving a misunderstanding or incorrect application of law.

Cheek v. United States

Tax evader (D) v. Federal government (P)

498 U.S. 192 (1991).

NATURE OF CASE: Appeal from a conviction for tax evasion.

FACT SUMMARY: When Cheek (D) was charged with willfully failing to file a federal income tax return and willfully attempting to evade his income tax, he argued that because he sincerely believed that the tax laws were invalid, he had acted without the willfulness required for conviction.

🏛 RULE OF LAW
Any person who willfully attempts to evade or defeat the requirement that he pay a tax on his income shall be guilty of a felony where it can be shown that he knows and understands the law.

FACTS: After attending various seminars, and based on his own study, Cheek (D) concluded that the income tax laws were being unconstitutionally enforced. He then ceased to file any income tax returns at all. As a result, he was indicted and charged with willfully failing to file a federal income tax and willfully attempting to evade his income tax. Cheek (D) represented himself at trial. Evidence showed that he had been involved in at least four civil cases that unsuccessfully challenged various aspects of the federal income tax system. An attorney had also advised Cheek (D) that the courts had rejected as frivolous the claim that wages are not income. The jury returned a verdict of guilty on all counts. The court of appeals affirmed. Cheek (D) appealed.

ISSUE: Shall any person who willfully attempts to evade or defeat the requirement that he pay a tax on his income be guilty of a felony where it can be shown that he knows and understands the law?

HOLDING AND DECISION: (White, J.) Yes. Any person who willfully attempts to evade or defeat the requirement that he pay a tax on his income shall be guilty of a felony where it can be shown that he knows and understands the law. Here, the evidence shows that Cheek (D) was aware of his duty to file a return and to treat wages as income. Moreover, claims that some of the provisions of the tax code are unconstitutional do not arise from innocent mistakes caused by the complexity of the Internal Revenue Code. Rather, they reveal full knowledge of the provisions at issue and a studied conclusion, however wrong, that those provisions are invalid and unenforceable. Under these circumstances, Cheek's (D) views on the validity of the tax statutes are irrelevant to the issue of willfulness, need not be heard by the jury, and if they are, an instruction to disregard them would be proper. It was

therefore not error in this case for the district judge to instruct the jury not to consider Cheek's (D) claims that the tax laws were unconstitutional.

▶ ANALYSIS

Cheek (D) was charged with violating 26 U.S.C. §§ 7201 and 7203. The statutory term "willfully," as used in the federal criminal tax statutes, carves out an exception to the traditional rule that ignorance of the law or mistake of law is no defense to a criminal prosecution. This special treatment is largely due to the complexity of the tax laws and the reluctance of Congress to penalize confused, but otherwise innocent, taxpayers.

Quicknotes

MISTAKE OF LAW An error involving a misunderstanding or incorrect application of law.

WILLFULLY An act that is undertaken intentionally, knowingly, and with the intent to commit an unlawful act without a justifiable excuse.

Lambert v. California
Felon (D) v. State (P)

355 U.S. 225 (1957).

NATURE OF CASE: Appeal from conviction for violation of registration statute.

FACT SUMMARY: Lambert (D) was convicted for violating a statute which required all persons who had previously been convicted of a felony to register with the police.

🏛 RULE OF LAW
Failure to act may not be punishable under a criminal statute unless it is shown that the defendant knew or should have known of the duty established by the statute and the penalty for failure to comply with the statute.

FACTS: A city ordinance defined a convicted person as any person who has been convicted of a felony in California, or convicted of any offense in any other state which would have been punishable as a felony under California law. Another ordinance required any convicted person who stayed more than five days in Los Angeles or who had visited Los Angeles more than five times within a 30-day period, to register with the Chief of Police; failure to register was a continuing offense, with each day's failure to register treated as a separate offense. Lambert (D) was arrested on suspicion of another crime and was charged with violating the registration statute.

ISSUE: Is it a violation of due process to apply a registration statute to a person who has no knowledge of his duty to register?

HOLDING AND DECISION: (Douglas, J.) Yes. It is a maxim of criminal law that ignorance of the law is no offense; but under this statute, the violation is wholly passive. Mere presence in the city is the test of violation, and there is no requirement that the convicted person have any knowledge of the registration statute. The only purpose of this ordinance was for the administrative convenience of the police. Due process requires notice of a possible offense, particularly in a situation where the mere failure to act will result in a penalty. Here, although Lambert's (D) failure to act was totally innocent, when she was informed of the existence of the statute, she was given no chance to comply with the requirement and avoid punishment. Therefore, to comply with due process, it must be shown that the defendant had actual knowledge of the duty to register, or that there was a probability of such knowledge. Otherwise, Lambert (D) cannot be punished for conduct which would have been innocent if done by other members of the community. Reversed.

DISSENT: (Frankfurter, J.) Many laws enacted under the police power of the state require no knowledge of the existence of the law on the part of the defendant. The majority bases its decision on a wholly untenable distinction between affirmative and passive acts.

▶ ANALYSIS

In such cases as this, which concern wholly passive acts, and in other cases which involve statutes concerning freedom of speech, the Court has readily read into such statutes a requirement of knowledge of the existence of the statute or some other form of scienter.

Quicknotes

DUE PROCESS The constitutional mandate requiring the courts to protect and enforce individuals' rights and liberties consistent with prevailing principals of fairness and justice and prohibiting the federal and state governments from such activities that deprive its citizens of a life, liberty or property interest.

FELONY A criminal offense of greater seriousness than a misdemeanor; felonies are generally defined pursuant to statute as any crime that is punishable by death or by a term of imprisonment exceeding one year.

POLICE POWER The power of a government to impose restrictions on the rights of private persons, as long as those restrictions are reasonably related to the promotion and protection of public health, safety, morals and the general welfare.

SCIENTER Knowledge of certain facts; often refers to "guilty knowledge," which implicates liability.

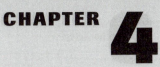
Quick Reference Rules of Law

State v. Rusk

State (P) v. Convicted rapist (D)

Md. Ct. App., 289 Md. 230, 424 A.2d 720 (1981).

NATURE OF CASE: Appeal from a rape conviction.

FACT SUMMARY: Rusk's (D) second-degree rape conviction was reversed by the court of special appeals, which said it could not see in any of the victim's testimony "any resistance on her part to the sex acts" and "no fear as would overcome her attempt to resist or escape."

🏛 RULE OF LAW
The lack of consent element essential to a rape conviction can be established by proof of resistance or by proof that the victim failed to resist because of a genuine, reasonably grounded fear.

FACTS: Rusk (D) was convicted of raping a 21-year-old. She testified that Rusk (D) took her car keys after she drove him at night to an unfamiliar part of the city where he lived. The "look" on his face when he told her to come up to his place scared her to the point that she complied instead of running, blowing her horn, or seeking some other method of escape. She also testified that she remained seated in his apartment, even though he left the room for one to five minutes, and that she did not notice a telephone in the room. Allegedly, he pulled her by the arms to the bed and began to undress her. She admitted to removing his pants because "he asked her to do it" and to engaging in sexual activity after Rusk (D) allegedly "began to lightly choke her" in response to her starting to cry after he gave no response to her query as to whether or not he would let her go without killing her if she did what he wanted. The court of special appeals reversed his conviction, stating it did not see in any of the "victim's" testimony "any resistance on her part to the sex acts" and "no fear as would overcome her attempt to resist or escape."

ISSUE: Can one establish that the sexual act was without the consent of the victim and thus constituted rape, by showing that the victim resisted or failed to resist because of a genuine, reasonably grounded fear?

HOLDING AND DECISION: (Murphy, C.J.) Yes. Lack of consent, which is an essential element of rape, is generally established through proof of resistance or by proof that the victim failed to resist because of fear. The degree of fear necessary to obviate the need to prove resistance, and thereby establish lack of consent, was defined in the following manner: "The kind of fear which would render resistance by a woman unnecessary to support a conviction of rape includes, but is not necessarily limited to, a fear of death or serious bodily harm, or a fear so extreme as to preclude resistance, or a fear which would

well nigh render her mind incapable of continuing to resist, or a fear that so overpowers her that she does not dare resist." It is clear that the fear had to be genuine, but undecided whether a real but unreasonable fear of imminent death or serious bodily harm would suffice. The vast majority of jurisdictions have required that the victim's fear be reasonably grounded in order to obviate the need for either proof of actual force on the part of the assailant or physical resistance on the part of the victim. In general, that is the correct standard. Such principles notwithstanding, it seems to this court that the court of special appeals was in error in this case in that it substituted its view of the evidence for that of the judge and jury. Just where persuasion ends and force begins in cases like the present is essentially a factual issue. Considering all of the evidence, with particular focus upon the actual force applied by Rusk (D) to the victim's neck, this court concludes that the jury could rationally find that the essential elements of second-degree rape had been established and that Rusk (D) was guilty of that offense beyond a reasonable doubt. Conviction affirmed.

DISSENT: (Cole, J.) In concluding that the reasonableness of the victim's fear was plainly a question of fact for the jury to determine, the majority has skipped over the crucial issue. It seems to me that whether the prosecutrix's fear is reasonable becomes a question only after the court determines that the defendant's conduct under the circumstances was reasonably calculated to give rise to a fear on her part to the extent that she was unable to resist. There is simply no evidence in this case to suggest that the actions taken by Rusk (D) were anything other than a pattern of conduct consistent with the ordinary seduction of a female acquaintance who at first suggests her disinclination. While the prosecutrix did claim she started to cry and that Rusk (D) "started lightly to choke" her, whatever that means it is obvious that the choking was not of any significance. There are no acts or conduct on the part of Rusk (D) to suggest that the prosecutrix's fears were created by Rusk (D) or that he made any objective, identifiable threats to her which would give rise to her failure to flee, summon help, scream, or make physical resistance. The State (P) simply failed to prove the essential element of force beyond a reasonable doubt. A prosecutrix cannot transform a seducer into a rapist by simply asserting that she was scared. While courts no longer require a female to resist to the utmost or to resist where resistance would be foolhardy, they do require her acquiescence in the act of intercourse to stem from fear generated by something of substance. A

Continued on next page.

female must resist unless the defendant has objectively manifested his intent to use physical force to accomplish his purpose. The law regards rape as a crime of violence. The majority today attenuates this proposition. It declares the innocence of an at best distraught young woman. It does not demonstrate the defendant's guilt of the crime of rape.

▶ *ANALYSIS*

There is no jurisdiction in this country that still adheres to the stringent traditional notion that the victim must have resisted "to the utmost." In its heyday, that notion led courts to insist that the victim resist to the extent of her physical capacity and that her struggle be continued throughout the encounter. The only case in which utmost resistance was not required was when the victim was in fear of grave harm. While lack of resistance might still be used by a defendant as evidence that the victim consented, some state codes and the Model Penal Code have taken the focus off of the victim's lack of consent and placed it on the actor's use of force in compelling her to submit to intercourse by defining the crime of rape in these terms.

■=■

Quicknotes

RAPE Unlawful sexual intercourse with a woman by a man by means of fear or force and without her consent.

REASONABLE DOUBT Standard of proof necessary to convict a defendant, requiring the absence of evidence that would cause a reasonable person to hesitate in making an important decision in his personal affairs.

■=■

State in the Interest of M.T.S.

State (P) v. Seventeen-year-old boy (P)

N.J. Sup. Ct., 129 N.J. 422, 609 A.2d 1266 (1992).

NATURE OF CASE: Appeal from reversal of a disposition of delinquency for the commission of sexual assault.

FACT SUMMARY: M.T.S. (D), a 17-year-old boy, engaged in sexual penetration of a 15-year-old girl to which she did not consent, but there was no evidence of unusual or extra force or threats to accomplish the act of penetration.

🏛 RULE OF LAW
The element of "physical force" in the crime of sexual assault is met simply by an act of nonconsensual penetration involving no more force than necessary to accomplish that result.

FACTS: M.T.S. (D), a 17-year-old boy, engaged in consensual kissing and heavy petting with a 15-year-old girl and thereafter engaged in actual sexual penetration of the girl to which she had not consented. There was no evidence or suggestion that M.T.S. (D) used any unusual or extra force or threats to accomplish the act of penetration. The trial court determined that M.T.S. (D) was delinquent for committing a sexual assault. The appellate court reversed the disposition of delinquency, concluding that nonconsensual penetration does not constitute sexual assault unless it is accompanied by some level of force more than that necessary to accomplish the penetration. The State (P) appealed.

ISSUE: Is the element of "physical force" in the crime of sexual assault met simply by an act of nonconsensual penetration involving no more force than necessary to accomplish that result?

HOLDING AND DECISION: (Handler, J.) Yes. The element of "physical force" in the crime of sexual assault is met simply by an act of nonconsensual penetration involving no more force than necessary to accomplish that result. Traditional rape law required that the state show both that force had been used and that the penetration had been against the woman's will. However, the New Jersey legislature has adopted new statutory provisions defining sexual assault as penetration accomplished by the use of "physical force" or "coercion" but without defining the two terms. Just as any unauthorized touching is a crime under traditional laws of assault and battery, so is any unauthorized sexual contact a crime under the reformed law of criminal sexual contact and so is any unauthorized sexual penetration a crime under the reformed law. Under the new law, the victim is no longer required to resist in order for the sexual penetration to be unlawful. Therefore, any act of sexual penetration engaged in by the defendant without the affirmative and freely given permission of the victim to the specific act of penetration constitutes the offense of sexual assault. A showing of force in addition to that entailed in the sexual contact itself is not required. Reversed.

▶ ANALYSIS

New Jersey is one of only a few states that permit non-consent, by itself, to be a sufficient showing of proof of sexual assault. Other states are not in agreement with the above decision. See, e.g., *Commonwealth v. Berkowitz*, 641 A.2d 1161 (Pa. 1994), in which the court determined that a victim of a rape need not resist but that a showing of physical force to establish lack of consent was still required. However, force need not be proved if the victim is under a certain age, is mentally incompetent, or has been deceived in some egregious fashion since under these circumstances, consent would be legally ineffective anyway.

■═■

Quicknotes

RAPE Unlawful sexual intercourse with a woman by a man by means of fear or force and without her consent.

■═■

M.C. v. Bulgaria

Bulgarian national (P) v. Bulgarian government (D)

Eur. Ct. H.R., 39272/98 (2003).

NATURE OF CASE: Application for damages by a Bulgarian national against the Bulgarian government for an alleged failure to enforce rape laws in conformity with international norms.

FACT SUMMARY: A Bulgarian girl who was almost 15-years-old claimed to have been raped by two men in Bulgaria. Bulgarian officials closed their investigation in her accusations when they found insufficient proof that she was physically forced to have sex with the men.

🏛 RULE OF LAW
A member state does not meet its obligations under the European Convention on Human Rights by closing a rape investigation for insufficient proof of physical force without also considering whether the victim was subjected to coercive circumstances.

FACTS: Two men, P. and A., allegedly raped M.C. (P), when she was 14 years and 10 months old. According to M.C. (P), the rapes occurred after she went to a disco one night with the two men and another man, and after they had taken her to a reservoir for a swim later that night despite her objections. Because M.C. (P) was older than 14 at the time of the alleged rapes, the criminal law in Bulgaria (D) defined rape as "sexual intercourse with a woman . . . who was compelled by force or threats." The Bulgarian authorities (D) closed their investigation into M.C.'s (P) allegations because they deemed the evidence of M.C.'s (P) physical resistance insufficient to warrant prosecution. M.C. (P) filed an application for damages against the Bulgarian government (D) in the European Court of Human Rights.

ISSUE: Does a member state meet its obligations under the European Convention on Human Rights by closing a rape investigation for insufficient proof of physical force without also considering whether the victim was subjected to coercive circumstances?

HOLDING AND DECISION: (Per curiam) No. A member state does not meet its obligations under the European Convention on Human Rights by closing a rape investigation for insufficient proof of physical force without out also considering whether the victim was subjected to coercive circumstances. The Bulgarian Supreme Court has interpreted the statute at issue in this case to include less than direct violence against a woman. That interpretation of Bulgarian law accords with international norms in both Europe and the United States: today, coercive circumstances, even in the absence of physical force, can make

sexual intercourse non-consensual as required in prosecutions for rape. The European Convention on Human Rights imposes positive obligations on member states to conform local law to the Convention's standards. In this case, Section 3 of the Convention provides that "[n]o one shall be subjected to torture or inhuman or degrading treatment or punishment," and Section 8 provides that "[e]veryone has the right to respect for his private . . . life. . . ." Requiring proof of physical resistance in a rape case, as the Bulgarian officials (D) did here, violates these provisions of the Convention. The authorities in this case did not pursue their investigation into circumstances that could have been sufficiently coercive to vitiate M.C.'s (P) consent under the recognized norms of international law and the Convention. In that failure, the Bulgarian authorities' (D) insufficient investigation played some role in causing M.C. (P) psychological trauma. [Damages awarded to the applicant.]

▶ ANALYSIS

In *M.C. v. Bulgaria*, the European Court of Human Rights awarded damages against a member state for failing to prosecute rape in compliance with contemporary international norms. The case does not turn on whether positive law in Bulgaria (D) was satisfactory; the Bulgarian Supreme Court's interpretation of the rape statute is acceptably broad. Instead, according to the European Court of Human Rights, the Bulgarian government's (D) shortcoming in this case was the narrow, outdated manner of enforcing the statute.

━━■

Quicknotes

DAMAGES Monetary compensation that may be awarded by the court to a party who has sustained injury or loss to his person, property or rights due to another party's unlawful act, omission or negligence.

RAPE Unlawful sexual intercourse with a woman by a man by means of fear or force and without her consent.

━━■

People v. Evans

State (P) v. Alleged rapist (D)

Sup. Ct., N.Y. County, Trial Term, 85 Misc. 2d 1088, 379 N.Y.S. 2d 912 (1975).

NATURE OF CASE: Prosecution for rape.

FACT SUMMARY: According to Evans (D), the words his "victim" misinterpreted as a threat by him—causing her to submit to sexual intercourse—were not so intended, but were part of his seduction of her.

🏛 RULE OF LAW
A defendant is not guilty of rape if words he uses in attempting to seduce a woman are misinterpreted as a threat by her so that she acquiesces to sexual intercourse.

FACTS: Evans (D) used the ruse that he was a psychologist doing an article and conducting a sociological experiment to persuade a 20-year-old college sophomore to come with him to an apartment. When she resisted his advances, he told her she had failed the experiment, pointing out she had come to a strange man's apartment and could not even be sure he was really a psychologist. He then made the statements, "I could kill you; I could rape you; I could hurt you physically." Trying another tactic, he gave her a story about how she reminded him of his lost love—who had driven her car off a cliff. Sexual intercourse took place, the girl later claiming Evans's (D) words had so frightened her that she had been afraid to resist. Evans (D) claimed he might be guilty of seduction, which was no crime, but was not guilty of rape in that he never intended to threaten her.

ISSUE: Is a defendant guilty of rape if the words he uses to seduce a woman are interpreted by her, but not meant by him, as a threat designed to "compel" her to engage in sexual intercourse without resistance?

HOLDING AND DECISION: (Greenfield, J.) No. If a defendant engages in fraud, trick, or stratagem to seduce a woman, it does not become rape because the words he used to achieve his goal are interpreted by her, but not meant by him, as a threat designed to "compel" her to engage in sexual intercourse without resistance. The controlling state of mind is that of the defendant who is charged with rape. If one who is attempting a seduction utters words which are taken as a threat by the person who hears them, but are not intended as a threat by the person who offers them, there would be no basis for finding the necessary criminal intent to establish culpability under the law. Since Evans's (D) statements are susceptible to diverse interpretations, the court cannot say beyond a reasonable doubt that the guilt of Evans (D) has been established with respect to the crime of rape. The court can find neither forcible compulsion nor threat beyond a reasonable doubt—despite Evans's (D) reprehensible conduct.

▶ ANALYSIS

Some jurisdictions abandoned the common-law approach, which was that seduction was not a criminal act, and made it a statutory offense. One primary difference between seduction and rape is that in seduction the woman's consent, either implied or explicit, is procured—although by artifice, deception, flattery, fraud, or promise.

Quicknotes

RAPE Unlawful sexual intercourse with a woman by a man by means of fear or force and without her consent.

REASONABLE DOUBT Standard of proof necessary to convict a defendant, requiring the absence of evidence that would cause a reasonable person to hesitate in making an important decision in his personal affairs.

Commonwealth v. Sherry

State (P) v. Convicted rapist (P)

Mass. Sup. Jud. Ct., 386 Mass. 682, 437 N.E. 2d 224 (1982).

NATURE OF CASE: Appeal of rape conviction.

FACT SUMMARY: Sherry (D), charged with rape, argued that he had believed the victim to have consented to intercourse.

🏛 RULE OF LAW
A subjective belief that the victim has consented is no defense to a rape charge.

FACTS: Sherry (D) and two male companions left a party with a woman. Whether she left voluntarily or was coerced was unclear. When the four arrived at the home of one of the men, they smoked marijuana and conversed for a while. Eventually the woman had intercourse with the three men, sequentially. The woman pressed charges, and the three were charged with rape. Sherry (D) and the other two defendants claimed that the woman had consented. The court refused to offer an instruction permitting a subjective belief in consent to be a defense. Sherry (D) and the others were convicted and appealed.

ISSUE: Is a subjective belief that the victim has consented, a defense to a rape charge?

HOLDING AND DECISION: (Liacos, J.) No. A subjective belief that the victim has consented is not a defense to a rape charge. It has never been held that the subjective mindset of an alleged perpetrator was crucial in passing upon consent; the prosecution would have a serious burden of proof were this so. Rather, it is proper for the jury to consider the entire sequence of events from an objective perspective. Here, the instruction the court gave did in fact create an objective standard, and this was proper. The defense of mistake of fact is not possible if the belief is unreasonable. Affirmed.

▶ ANALYSIS

There is no uniform rule on this issue among the jurisdictions. A fully subjective approach is found in few, if any, jurisdictions. Some permit a good-faith-belief-in-consent defense, but those that do require the good-faith belief to be reasonable.

━━━

Quicknotes

OBJECTIVE STANDARD A standard that is not personal to an individual but is dependent on some external source.

RAPE Unlawful sexual intercourse with a woman by a man by means of fear or force and without her consent.

SUBJECTIVE BELIEF A belief that is personal to an individual.

━━━

Commonwealth v. Fischer

State (P) v. Student rapist (D)

Pa. Super. Ct., 721 A.2d 1111 (1998).

NATURE OF CASE: Appeal on ruling in favor of rape victim on the issue of mens rea.

FACT SUMMARY: Fischer (D), a college student, engaged in intimate contact in a dorm room after which Fischer (D) was charged with and convicted of sexual assault, a decision which he later appealed on the basis that he should not be convicted if he believed the victim had given her consent.

🏛 RULE OF LAW
A defendant's subjective belief that a victim consented to sexual conduct is not a defense to the crime of rape.

FACTS: Fischer (D) and the victim were freshman students at the same college. They went into Fischer's (D) dorm room and engaged in intimate contact for a brief period before parting ways to eat dinner with separate groups of friends. Fischer (D) characterized this encounter as "rough sex" involving intimate contact, while the victim described the activity as light "kissing and fondling." After dinner, the two met again in Fischer's (D) room. Fischer (D) alleges he was encouraged by the victim to continue with the activity from the previous encounter, while the victim asserts that she was forcibly pushed onto the bed after protesting. Fischer (D) was charged with sexual assault. At trial, he asserted that he was sexually inexperienced and believed that the victim was a willing participant in the sexual encounters. In addition, Fischer (D) asserted that the victim's willing conduct did not make his actions "forcible" and that he desisted once the victim protested. The jury found Fischer (D) guilty, after which he filed this appeal, suggesting that his counsel at trial had provided ineffective assistance because he had failed to assert a mistake of fact defense based on Fischer's (D) belief that the victim had given her consent.

ISSUE: Is a defendant's subjective belief that a victim consented to sexual conduct a defense to the crime of rape?

HOLDING AND DECISION: (Beck, J.) No. A defendant's subjective belief that a victim consented to sexual conduct is not a defense to the crime of rape. When an individual uses threats or force to have sex with another person without that person's consent, that person commits the crime of rape. The issues of consent and forcible compulsion are complex, requiring an analysis of the psychological and physiological dimensions of the encounter. The degree of force required to constitute rape depends on the facts and particular circumstances of each case. Force vitiating consent may include psychological, moral, and intellectual force. In addition, the young age of a victim may void consent regardless of the circumstances. However, we cannot find support for Fischer's (D) assertion that the subjective belief of a defendant that consent has been given is an adequate defense, based on the applicable and binding precedent as enunciated in *Commonwealth v. Williams*, 439 A.2d 765 (Pa. Super. Ct. 1982). There, the court refused to create such a defense. This case is distinguishable from *Williams* because it involves intimate contact between acquaintances, where *Williams* involved a sexual encounter between a victim and a stranger. However, in both cases the victim alleged physical force and the defendant claimed he reasonably believed he had consent. As with the court in *Williams*, we do not recognize Fischer's (D) belief as an adequate basis for a defense based on mistake of fact, and are not persuaded that defense counsel performed ineffectively during trial. Affirmed.

▸ *ANALYSIS*

Although Fisher (D) failed to convince the court otherwise, the opinion does note that courts elsewhere have provided jury instructions regarding the reasonableness of a defendant's belief as to the consent of the victim. The court in the present case found these opinions convincing, but procedurally refused to depart from the specific ruling in *Williams*, which it found binding based on the aforementioned similarity of facts. As was mentioned in the opinion, the *Williams* court recognized that creation of laws and defenses were tasks for the legislature, and so refused to create what amounted to a new law. In cognizance of this, the court in the present case affirmed Fischer's (D) conviction because it could not fault Fischer's (D) attorney for failing to predict that such a law should be created.

■═■

Quicknotes

MENS REA Criminal intent.

MISTAKE OF FACT An unintentional mistake in knowing or recalling a fact without the will to deceive.

RAPE Unlawful sexual intercourse with a woman by a man by means of fear or force and without her consent.

■═■

State v. DeLawder

State (P) v. Convicted rapist (D)

Md. Ct. Spec. App., 28 Md. App. 212, 344 A.2d 446 (1975).

NATURE OF CASE: Action seeking post-conviction relief.

FACT SUMMARY: DeLawder (D) had tried to introduce evidence of the prosecutrix's prior sexual activity with others to show she was pregnant and fabricated the rape story out of fear of her mother's reaction.

RULE OF LAW
A defendant's constitutional right to engage in effective cross-examination is denied when he is not permitted to introduce evidence of the prosecutrix's prior sexual activities so as to establish an alleged bias, prejudice, or ulterior motive and thus attack her credibility as a witness.

FACTS: After being convicted of having carnal knowledge of a female under 14 years of age, DeLawder (D) sought post conviction relief. At his trial, he had not been permitted to introduce evidence of the "victim's" prior acts of sexual intercourse to support his contention that at the time of their alleged encounter, she was already pregnant as the result of voluntary sexual activity with others, that she feared telling her mother this, and that she therefore fabricated the story that DeLawder (D) had raped her.

ISSUE: Is it unconstitutional to deny a rape defendant the right to introduce evidence of the prosecutrix's prior sexual activities as they relate to an alleged bias, prejudice, or ulterior motive that would undermine her credibility as a witness?

HOLDING AND DECISION: (Orth, C.J.) Yes. A defendant has a constitutional right to engage in effective cross-examination of the witnesses against him. That right is denied when, as here, a defendant is kept from introducing evidence or asking questions concerning the past sexual activity of the prosecutrix as they relate to an alleged bias, prejudice, or ulterior motive that would undermine her credibility as a witness. Defense counsel should have been permitted to expose to the jury the facts from which jurors, as the sole triers of fact and credibility, could appropriately draw inferences relating to the reliability of the prosecutrix as a witness. The desirability that the prosecutrix fulfill her public duty to testify, free from embarrassment and with her reputation unblemished, must fall before the right of an accused to seek out the truth in the process of defending himself. The conviction must not be permitted to stand.

ANALYSIS

A Wisconsin court did not accept the same type of argument when advanced by a defendant who sought to introduce prior sexual history to show the prosecutrix had contracted a venereal disease from others and fabricated the rape accusation because she was afraid she had infected her boyfriend, *Milenovic v. State*, 86 Wis. 2d 272 (1978). In fact, it criticized the *DeLawder* court's "unwarranted assumption" that the prosecutrix's mother was unaware of her daughter's pregnancy at the time of the alleged encounter with the defendant.

Quicknotes
CREDIBILITY Believability; plausibility; whether or not a witness's testimony is believable.

RAPE Unlawful sexual intercourse with a woman by a man by means of fear or force and without her consent.

Government of the Virgin Islands v. Scuito

Government (P) v. Convicted rapist (D)

623 F.2d 869 (3d Cir. 1980).

NATURE OF CASE: Appeal from a conviction for forcible rape.

FACT SUMMARY: Scuito (D) charged that the trial judge had abused his discretion in not ordering a psychiatric examination of the woman who claimed that Scuito (D) had forcibly raped her.

🏛 RULE OF LAW
The decision whether or not to order a psychiatric examination of the prosecutrix in a rape case is one that is entrusted to the sound discretion of the trial judge.

FACTS: In appealing his conviction for forcible rape, Scuito (D) maintained that the trial judge abused or failed to exercise his discretion in denying his motion for a psychiatric examination of the prosecutrix. In an affidavit supporting the motion, Scuito's (D) attorney had made specific representations that community members had witnessed her "spaced out" behavior and knew she was in the habit of using controlled substances; that she had admitted at the first trial a devotion to the writings of Timothy Leary; that she habitually appeared in public in see-through top garments; and that this was all behavior indicative of a personality that fantasizes to extremes and indulges in and seeks altered states of consciousness.

ISSUE: Is it within the judge's discretion to decide whether the prosecutrix in a rape case should be ordered to undergo a psychiatric examination?

HOLDING AND DECISION: (Adams, J.) Yes. The decision to order an examination of the prosecutrix in a rape case is one that has been entrusted to the sound discretion of the trial judge in light of the particular facts of each case. It is not an unbounded discretion, for there are countervailing considerations weighing heavily against such an order: it may seriously impinge on a witness's right to privacy; the trauma that attends the role of complainant to sex offense charges is sharply increased by the indignity of such an examination; it could serve as a tool of harassment; and the impact of all these considerations may well deter the victim of such a crime from lodging any complaint at all. The trial judge did not abuse his discretion or fail to exercise it in this case when, in refusing to order such an examination, he relied on the spirit of Fed. R. Evid. 412—whose letter does not apply to the motion that was made, but whose purpose was to protect rape victims from the degrading and embarrassing disclosure of intimate details about their private lives. To the extent admissible, evidence of the prosecutrix's indulging in drugs or dressing provocatively could be introduced by direct evidence rather than expert testimony of a psychiatrist. Affirmed.

▶ ANALYSIS

Wigmore has taken the extreme position that "No judge should let a sex offense charge go to the jury unless the female complainant's social history and mental makeup have been examined and testified by a qualified physician." No jurisdiction has followed his suggestion.

■=■

Quicknotes

RAPE Unlawful sexual intercourse with a woman by a man by means of fear or force and without her consent.

RIGHT TO PRIVACY The violation of an individual's right to be protected against unwarranted interference in his personal affairs, falling into one of four categories: (1) appropriating the individual's likeness or name for commercial benefit; (2) intrusion into the individual's seclusion; (3) public disclosure of private facts regarding the individual; and (4) disclosure of facts placing the individual in a false light.

■=■

Homicide

Quick Reference Rules of Law

Commonwealth v. Carroll

State (P) v. Murderer (D)

Pa. Sup. Ct., 412 Pa. 525, 194 A.2d 911 (1963).

NATURE OF CASE: Murder trial.

FACT SUMMARY: Carroll (D) shot his wife in the back of the head following a violent argument.

🏛 RULE OF LAW
The specific intent to kill, which is necessary to prove first-degree murder, may be found from a defendant's words or conduct or from the attendant circumstances together with all reasonable inferences therefrom, and from the intentional use of a deadly weapon on a vital part of the body of another human being.

FACTS: Carroll's (D) wife suffered a fractured skull while attempting to leave his car during the course of an argument. This allegedly led to a mental disorder, which was diagnosed as a schizoid personality type. When he selected to attend an electronics school requiring him to be absent for nine days, the couple had a violent argument. Later that night he shot her in the back of the head. Carroll (D) pled guilty to a murder indictment. He was found guilty of first-degree murder and sentenced to life imprisonment. Carroll (D) appealed.

ISSUE: May the specific intent to kill, which is necessary to prove first-degree murder, be found from a defendant's words or conduct or from the attendant circumstances together with all reasonable inferences therefrom, and from the intentional use of a deadly weapon on a vital part of the body of another human being?

HOLDING AND DECISION: (Bell, C.J.) Yes. The specific intent to kill, which is necessary to prove first-degree murder, may be found from a defendant's words or conduct or from the attendant circumstances together with all reasonable inferences therefrom, and from the intentional use of a deadly weapon on a vital part of the body of another human being. Carroll (D) argued that the crime amounted only to second-degree murder. Here the evidence clearly supports a finding of first-degree murder. Whether the intent to kill and the killing were within a brief space of time or a long space of time is immaterial if the killing was in fact intentional, willful, deliberate and premeditated. Affirmed.

▎ ANALYSIS

This case stands for the proposition that "no time is too short" to prove premeditation.

Quicknotes

FIRST-DEGREE MURDER The willful killing of another person with deliberation and premeditation; first-degree murder also encompasses those situations in which a person is killed within the perpetration of, or attempt to perpetrate, specified felonies.

PREMEDITATION The contemplation of undertaking an activity prior to action; any length of time is sufficient.

SECOND-DEGREE MURDER The unlawful killing of another person, without premeditation, and characterized by either an intent to kill or by a reckless disregard for human life.

State v. Guthrie

State (P) v. Murderer (D)

W.Va. Sup. Ct. of App., 194 W.Va. 657, 461 S.E.2d 163 (1995).

NATURE OF CASE: Murder case.

FACT SUMMARY: Guthrie (D) stabbed a co-worker who poked fun at him.

🏛 RULE OF LAW
There must be some evidence that the defendant considered and weighed his decision to kill in order for the state to establish premeditation and deliberation under the West Virginia first-degree murder statute.

FACTS: Farley, a co-worker of defendant, poked fun at Guthrie (D) who appeared to be in a bad mood. Farley snapped him with a dishtowel several times on the nose and Guthrie (D) became enraged. He stabbed Farley in the neck and killed him. He appealed the jury verdict finding him guilty of first-degree murder on the basis that the jury instructions were improper because the terms willful, deliberate, and premeditated were equated with a mere intent to kill.

ISSUE: Must there be some evidence that the defendant considered and weighed his decision to kill in order for the state to establish premeditation and deliberation under the West Virginia first-degree murder statute?

HOLDING AND DECISION: (Cleckley, J.) Yes. There must be some evidence that the defendant considered and weighed his decision to kill in order for the state to establish premeditation and deliberation under the West Virginia first-degree murder statute. Here the jury instructions confuse premeditation with the intent to kill. Although premeditation and deliberation are not measured by any particular time period, there must be some period between the formation of the intent to kill and the actual killing, which indicates that the killing is by prior calculation and design. Reversed and remanded for a new trial.

▶ ANALYSIS

Compare this case with the decision in *Commonwealth v. Carroll*, 412 Pa. 525 (1963). There the court concluded that "no time is too short" to form the requisite premeditation for a finding of first-degree murder.

Quicknotes

DELIBERATION Reflection; the pondering and weighing of the consequences of an action.

FIRST-DEGREE MURDER The willful killing of another person with deliberation and premeditation; first-degree murder also encompasses those situations in which a person is killed within the perpetration of, or attempt to perpetrate, specified felonies.

PREMEDITATION The contemplation of undertaking an activity prior to action; any length of time is sufficient.

Girouard v. State

Convicted murderer (D) v. State (P)

Md. Ct. App., 321 Md. 532, 583 A.2d 718 (1991).

NATURE OF CASE: Appeal from conviction of second-degree murder.

FACT SUMMARY: Girouard (D) was convicted of second-degree murder after killing his wife during an argument in which only words were exchanged.

🏛 RULE OF LAW
Words alone do not constitute adequate provocation to mitigate murder to manslaughter.

FACTS: Girouard (D) stabbed and killed his wife after an angry argument in which his wife ridiculed his sexual ability, told him that she did not love him, and demanded a divorce. She also told him that she had filed charges against him and that he would likely be court-martialed. After this, Girouard (D) lunged at his wife with a kitchen knife and stabbed her nineteen times. He was convicted of second-degree murder and appealed.

ISSUE: Do words alone constitute adequate provocation to mitigate murder to manslaughter?

HOLDING AND DECISION: (Cole, J.) No. Words alone do not constitute adequate provocation to mitigate murder to manslaughter. Traditionally the provocation to mitigate murder to manslaughter has been limited only to the circumstances of extreme assault or battery upon the defendant; mutual combat; defendant's illegal arrest; injury or serious abuse of a close relative of the defendant; or the sudden discovery of a spouse's adultery. Provocation in this case was not enough to cause a reasonable man to stab his provoker nineteen times. There must be not simply provocation in psychological fact, but one of certain fairly well-defined classes of provocation recognized as being adequate as a matter of law. There is no reason for a holding in favor of those who find that the easiest way to end a domestic dispute is by killing the offending spouse. Affirmed.

▶ *ANALYSIS*

Only a few types of provocation were considered adequate at early common law because "adequate provocation" was an issue of law to be determined by the judge. The current trend is to treat "adequate provocation" as an issue of fact that would then be determined by a jury. This would allow a jury to decide on a case-by-case basis what provocation would be sufficient to cause the ordinary person to act rashly.

Quicknotes

ADEQUATE PROVOCATION Provocation such that would cause an ordinary reasonable man to set aside his judgment; a defense to a claim of premeditation.

MANSLAUGHTER The killing of another person without premeditation, deliberation or with the intent to kill or to commit a felony, which may be reasonably expected to result in death or serious bodily injury; manslaughter is characterized by reckless conduct or by some adequate provocation on the part of the actor, as determined by a subjective standard.

REASONABLE PERSON STANDARD The standard of care exercised by a hypothetical person who possesses the intelligence, education, knowledge, attention, and judgment required by society of its members when governing behavior; the standard applies to a person's judgment when determining breach of a duty under the theory of negligence.

SECOND-DEGREE MURDER The unlawful killing of another person, without premeditation, and characterized by either an intent to kill or by a reckless disregard for human life.

Maher v. People

Assailant (D) v. State (P)

Mich. Sup. Ct., 10 Mich. 212, 81 Am. Dec. 781 (1862).

NATURE OF CASE: Appeal from conviction for assault with intent to kill.

FACT SUMMARY: The court rejected evidence offered by Maher (D) which tended to show that shortly before the assault, Hunt, the victim, had intercourse with Maher's (D) wife.

🏛 RULE OF LAW
If a killing, though intentional, is committed in the heat of passion produced by a reasonable provocation before a reasonable time has lapsed for the passion to cool and is the result of temporary excitement rather than one's personal depravity, it is manslaughter rather than murder.

FACTS: Maher (D) was charged with an assault with an intent to kill Hunt. Maher (D) offered evidence showing that he saw his wife and Hunt go into the woods half an hour before he assaulted Hunt. When they came out, he followed Hunt and attacked him. On his way to do so, a friend informed him that Hunt and Maher's (D) wife had had sexual intercourse in the woods the preceding day. The evidence was rejected by the court. Maher (D) was charged with assault with intent to kill.

ISSUE: Is the question of what constitutes a reasonable provocation sufficient to reduce a killing from murder to manslaughter a question of fact to be determined by the facts of each case?

HOLDING AND DECISION: (Christiancy, J.) Yes. If a killing, though intentional, is committed in the heat of passion, produced by a reasonable provocation and before a reasonable time has lapsed for the passion to cool and is the result of temporary excitement rather than one's personal depravity, it is manslaughter rather than murder. In determining what constitutes reasonable provocation, the standard to be used is that of the average reasonable person. This is essentially a question of fact and is to be decided with reference to the facts of each case. The rejected evidence in this case tends to show adulterous relations between Hunt and Maher's (D) wife shortly before the assault. This is sufficient evidence of provocation to go to the jury. Judgment reversed. A new trial is granted.

DISSENT: (Manning, J.) To reduce a homicide to manslaughter, the provocation must have occurred in the defendant's presence.

▌ ANALYSIS

Contrary to *Maher*, the traditional common-law view did not permit a jury to return a verdict of manslaughter in all situations in which it found reasonable provocation. Only in certain narrowly-defined circumstances could a jury find "legally sufficient" provocation. The principal "legally sufficient" provocation was an actual physical battery, although there were others such as personal witnessing of a wife in the act of adultery. This view is generally followed in the United States, although there is some movement toward expanding legally sufficient provocation to include words.

Quicknotes

ASSAULT The intentional placing of another in fear of immediate bodily injury.

HEAT OF PASSION DEFENSE A defense utilized in order to reduce a charge of murder to manslaughter, based on the theory that the perpetrator was under adequate provocation so that he was incapable of forming the premeditation necessary for first-degree murder.

MANSLAUGHTER The killing of another person without premeditation, deliberation or with the intent to kill or to commit a felony, which may be reasonably expected to result in death or serious bodily injury; manslaughter is characterized by reckless conduct or by some adequate provocation on the part of the actor, as determined by a subjective standard.

REASONABLE PROVOCATION Provocation such that would cause an ordinary reasonable man to set aside his judgment; a defense to a claim of premeditation.

People v. Casassa

State (P) v. Convicted murderer (D)

N.Y. Ct. App., 49 N.Y.2d 668, 404 N.E.2d 1310 (1980).

NATURE OF CASE: Appeal of conviction for second-degree murder.

FACT SUMMARY: Casassa (D), charged with murder, contended that whether he was under extreme disturbance should be analyzed subjectively.

🏛 RULE OF LAW
Whether a defendant was so emotionally disturbed as to lessen murder to manslaughter involves both an objective and subjective analysis.

FACTS: Casassa (D) became romantically obsessed with a neighbor. After she consistently rejected his advances, he confronted her with a knife, stabbing her to death. He was charged with murder. The trial court rejected his argument that whether he was under an extreme emotional disturbance sufficient to mitigate the homicide to manslaughter should be viewed from an entirely subjective viewpoint. Instead, the court, sitting without a jury, found the reaction to have been so peculiar to Casassa (D) that it would have been unreasonable to mitigate the crime. The court therefore convicted Casassa (D) of second-degree murder. Casassa (D) appealed.

ISSUE: Does the question of whether a defendant was so emotionally disturbed as to lessen murder to manslaughter involve both an objective and subjective analysis?

HOLDING AND DECISION: (Jasen, J.) Yes. Whether a defendant was so emotionally disturbed as to lessen murder to manslaughter involves both an objective and subjective analysis. The applicable penal code provision permits the affirmative defense where "the defendant acted under the influence of extreme emotional disturbance for which there was a reasonable explanation or excuse." This language clearly introduces both subjective and objective elements into the analysis. It is subjective as to whether or not the defendant was in fact under an extreme emotional disturbance. It is objective as to whether or not the disturbance was reasonable. The court here appears to have used this standard, and found Casassa's (D) disturbance not to have been based on reasonable grounds. This was a proper analysis. Affirmed.

▌ ANALYSIS

The language adopted by the New York Legislature here basically comports with the Model Penal Code. The test here can be seen to have grown out of the classic "heat of passion" manslaughter test. The test here differs from heat of passion mainly in that the homicide does not necessarily have to be basically contemporaneous to the triggering event, as heat of passion almost always requires.

■≡■

Quicknotes

AFFIRMATIVE DEFENSE A manner of defending oneself against a claim not by denying the truth of the charge but by the introduction of some evidence challenging the plaintiff's right to bring the claim.

HEAT OF PASSION DEFENSE A defense utilized in order to reduce a charge of murder to manslaughter, based on the theory that the perpetrator was under adequate provocation so that he was incapable of forming the premeditation necessary for first-degree murder.

MANSLAUGHTER The killing of another person without premeditation, deliberation or with the intent to kill or to commit a felony, which may be reasonably expected to result in death or serious bodily injury; manslaughter is characterized by reckless conduct or by some adequate provocation on the part of the actor, as determined by a subjective standard.

SECOND-DEGREE MURDER The unlawful killing of another person, without premeditation, and characterized by either an intent to kill or by a reckless disregard for human life.

■≡■

Commonwealth v. Welansky

State (P) v. Convicted murderer (D)

Mass. Sup. Jud. Ct., 316 Mass. 383, 55 N.E.2d 902 (1944).

NATURE OF CASE: Appeal from conviction for involuntary manslaughter.

FACT SUMMARY: Welansky (D), owner of a nightclub, had failed to alleviate serious fire hazards that existed prior to a deadly blaze that erupted one night.

RULE OF LAW
A manslaughter conviction may be based on omissions as well as affirmative acts.

FACTS: Welansky (D) owned a fashionable Boston nightclub. Access was limited, with only one main door, and the few emergency exits were either blocked or barred so as to prevent dinner patrons from leaving without paying. One evening a fire broke out, which quickly swept through the overcrowded facilities. Escape proved impossible for many, and dozens of patrons and employees were killed. Welansky (D) was convicted of involuntary manslaughter, and he appealed.

ISSUE: May a manslaughter conviction be based on omissions as well as affirmative acts?

HOLDING AND DECISION: (Lummus, J.) Yes. A manslaughter conviction may be based on omissions as well as affirmative acts. Involuntary manslaughter consists of wanton or reckless conduct resulting in a homicide. Where one has a duty to act, such recklessness may exist in the failure to perform the duty. Here, Welansky (D) was under a duty to provide for the safety of his patrons. The jury found his failure to have done so to have gone beyond mere negligence into recklessness. Considering the numerous safety hazards that existed at the club, the record supports the verdict. Affirmed.

ANALYSIS

The "wanton and reckless" standard is a common one among the jurisdictions for supporting manslaughter. It implies something worse than a mere failure to act prudently, yet falls short of intentional behavior. It is often defined as a conscious disregard of a known risk.

Quicknotes

INVOLUNTARY MANSLAUGHTER The killing of another person without premeditation or deliberation or with the intent to kill or to commit a felony, which may be reasonably expected to result in death or serious bodily injury; involuntary manslaughter is characterized by reckless conduct in the commission of a lawful act, or by the commission of an unlawful act that is not a felony, but which leads to the killing of another.

OMISSION The failure to perform an act or obligation that one is required to perform by law.

RECKLESSNESS The conscious disregard of substantial and justifiable risk.

People v. Hall

State (P) v. Manslaughter defendant (D)

Colo. Sup. Ct., 999 P.2d 207 (2000).

NATURE OF CASE: A state's appeal from the trial court's dismissal of a charge of felony reckless manslaughter.

FACT SUMMARY: A trained, experienced skier collided with and killed another skier on Vail Mountain in Colorado.

🏛 RULE OF LAW
The People have probable cause to charge felony reckless manslaughter where a death caused by a defendant who was a trained, experienced skier occurred while the defendant was clearly skiing too fast for the circumstances.

FACTS: Hall (D), an employee of a ski resort and a very experienced skier, killed another skier when the two collided on Vail Mountain. The People (P) charged Hall (D) with felony reckless manslaughter, and Hall (D) moved to dismiss. The trial court granted the motion, finding that the charged conduct was not sufficiently dangerous to support the charge. The intermediate appellate court affirmed, reasoning that Hall's (D) conduct was not "reckless" because his skiing too fast for conditions did not make the victim's death "at least more likely than not." The two lower courts, in other words, agreed with Hall (D) that the People (P) lacked probable cause to charge felony reckless manslaughter. The People (P) requested further review in the Colorado Supreme Court.

ISSUE: Do the People have probable cause to charge felony reckless manslaughter where a death caused by a defendant who was a trained, experienced skier occurred while the defendant was clearly skiing too fast for the circumstances?

HOLDING AND DECISION: (Bender, J.) Yes. The People have probable cause to charge felony reckless manslaughter where a death caused by a defendant who was a trained, experienced skier occurred while the defendant was clearly skiing too fast for the circumstances. Colorado statute defines reckless manslaughter as "recklessly caus[ing] the death of another person." By statute, conduct is "reckless" when the alleged actor must have consciously disregarded a substantial and unjustifiable risk that death could result from the person's actions. Interpreting the evidence most favorably to the People (P) [as review on the non-movant's appeal following dismissal requires], the record shows that the People (P) did have probable cause to charge Hall (D) with felony reckless manslaughter. Even a less-than-50-percent risk of death can be sufficiently substantial if the case's particular circumstances so warrant. Here, Hall's (D) clearly excessive speed, lack of control, and bad technique constitute the rare but substantial risk that death would result from skiing. Second, because Hall's (D) fast skiing served no purpose but his own pleasure, the substantial risk of death was not justified. Third, Hall's (D) extreme violation of his statutory duty of care while skiing could constitute the gross deviation from the standard of care required for the charge. Finally, fourth, Hall's (D) experience and training could support a reasonable inference that he consciously disregarded the substantial risk of death. Reversed.

▶ ANALYSIS

The Colorado Supreme Court's first holding in *Hall*—that a risk of death can be sufficiently "substantial" even if it is less than 50 percent probable—establishes that less than preponderance of evidence on the recklessness element can support probable cause to charge felony reckless manslaughter. That holding, however, was also qualified by requiring an analysis of each case's particular facts.

■=■

Quicknotes

MANSLAUGHTER The killing of another person without premeditation, deliberation or with the intent to kill or to commit a felony, which may be reasonably expected to result in death or serious bodily injury; manslaughter is characterized by reckless conduct or by some adequate provocation on the part of the actor, as determined by a subjective standard.

PROBABLE CAUSE A reasonable basis for believing that a crime has been committed.

■=■

State v. Williams

State (P) v. Convicted murderer (D)

Wash. Ct. App., 4 Wash. App. 908, 484 P.2d 1167 (1971).

NATURE OF CASE: Appeal of manslaughter conviction.

FACT SUMMARY: Mr. and Mrs. Williams (D) failed to obtain medical aid for their 17-month-old child and, as a result, he died.

🏛 RULE OF LAW
Where the failure of a person to act while under the duty to do so is the proximate cause of the death of another, that person may be convicted of involuntary manslaughter, even though his conduct was no more than ordinary negligence.

FACTS: Mrs. Williams (D) had a son by a previous marriage before she married Mr. Williams (D). When the lad, only 17 months old, developed a toothache, neither she nor her husband considered it serious enough to seek out medical help. As the tooth became worse and abscessed, however, the Williamses (D) became apprehensive but did not seek medical (or dental) care for the boy, fearing that the welfare department might take him away if they saw how bad he looked. Eventually, the boy developed gangrene (the smell from which was clearly noticeable), and pneumonia, from which he died about ten days later. The Williamses (D) were convicted of manslaughter on these facts. They appealed.

ISSUE: May ordinary negligence serve as the basis for convicting someone of involuntary manslaughter?

HOLDING AND DECISION: (Horowitz, C.J.) Yes. Where the failure of a person to act while under a duty to do so is the proximate cause of the death of another, that person may be convicted of involuntary manslaughter, even though his conduct was no more than ordinary negligence. There is no question but that the Williamses (D) were under a duty to obtain medical care for their seriously ill son, and their fear of the welfare department does not excuse this duty. The tough question here is whether the seriousness of the child's illness became sufficiently apparent to them early enough for their failure to do anything about it to be declared the proximate cause of the boy's death. Medical experts, however, testified that the gangrenous condition of the boy's cheek must have been apparent (both by sight and smell) to his parents for some ten days before he died. Clearly, they were on notice as to the seriousness of their son's illness in time to prevent him from dying of it. Conviction affirmed.

▶ ANALYSIS

This case points up a modern departure from the common-law rule that involuntary manslaughter required an act of gross negligence (i.e., criminal negligence). Ordinary negligence may arise either by act or, as above, by omission while under a duty to act. As in tort, its general formulation is the "failure of a man of reasonable prudence to exercise due care under the circumstances." Note, however, that this "objective" (i.e., what a reasonable man would do) standard runs the risk of undermining individualized justice by sanctioning punishment, regardless of the subjective knowledge of the wrongdoer. In *Williams*, for example, it appeared that the parents were illiterates—wholly ignorant of the most rudimentary principles of health care—who honestly did not know their son was in trouble.

Quicknotes

GROSS NEGLIGENCE The intentional failure to perform a duty with reckless disregard of the consequences.

INVOLUNTARY MANSLAUGHTER The killing of another person without premeditation or deliberation or with the intent to kill or to commit a felony, which may be reasonably expected to result in death or serious bodily injury; involuntary manslaughter is characterized by reckless conduct in the commission of a lawful act, or by the commission of an unlawful act that is not a felony, but which leads to the killing of another.

NEGLIGENCE Conduct falling below the standard of care that a reasonable person would demonstrate under similar conditions.

OMISSION The failure to perform an act or obligation that one is required to perform by law.

PROXIMATE CAUSE The natural sequence of events without which an injury would not have been sustained.

Commonwealth v. Malone

State (P) v. Convicted murderer (D)

Pa. Sup. Ct., 354 Pa. 180, 47 A.2d 445 (1946).

NATURE OF CASE: Appeal from conviction of second-degree murder.

FACT SUMMARY: Malone (D), aged 17, killed his friend by shooting him in the head during a game of "Russian poker."

🏛 RULE OF LAW

When an individual commits an act of gross recklessness for which he must reasonably anticipate that death to another is likely to result, he exhibits that wickedness of disposition and cruelty that constitutes the malice required for a charge of second-degree murder.

FACTS: Malone (D), aged 17, obtained a gun. His friend, Long, aged 13, obtained a cartridge. Malone (D) suggested they play Russian poker and Long consented. Malone (D) put the gun to Long's head, fired three times, and killed him. They were on friendly terms at the time, and Malone (D) testified that he had no intention of harming Long. Malone (D) contended he was only guilty of involuntary manslaughter.

ISSUE: When an individual commits an act of gross recklessness for which he must reasonably anticipate that death to another is likely to result, does he exhibit that wickedness of disposition and cruelty that constitutes the malice required for a charge of second-degree murder?

HOLDING AND DECISION: (Maxey, C.J.) Yes. When an individual commits an act of gross recklessness for which he must reasonably anticipate that death to another is likely to result, he exhibits that wickedness of disposition and cruelty that constitutes the malice required for a charge of second-degree murder. The malice on the part of a killer is not necessarily malevolent to the deceased particularly but "any evil design in general, the dictate of a wicked, depraved and malignant heart." The killing of Long by Malone (D) resulted from an act intentionally done by Malone (D) in reckless and wanton disregard of the consequences. The killing was therefore murder, for malice is evidenced by the intentional doing of an uncalled-for act in callous disregard of its likely effect on others. The fact that there was no motive for this murder does not exculpate Malone (D). Affirmed.

▶ ANALYSIS

Malone (D) had argued for a lesser charge of manslaughter. Most jurisdictions apply the rule here that second-degree murder occurs when the defendant acted without premeditation but with extreme disregard for human life.

■■■

Quicknotes

MALICE The intention to commit an unlawful act without justification or excuse.

SECOND-DEGREE MURDER The unlawful killing of another person, without premeditation, and characterized by either an intent to kill or by a reckless disregard for human life.

■■■

United States v. Fleming

Federal government (P) v. Convicted murderer (D)

739 F.2d 945 (4th Cir. 1984).

NATURE OF CASE: Appeal from conviction for second-degree murder.

FACT SUMMARY: Fleming (D) was convicted of murder subsequent to a vehicular homicide without evidence of intent to kill.

🏛 RULE OF LAW
Second-degree murder does not require an intent to kill.

FACTS: Fleming (D), with a blood alcohol level of over .30, drove for several miles at speeds of over 50 mph in excess of the posted limit, at times driving on the wrong side of the road to avoid traffic. He lost control of his vehicle and hit another vehicle head-on, killing the occupant. He was tried and convicted of second-degree murder. He appealed, contending that the record could support only a manslaughter conviction.

ISSUE: Does second-degree murder require an intent to kill?

HOLDING AND DECISION: (Winter, C.J.) No. Second-degree murder does not require an intent to kill. The mental state required for murder is "malice aforethought." This standard does not require an intent to kill; it may also be satisfied by wanton conduct grossly deviating from a reasonable standard of care such that it may be inferred that the defendant was aware of a serious risk of death or serious bodily harm. Here, the record is clear that Fleming's (D) conduct went beyond merely driving under the influence; the driving was so reckless that a serious accident was highly probable. The jury found this to constitute malice aforethought, and the record supports this finding. Affirmed.

▌ *ANALYSIS*

There is a good deal of overlap between involuntary manslaughter and second-degree murder. They both involve wanton and reckless conduct. The distinction is not clear and varies among the jurisdictions. The risk of harm and the defendant's awareness thereof appear to be the crucial factors, but where involuntary manslaughter ends and second-degree murder begins is not clear.

■■■

Quicknotes

MALICE AFORETHOUGHT The intention to commit an unlawful act without justification or excuse.

MANSLAUGHTER The killing of another person without premeditation, deliberation or with the intent to kill or to commit a felony, which may be reasonably expected to result in death or serious bodily injury; manslaughter is characterized by reckless conduct or by some adequate provocation on the part of the actor, as determined by a subjective standard.

SECOND-DEGREE MURDER The unlawful killing of another person, without premeditation, and characterized by either an intent to kill or by a reckless disregard for human life.

WANTON AND RECKLESS Unlawful intentional or reckless conduct without regard to the consequences.

■■■

Regina v. Serné

Government (P) v. Arsonist (D)

Central Criminal Court, 16 Cox Crim. Cas. 311 (1887).

NATURE OF CASE: Indictment for murder.

FACT SUMMARY: It was alleged that Serné (D) set a house on fire and caused his son to burn to death.

🏛 RULE OF LAW
Any act known to be dangerous to life and likely, in itself, to cause death, done for the purpose of committing a felony, and which causes death, is murder.

FACTS: It was alleged that Serné (D) deliberately set his house on fire to collect insurance on it. Serné (D), his wife, two daughters, two sons, and a servant were in the house at the time of the fire. One son burned to death.

ISSUE: Is one guilty of murder who commits an act, known to be dangerous to life and likely to cause death, when the act is a felony and when the commission of that act causes death?

HOLDING AND DECISION: (Stephen, J.) Yes. The law that says any act done with the intent to commit a felony and which causes death amounts to murder should be narrowed. It is more reasonable to say that any act known to be dangerous to life and likely to cause death, done for the purpose of committing a felony, and which causes death, should be murder. It is alleged that Serné (D) deliberately set fire to his house while other people were sleeping in it and that he must have known that he was placing all of those people in a deadly risk. If these alleged facts are true, it does not matter whether Serné (D) set fire to his house with his family in it and a boy burned to death. He is as guilty of murder as if he had stabbed the boy. [Verdict, not guilty.]

▌ *ANALYSIS*

At early common law one whose conduct brought about an unintended death in the commission of a felony was guilty of murder. Today, the law of felony murder varies substantially throughout the United States, largely as a result of efforts to limit the scope of the rule. Some U.S. jurisdictions have limited the rule by permitting its use only as to certain types of felonies. Others have done so by a more strict interpretation of the requirement of proximate cause. Some give a narrower construction of the time period during which the felony is being committed, and others require that the underlying felony be independent of the homicide.

Quicknotes

MURDER Unlawful killing of another person either with deliberation and premeditation or by conduct demonstrating a reckless disregard for human life.

PROXIMATE CAUSE The natural sequence of events without which an injury would not have been sustained.

People v. Phillips

State (P) v. Chiropractor (D)

Cal. Sup. Ct., 64 Cal.2d 574, 414 P.2d 553 (1966).

NATURE OF CASE: Appeal from conviction for second-degree murder.

FACT SUMMARY: Phillips (D), a chiropractor, persuaded a child's parents not to have her submit to an operation for cancer, but to have her treated by him. She died as a result.

RULE OF LAW
Only felonies which are inherently dangerous to human life can support the application of the felony murder rule.

FACTS: A medical center told a child's parents that immediate removal of the child's cancerous eye was necessary to save or prolong her life. Phillips (D), a chiropractor, induced the parents not to consent to the operation and told them he could cure the child without surgery. He charged $700 for his treatment. The child died. It is argued that since the death occurred in the perpetration of a felony (i.e., grand theft) Phillips (D) is guilty of felony murder.

ISSUE: Can one be found guilty of felony murder for death caused by the perpetration of a felony which is not inherently dangerous?

HOLDING AND DECISION: (Tobriner, J.) No. Only felonies which are in themselves, inherently dangerous to human life can support the application of the felony murder rule. Grand theft by false pretenses is not such a felony. The prosecution argued that in determining whether the felony committed by Phillips (D) was inherently dangerous, the court should look to the facts of this case and hold that Phillips's (D) conduct was inherently dangerous. To do so would mean that the felony murder rule could be applied to the perpetration of any felony during which a defendant may have acted in such a manner as to endanger life. In assessing the danger to human life inherent in any felony, we look to the elements of the felony in the abstract, not the particular facts of the case. Reversed.

ANALYSIS

According to Professor LaFave, the approach applied in *Phillips* is incorrect if the purpose of the felony murder rule is to hold felons accountable for unintended deaths caused by their dangerous conduct. "If the armed robber is to be held guilty of felony murder because of a death caused by the accidental firing of her gun, it seems no more harsh to apply the felony murder rule to the thief whose fraudulent scheme includes inducing the victim to forego a life-prolonging operation." He adds, however, that

the rule is more understandable if viewed as an attempt by courts to limit the scope of the felony murder rule.

Quicknotes

FELONY MURDER RULE Common law rule that the unlawful killing of another human being while in the commission of, or attempted commission of, specified felonies constitutes murder.

INHERENTLY DANGEROUS FELONY In some jurisdictions, invocation of the felony murder rule will only occur if the underlying felony being committed is inherently dangerous.

SECOND-DEGREE MURDER The unlawful killing of another person, without premeditation, and characterized by either an intent to kill or by a reckless disregard for human life.

Hines v. State

Felony murderer (D) v. State (P)

Ga. Sup. Ct., 578 S.E.2d 868 (2003).

NATURE OF CASE: Appeal from a conviction for felony murder.

FACT SUMMARY: While hunting with a friend, a man mistook his friend for a turkey and shot and killed him.

🏛 RULE OF LAW
Possession of a firearm by a convicted felon can be an inherently dangerous felony that serves as the predicate felony for felony murder.

FACTS: Robert Lee Hines (D), a convicted felon, went turkey hunting with several of his friends and relatives. Toward dusk, Hines (D) heard a turkey gobble in heavy foliage about eighty feet away and saw it fan out. He shot—and only then learned that he had mistaken one of his friends for a turkey. Hines's (D) friend died from the shot. The State (P) charged Hines (D) with felony murder, using a charge of possession of a firearm by a convicted felon as the predicate felony supporting the felony-murder charge. At trial, evidence showed that Hines (D) had been drinking both before and during the hunting trip, that he knew that other hunters were nearby but did not know exactly where they were, and that he did not completely identify the object of shot as a turkey before he fired the shot. The jury convicted Hines (D) of felony murder. Hines (D) appealed.

ISSUE: Can possession of a firearm by a convicted felon be an inherently dangerous felony that serves as the predicate felony for felony murder?

HOLDING AND DECISION: (Fletcher, C.J.) Yes. Possession of a firearm by a convicted felon can be an inherently dangerous felony that serves as the predicate felony for felony murder. This case differs from *Ford v. State*, 423 S.E.2d 255 (Ga. 1992), in several ways: Hines (D) intentionally fired the fatal shot, he was drinking before and during the course of conduct that resulted in the death, he knew that potential victims were nearby, and he knew that the shot he took was not safe. These circumstances demonstrate that Hines's (D) possession of a firearm as a convicted felon was an inherently dangerous activity that can support felony murder. Affirmed.

DISSENT: (Sears, J.) Hines's (D) possession of a firearm here was not an inherently dangerous activity within the meaning of *Ford*, a case that did not establish a test for identifying inherently dangerous activities. Properly understood, a predicate felony for felony murder is an inherently dangerous activity if it causes "a high probability that a human death will result." Here, Hines's (D) possession of

the firearm was not inherently dangerous, though it could be seen as negligent. The sentence of life in prison should be reserved for persons whose moral culpability warrants such severe punishment. This case does not merit that result.

▶ ANALYSIS

Hines turns on a subtle distinction that is not stated in the casebook excerpt. Neither the majority nor the dissent focuses on the mere act of possessing a firearm, as the face of the felony-murder charge suggests that they should do. Instead, the justices focus on the manner in which Hines (D) possessed a firearm. The former, very limited analysis would almost certainly support Hines's (D) challenge to the charge because the mere possession of a firearm, even if by a convicted felon, cannot possibly be an inherently dangerous activity. On the other hand, the more nuanced analysis of the manner in which he possessed a firearm can, as this case shows, support a finding of an inherently dangerous activity.

■═■

Quicknotes

FELONY MURDER The unlawful killing of another human being while in the commission of, or attempted commission of, specified felonies.

■═■

People v. Burton

State (P) v. Felony murderer (D)

Cal. Sup. Ct., 491 P.2d 793 (1971).

NATURE OF CASE: Appeal from a conviction for first-degree felony murder.

FACT SUMMARY: An armed robber killed a person during the armed robbery.

> 🏛 **RULE OF LAW**
> Armed robbery is not included within the offense of murder such that armed robbery cannot serve as the predicate felony for felony murder.

FACTS: Burton (D) killed a person while Burton (D) was committing an armed robbery. He (D) was charged with and convicted of first-degree felony murder, and he appealed.

ISSUE: Is armed robbery included within the offense of murder such that armed robbery cannot serve as the predicate felony for felony murder?

HOLDING AND DECISION: (Sullivan, J.) No. Armed robbery is not included within the offense of murder such that armed robbery cannot serve as the predicate felony for felony murder. The rule developed in *People v. Ireland*, 450 P.2d 580 (Cal. 1960), and *People v. Wilson*, 462 P.2d 22 (Cal. 1969), does not mean that armed robbery is an offense included within murder. *Ireland* rejected an instruction that would have permitted assault with a deadly weapon to be a predicate felony where the defendant's entire defense was that he lacked the requisite mental state for murder; treating assault with a deadly weapon as the predicate offense thus would have imported a mental state that negated the defendant's entire case. Burglary with intent to commit assault with a deadly weapon was the predicate offense in *Wilson*. Burglary was listed in the Penal Code as an offense supporting felony murder, but this court excluded burglary in cases involving an intended felony of assault with a deadly weapon. Burton's (D) case here differs, however, because the deaths in a felony murder based on armed robbery result from conduct that has an independent felonious purpose; as discussed in *Ireland* and *Wilson*, assault with a deadly weapon was an included offense because it did not have an independent felonious purpose. Burton's (D) armed robbery therefore brought him within the category of persons who may face criminal charges for felony murder. [Reversed on other grounds.]

▶ *ANALYSIS*

In *Burton*, the California Supreme Court distinguished between included and independent felonious purposes. The merger doctrine requires that crimes factually included within the actual causation of death be "merged" with the resulting death such that there is no predicate felony supporting felony murder, and the State must seek conviction on a lesser charge.

∎━∎

Quicknotes

FELONY MURDER The unlawful killing of another human being while in the commission of, or attempted commission of, specified felonies.

ROBBERY The unlawful taking of property from the person of another through the use of force or fear.

∎━∎

People v. Chun

State (P) v. Individual (D)

Cal. Sup. Ct., 203 P.3d 425 (2009).

NATURE OF CASE: Appeal from jury verdict convicting defendant of second-degree felony murder.

FACT SUMMARY: Chun (D) admitted he discharged a firearm during a shooting that left one person dead and two others seriously injured. Chun (D) testified that he did not point his weapon at a person but only discharged his weapon to scare the victims.

> **RULE OF LAW**
> When the underlying felony in a felony murder case is assaultive in nature, the felony merges with the homicide and cannot serve as a basis for a felony murder jury instruction.

FACTS: Chun (D) was sitting in the back seat of a vehicle driven by another person, Chan. When the vehicle pulled up next to the victims' vehicle, gunshots were fired from Chun's (D) vehicle, resulting in the death of one of the passengers in the other vehicle and serious injuries to two other people. Chun (D) testified that he never pointed his weapon at anyone, but only discharged his weapon to scare the victims. The court instructed the jury on a second-degree felony murder based upon Chun's (D) underlying felony of shooting at an occupied motor vehicle. The jury acquitted Chun (D) of attempted murder but found him guilty of second-degree felony murder. Chun (D) appealed.

ISSUE: When the underlying felony in a felony murder case is assaultive in nature, does the felony merge with the homicide and fail to serve as a basis for a felony murder jury instruction?

HOLDING AND DECISION: (Chin, J.) Yes. When the underlying felony in a felony murder case is assaultive in nature, the felony merges with the homicide and cannot serve as a basis for a felony murder jury instruction. An assaultive felony is one that includes the threat of immediate violent injury. To determine whether the felony charge merges with the homicide, the court looks to the elements of the crimes rather than the facts at issue. If the elements of the underlying felony have an assaultive aspect, the crime will merge with the homicide. Here, the felony charge of shooting at an occupied vehicle is assaultive in nature and therefore cannot serve as the basis for a second-degree felony murder charge. [The court went on to find the instruction was harmless error, as no reasonable juror could have found that Chun (D) acted without implied malice, an element necessary to support the second-degree murder charge.] Affirmed.

CONCURRENCE: (Moreno, J.) The second-degree felony murder rule should be abolished in its entirety. Juries are competent enough to recognize those scenarios when a defendant commits second-degree murder during the commission of a felony that includes the threat of immediate violent injury.

ANALYSIS

The first-degree felony murder rule holds that any death that occurs during the commission of particular felonies, including arson, rape or other sexual offenses, burglary, robbery or kidnapping, constitutes first-degree murder and all participants in the felony can be held criminally liable, including those who did no harm and did not intend to hurt anyone. Intent only needs to be proven for the underlying felony. The second-degree felony murder rule applies to all other felonies that are inherently dangerous to human life and not included in the list of felonies that qualify under the first-degree felony murder rule. States define first-degree felony murder and second-degree felony murder differently.

Quicknotes

FELONY MURDER The unlawful killing of another human being while in the commission of, or attempted commission of, specified felonies.

State v. Canola

State (P) v. Armed robber (D)

N.J. Sup. Ct., 73 N.J. 206, 374 A.2d 20 (1977).

NATURE OF CASE: Appeal from affirmation of a felony murder conviction.

FACT SUMMARY: Canola (D) was convicted of felony murder because one of his cohorts in the commission of an armed robbery was killed by a bullet fired by the owner of the store being robbed.

🏛 **RULE OF LAW**
The felony murder rule does not extend to render a felon liable for the death of a co-felon affected by one resisting the felony.

FACTS: While Canola (D) and three confederates were in the process of robbing a store, the store owner and an employee engaged one of the robbers in a physical skirmish in an effort to resist the robbery. Hearing a call for assistance, another of the robbers began shooting. The store owner returned the gunfire. In the exchange, both the owner and one of the robbers, Lloredo, were fatally shot, the latter by the firearm of the owner. The appellate division upheld Canola's (D) conviction under the felony murder rule for the murder of the store owner and his conviction under the same rule for the murder of his co-felon, Lloredo. The Supreme Court of New Jersey granted a petition for certification addressed to the latter count.

ISSUE: Does the felony murder rule apply to make a felon liable for the death of his co-felon at the hands of the intended victim of the felony?

HOLDING AND DECISION: (Conford, J.) No. The English courts never applied the felony murder rule to hold a felon guilty of the death of his co-felon at the hands of the intended victim of the felony. Traditionally, it is concerned solely with situations where the felon or a confederate does the actual killing. It appears to this court to be regressive to extend the application of the rule beyond its classic common-law limitation to acts by the felon and his accomplices, to lethal acts of third persons not in furtherance of the felonious scheme. Judgment modified to strike the conviction.

CONCURRENCE: (Sullivan, J.) The result is correct, but not the reasoning. The thrust of our felony murder statute is to hold the criminal liable for any killing which ensues during the commission of a felony, even though the felon, or a confederate, did not commit the actual killing. The only exception that should be recognized is the death of a co-felon, which could be classified as a justifiable homicide and not within the purview of the statute.

▶ **ANALYSIS**

This case expresses the majority rule—that the felony murder rule renders a defendant guilty for a killing that grows out of the commission of the felony only if it is directly attributable to the act of the defendant or those associated with him in the felonious scheme. Acceptance has not been forthcoming as to the opposing view, which would extend the rule to cover any death proximately resulting from the unlawful activity, including the death of a co-felon.

━━■

Quicknotes

FELONY MURDER RULE Common law rule that the unlawful killing of another human being while in the commission of, or attempted commission of, specified felonies constitutes murder.

JUSTIFIABLE HOMICIDE The intentional killing of another individual without malice and under such circumstances as to relieve the party from criminal liability therefor.

━━■

Gregg v. Georgia

Convicted murderer (D) v. State (P)

428 U.S. 153 (1976).

NATURE OF CASE: Appeal from a death sentence.

FACT SUMMARY: Gregg (D) alleged that the death penalty was per se unconstitutional.

🏛 RULE OF LAW
The death penalty is not per se unconstitutional and is permissible if the statute has sufficient controls to avoid capricious or indiscriminate sentencing.

FACTS: Gregg (D) was convicted of murder and was sentenced to death. Gregg (D) argued that the death sentence was cruel and inhuman punishment and was a per se violation of the Eighth Amendment. Gregg (D) relied on *Furman v. Georgia*, 408 U.S. 238 (1972), which struck down the Georgia death penalty statute on the grounds that there were inadequate standards and guidelines to avoid capricious and indiscriminate impositions of a death sentence. The State (P) argued that it had cured the constitutional defects by requiring the jury to find that one of ten specific factors exist before the penalty is imposed. The statute also provided for review of all such sentences by the Supreme Court to determine if the sentence was justified and if one of the statutory factors was present. Gregg (D) argued that several of the factors were vague, and the ability to plea bargain and the vagaries of jury sentencing practices rendered the statute unconstitutional.

ISSUE: Is the imposition of the death penalty cruel and unusual punishment constituting a per se violation of the Eighth Amendment?

HOLDING AND DECISION: (Stewart, J.) No. The Eighth Amendment merely requires that punishments not be excessive, i.e. unnecessary and wanton infliction of pain, and that the punishment not be grossly out of proportion with the crime. The Eighth Amendment reflects current social trends. Legislatures, and not the courts, are the determiners of such trends in most cases. Almost every state revised their capital offense statutes after *Furman* and retained, in some form or another, a death penalty. *Furman* merely stated that there must be standards and guidelines to prevent indiscriminate or capricious sentencing. It did not prohibit the imposition of the death penalty. Traditionally, we have recognized death penalties for specific crimes since the beginning of the country and even before. The retention of the penalty by most states after *Furman* indicates that current social trends and morality still favor it. It may have a deterrent effect on some who might otherwise commit murder. The Georgia (P) statute contains sufficient safeguards to prevent capricious or indiscriminate results. Prior cases involving ambiguous portions of the statute have established that the state supreme court is carefully construing these requirements to prevent abuses, and one of the factors was even declared unconstitutionally vague. The fact that in the interests of justice and compassion some individuals are shown mercy will not invalidate the statute. The conviction is affirmed, as death penalties are not, per se, unconstitutional and the Georgia (P) statute gives defendants adequate protection.

DISSENT: (Marshall, J.) If the American people were adequately acquainted with the information critical to a judgment on the morality of the death penalty, they would consider that penalty shocking, unjust, and unacceptable. As to the two purposes the death penalty supposedly serves—general deterrence and retribution—the evidence shows that capital punishment is not necessary to deter crime in our society and it simply defies belief to suggest that the death penalty is necessary to prevent the American people from taking the law into their own hands.

▶ *ANALYSIS*

In *Jurek v. Texas*, 428 U.S. 262 (1976), the defendant challenged the death penalty statute of Texas. The procedure limited capital punishment to five knowing types of homicide. The jury had to also find that the murder was deliberate and with reasonable expectation of death; whether the defendant was a likely continuing threat to the community; and whether any justification or provocation was present. The Court found that the sentencing procedure satisfied the demands of the Eighth Amendment.

Quicknotes

CRUEL AND INHUMAN PUNISHMENT Punishment that is excessive or disproportionate to the offense committed and which is prohibited by the Eighth Amendment to the United States Constitution.

EIGHTH AMENDMENT The Eighth Amendment to the federal Constitution prohibiting the imposition of excessive bail, fines and cruel and unusual punishment.

PER SE VIOLATION Business transactions that in themselves constitute restraints on trade, obviating the need to demonstrate an injury to competition in making out an antitrust case.

Atkins v. Virginia

Murderer (D) v. State (P)

536 U.S. 304 (2002).

NATURE OF CASE: Appeal from a sentence of death.

FACT SUMMARY: When Atkins (D), who had an IQ of 59, was sentenced to death for committing a murder, he argued that the execution of a mentally retarded criminal would constitute cruel and unusual punishment in violation of the Eighth Amendment.

⚖ RULE OF LAW
Capital punishment of a mentally retarded criminal constitutes cruel and unusual punishment under the Eighth Amendment.

FACTS: Daryl Atkins (D) was convicted of abduction, armed robbery, and capital murder, and he was sentenced to death for robbing and shooting a patron of an automated teller machine. During the penalty phase of the trial, a forensic psychologist testified that Atkins (D) was "mildly mentally retarded" based upon interviews with Atkins (D), interviews with people who knew Atkins (D), a review of school and court records of other crimes, and the administration of a standard intelligence test which indicated that Atkins (D) had a full scale IQ of 59. Atkins (D) appealed, arguing that the capital punishment of a mentally retarded criminal constitutes cruel and unusual punishment under the Eighth Amendment.

ISSUE: Does capital punishment of a mentally retarded criminal constitute prohibited cruel and unusual punishment under the Eighth Amendment?

HOLDING AND DECISION: (Stevens, J.) Yes. Capital punishment of a mentally retarded criminal constitutes cruel and unusual punishment under the Eighth Amendment. Mentally retarded persons who meet the law's requirements for criminal responsibility should be tried and punished when they commit crimes. However, because of their disabilities in areas of reasoning, judgment, and control of their impulses, they do not act with the level of moral culpability that characterizes the most serious adult criminal conduct. Moreover, their impairments can jeopardize the reliability and fairness of capital proceedings against mentally retarded defendants. In recent years, more and more jurisdictions have emulated the federal government by expressly exempting the mentally retarded from execution. It is not so much the number of these states, but the consistency of the direction of change, that is significant. These enactments provide powerful evidence that today our society views mentally retarded offenders as less culpable than the average criminal. Additionally, mentally retarded defendants can be less capable of assisting their counsel, they are usually poor witnesses, and their demeanor might unjustifiably suggest that they lack remorse for their crimes. Reversed and remanded.

DISSENT: (Scalia, J.) This decision takes the Court's death-is-different jurisprudence to the extreme: this ruling has no basis in the Eighth Amendment's text or history, it has no basis in contemporary attitudes toward the death penalty, and ultimately it rests on nothing more than the personal preferences of the members of today's majority. Of the 38 states that have the death penalty, only 18 (47 percent of all states) prohibit executing mentally retarded persons—a number that does not even represent a majority of the states, let alone a "consensus." The decision also finds no support in the changing legislation on the death penalty because changing toward more lenient standards for mentally retarded persons was the only direction in which the law could have changed. Also unavailing are the opinions of professional and religious organizations, the results of opinion polls, and standards that might prevail in the "world community." The real basis of today's decision, then, is merely the feelings and intuitions of the Justices who make up today's majority. Furthermore, the majority's retribution argument is misplaced because culpability also depends on the depravity of each particular crime—and such matters, along with mental capacity, may be weighed in the sentencing phase of a capital trial. Likewise, the majority's deterrence argument does not hold up because mentally retarded persons are not more likely to kill, and because the purpose of deterrence is served if the penalty deters only many, though not all, members of the class targeted by the penalty. Abolishing the death properly belongs to the legislatures; this Court should not seek to abolish it one small increment at a time.

▶ ANALYSIS

In *Atkins*, the Supreme Court, observing that even in those states that allow the execution of a mentally retarded criminal the practice is uncommon, noted that the practice of such executions "has become truly unusual" and that it was fair to say that a "national consensus" had developed against it.

■══■

Quicknotes

CAPITAL PUNISHMENT Punishment by death.

Continued on next page.

CRUEL AND UNUSUAL PUNISHMENT Punishment that is excessive or disproportionate to the offense committed and which is prohibited by the Eighth Amendment to the United States Constitution.

EIGHTH AMENDMENT The Eighth Amendment to the federal Constitution prohibiting the imposition of excessive bail, fines and cruel and unusual punishment.

McCleskey v. Kemp

Convicted murderer (D) v. State (P)

481 U.S. 279 (1987).

NATURE OF CASE: Review of death sentence imposed after a murder conviction.

FACT SUMMARY: In challenge to a death penalty, McCleskey (D) produced statistics demonstrating a tendency toward bias in its application.

🏛 **RULE OF LAW**
The death penalty is not unconstitutional because of statistics demonstrating a tendency toward racial bias in its application.

FACTS: McCleskey (D), a black man, was convicted of killing a white police officer. The jury recommended the death penalty which the court imposed. McCleskey (D) appealed, producing statistical studies tending to prove that the penalty was imposed much more frequently on blacks than whites, particularly when the victim was white. The penalty was affirmed. The district court refused to grant habeas corpus, and the court of appeals affirmed. The United States Supreme Court granted certiorari.

ISSUE: Is the death penalty unconstitutional because of statistics demonstrating a tendency toward racial bias in its application?

HOLDING AND DECISION: (Powell, J.) No. The death penalty is not unconstitutional because of statistics demonstrating a tendency toward racial bias in its application. To prove an Equal Protection Clause violation, a person must prove he was the victim of purposeful discrimination. Evidence of statistical tendencies does not prove that the decision makers in his case were biased. In terms of Eighth Amendment analysis, the discretion that this Court has mandated in the application of the death penalty necessarily leaves room for bias. However, the only other alternative, mandatory application of the penalty is antithetical to the fundamental role of discretion in our penal system. Finally, to hold that statistical evidence of bias in death penalty application makes it unconstitutional would open the door to a broad range of challenges to various aspects of the criminal justice system, which would impose unacceptable costs thereon. Here, as the only challenge McCleskey (D) has made is based on statistical analysis, his challenge is insufficient. Affirmed.

DISSENT: (Brennan, J.) The proper analysis is not whether an arbitrary sentence has been imposed, but whether there is an unacceptable risk thereof. The studies here demonstrate this to be the case.

DISSENT: (Blackmun, J.) In terms of equal protection analysis, one challenging a particular system need only show that the totality of relevant facts gives rise to an inference of a discriminatory purpose, a burden McCleskey (D) has met here.

DISSENT: (Stevens, J.) The Court appears to base its conclusion on a fear that holding otherwise would ring the death knell for capital punishment in America. This is not so. Certain categories of crimes in the statistical studies show no tendency toward racial bias, and are not subject to constitutional attack.

▌ *ANALYSIS*

As the dissent of Justice Blackmun suggests, discrimination cases have been made based on statistical data. Examples include venue-selection cases and employment situations. However, even in instances of this nature, the variables were significantly fewer than in death penalty cases, and causation was much easier to demonstrate.

■=■

Quicknotes

EIGHTH AMENDMENT The Eighth Amendment to the federal Constitution prohibiting the imposition of excessive bail, fines and cruel and unusual punishment.

EQUAL PROTECTION CLAUSE A constitutional guarantee that no person should be denied the same protection of the laws enjoyed by other persons in like circumstances.

■=■

CHAPTER 6

The Significance of Resulting Harm

Quick Reference Rules of Law

People v. Acosta

State (P) v. Convicted murderer (D)

Cal. Ct. App., 284 Cal. Rptr. 117 (1991).

NATURE OF CASE: Appeal from conviction of three counts of second-degree murder.

FACT SUMMARY: Due to Acosta's (D) fleeing from police, a high-speed chase ensued which resulted in the collision of two helicopters and the deaths of three occupants of one of the helicopters.

🏛 RULE OF LAW
Unless an act is an actual cause of an injury, it will not be considered a proximate cause of a result for which an actor will be held responsible.

FACTS: Police officers saw Acosta (D) in a stolen car parked on a street. After the officers identified themselves to Acosta (D), he sped away. During the chase, two police helicopters that were assisting in tracking Acosta (D) collided. Both helicopters fell to the ground, resulting in the deaths of three occupants of one of the helicopters. During the trial an expert testified that the accident occurred as a result of the reckless maneuvering of one of the helicopter pilots. Furthermore, the expert testified that he had never heard of a midair collision between two police helicopters involved in tracking a ground pursuit. Acosta (D) was convicted on three counts of second-degree murder. He appealed, arguing that there was insufficient evidence that he proximately caused the deaths of the victims.

ISSUE: If an act is not the actual cause of an injury, will it be considered a proximate cause of a result for which an actor will be held responsible?

HOLDING AND DECISION: (Wallin, J.) No. Unless an act is an actual cause of an injury, it will not be considered a proximate cause of a result for which an actor will be held responsible. In this case, deaths resulting from the collision of helicopters during a high-speed ground chase are reasonably foreseeable. The threshold question in examining causation is whether the defendant's act was an "actual cause" of the victim's injury. Extremely remarkable or unusual results are excluded from the purview of proximate cause. Here, but for Acosta's (D) conduct of fleeing the police, the helicopters would never have been in position for the crash. Applying the "highly extraordinary result" standard, the result was not highly extraordinary. Although a two-helicopter collision was unknown to the expert witness and no reported cases describe one, it was a possible consequence that reasonably might have been contemplated. Therefore, a finding of proximate cause was appropriate. [The court reversed the lower court ruling, on a different basis, finding insufficient evidence of malice to support a conviction for murder.]

DISSENT: (Crosby, J.) The occupants of these helicopters were not within the range of apprehension of a fleeing criminal on the ground. This was a "highly extraordinary result," and the defendant may not be held criminally culpable for deaths which are not foreseeable.

▶ ANALYSIS

At common law, and under the Model Penal Code, if the result that comprises the criminal offense would not have occurred but for the defendant's voluntary act or omission, then "actual cause" exists. This analysis determines who the potential candidates are for causal responsibility for a certain result. The analysis for "proximate causation" is to determine who among these candidates should be held causally accountable for the harm.

▬▬■

Quicknotes

FORESEEABILITY A reasonable expectation that an act or omission would result in injury.

PROXIMATE CAUSE The natural sequence of events without which an injury would not have been sustained.

SECOND-DEGREE MURDER The unlawful killing of another person, without premeditation, and characterized by either an intent to kill or by a reckless disregard for human life.

▬▬■

People v. Arzon
State (P) v. Arsonist (D)

Sup. Ct., N.Y. County, 92 Misc. 2d 739, 401 N.Y.S. 2d 156 (1978).

NATURE OF CASE: Motion to dismiss murder counts in an indictment.

FACT SUMMARY: A fireman died from injuries sustained when he attempted to evacuate from a building under the hazardous conditions created by the fire Arzon (D) set plus smoke from another fire.

🏛 RULE OF LAW
A defendant's conduct can support a charge of homicide only if it was a sufficiently direct cause of the death and the ultimate harm was something which should have been foreseen as being reasonably related to his acts.

FACTS: The firemen who were called to the fifth floor fire allegedly set by Arzon (D) decided to withdraw from the building because they were making no progress in controlling it. A combination of that fire and dense smoke they encountered (which was later discovered to have been caused by another fire on the second floor with which Arzon (D) was not connected by any evidence) made evacuation from the building extremely hazardous. One fireman, in attempting to evacuate, sustained injuries from which he later died. An indictment was returned charging Arzon (D) with second-degree murder for having, "Under circumstances evincing a depraved indifference to human life, recklessly engaged in conduct which created a grave risk of death to another person," thereby causing the death of the fireman, and with felony murder. He moved to dismiss these counts, maintaining that the required causal link between the underlying crime and the death was lacking.

ISSUE: To be guilty of homicide, must the defendant's conduct have been a sufficiently direct cause of the death and must the ultimate harm be something which should have been foreseen as being reasonably related to his acts?

HOLDING AND DECISION: (Milonas, J.) Yes. While there is remarkably little authority on precisely what sort of behavior constitutes "depraved indifference to human life," it is clear that an obscure or merely probable connection between a defendant's conduct and another person's death is not enough to support a charge of homicide. Although the defendant's conduct need not be the sole and exclusive factor in the victim's death, to be criminally liable his conduct must have been a sufficiently direct cause of the death and the ultimate harm must be something which should have been foreseen as being reasonably related to his acts. The defendant's motion to dismiss the murder charges is denied.

▶ ANALYSIS

The standard adopted by requiring that the defendant's actions be a "sufficiently direct cause of the ensuing death" is "greater than that required to serve as a basis for tort liability." That is, it is not a but-for-causation test, and it does not sanction an "expanded application of proximate cause principles lifted from the civil law of torts." *People v. Warner-Lambert Co.*, 51 N.Y. 2d 295 (1980).

■=■

Quicknotes

FELONY MURDER The unlawful killing of another human being while in the commission of, or attempted commission of, specified felonies.

PROXIMATE CAUSE The natural sequence of events without which an injury would not have been sustained.

SECOND-DEGREE MURDER The unlawful killing of another person, without premeditation, and characterized by either an intent to kill or by a reckless disregard for human life.

■=■

People v. Campbell

State (P) v. Alleged murderer (D)

Mich. Ct. App., 124 Mich. App. 333, 335 N.W.2d 27 (1983).

NATURE OF CASE: Appeal from denial of a motion to quash information and to dismiss a charge of murder.

FACT SUMMARY: After Basnaw committed suicide with a gun sold to him by Campbell (D), Campbell was charged with murder.

RULE OF LAW
Juries can convict of murder only when they are convinced beyond a reasonable doubt that the defendant intended to kill.

FACTS: Campbell (D) and Basnaw were drinking heavily when Basnaw began to talk about committing suicide but said he did not have a gun. About two weeks earlier, Campbell (D) had caught Basnaw in bed with Campbell's (D) wife. Campbell (D) told Basnaw that he would sell him a gun for whatever money he had in his possession. They drove to Campbell's (D) parents' home to get the weapon, returning to Basnaw's with the gun and five shells. When Campbell (D) and Basnaw's girlfriend left Basnaw's, Campbell (D) told her that the shells were blanks and that the firing pin on the gun didn't work. The next morning, Basnaw was found dead from a wound to the temple, with the gun in his hand. The cause of death was listed as suicide. Campbell (D) was charged with murder. He moved to quash the information and moved for dismissal on the ground that providing a weapon to a person, who subsequently commits suicide with it, is not murder. The motion was denied. This appeal followed.

ISSUE: Can juries convict of murder only when they are convinced beyond a reasonable doubt that the defendant intended to kill?

HOLDING AND DECISION: (Hoehn, J.) Yes. Juries can convict of murder only when they are convinced beyond a reasonable doubt that the defendant intended to kill. The term suicide, by definition, excludes a homicide. Moreover, Campbell (D) had no present intention to kill. He provided the weapon and departed. Campbell (D) hoped Basnaw would kill himself, but hope alone is not the degree of intention requisite to a charge of murder. No legislature has classified such conduct as murder. Further, whether incitement to suicide is a crime under the common law is extremely doubtful. While Campbell's (D) conduct was morally reprehensible, it is not criminal under the present state of the law. Reversed and remanded with instructions to quash the information and discharge Campbell (D).

ANALYSIS

The Model Penal Code and a number of legislatures have enacted legislation which may be accepted as evidence of present-day social values in this area since they have made aiding or soliciting suicide a crime. However, those states are in the minority. Where it has been held to be a crime, there has been no unanimity as to the nature of the severity of the crime. The *Campbell* court noted that the legislature could remedy the lack of criminality under the present law and invited the legislature to adopt legislation on the subject.

Quicknotes

MOTION TO QUASH To vacate, annul, void.

MURDER Unlawful killing of another person either with deliberation and premeditation or by conduct demonstrating a reckless disregard for human life.

REASONABLE DOUBT Standard of proof necessary to convict a defendant, requiring the absence of evidence that would cause a reasonable person to hesitate in making an important decision in his personal affairs.

People v. Kevorkian

State (P) v. Doctor (D)

Mich. Sup. Ct., 447 Mich. 436, 527 N.W.2d 714 (1994).

NATURE OF CASE: A state's appeal from the dismissal of murder charges.

FACT SUMMARY: A doctor allegedly helped two people commit suicide, and he was charged with two counts of murder.

RULE OF LAW
The common-law equation of assisted suicide and murder has become obsolete.

FACTS: Kevorkian (D) allegedly helped two women commit suicide. He allegedly did so by providing the necessary instruments to the women and showing them how to use the instruments to kill themselves. Both women died after using the instruments and following Kevorkian's (D) directions, and Kevorkian (D) was charged with two counts of murder. He moved to dismiss, and the trial court granted the motion, reasoning that assisted suicide was not a form of murder. The intermediate appellate court reversed, and Kevorkian (D) appealed to the Michigan Supreme Court.

ISSUE: Has the common-law equation of assisted suicide and murder become obsolete?

HOLDING AND DECISION: (Cavanagh, C.J.) Yes. The common-law equation of assisted suicide and murder has become obsolete. The early common-law view illustrated by *People v. Roberts*, 178 N.W. 690 (Mich. 1920), is now in the minority. Most jurisdictions today criminalize assisted suicide separately from murder, and distinctions between the two crimes focus on actively participating in a suicide and merely being involved in events preceding a suicide. Thus, under contemporary principles, a defendant may be convicted of murder if he participates in the final overt act that results in death. *Roberts* therefore should be overruled insofar as it supports a murder charge for mere prior involvement in events leading up to a suicide. [Vacated and] remanded.

CONCURRENCE AND DISSENT: (Boyle, J.) Today's new distinction between active participation and indirect preliminary involvement will only lead to examinations of defendants' motives for killing. The test announced today does not work: Kevorkian (D), for example, did not actively participate in the final acts here; he was only indirectly involved before the final acts of the persons who committed suicide. Such a test gives no principled means of modifying the earlier common-law view.

ANALYSIS

Under *Kevorkian*, preliminary conduct that merely assists in the commission of a suicide does not have sufficient culpability to deserve a murder charge. Conversely, actively participating in the final act that does cause the person's death qualifies, not as a suicide, but as a murder committed by the person assisting the person who wishes to die.

Quicknotes

MURDER Unlawful killing of another person either with deliberation and premeditation or by conduct demonstrating a reckless disregard for human life.

Stephenson v. State

Abductor (D) v. State (P)

Ind. Sup. Ct., 205 Ind. 141, 179 N.E. 633 (1932).

NATURE OF CASE: Appeal from conviction for second-degree murder.

FACT SUMMARY: As a result of Stephenson's (D) acts, a woman took a drug to commit suicide.

🏛 RULE OF LAW
If an accused committed a felony such as rape or attempted rape and inflicted on the victim both mental and physical injuries as a result of which the victim was rendered mentally irresponsible and suicide followed, the accused would be guilty of murder.

FACTS: Stephenson (D) was the Grand Dragon of the Ku Klux Klan. He abducted a woman from her house and detained her on a train. He beat her and attempted to rape her on the train. Later, he forced her to get off the train, and they registered in a hotel. The woman managed to procure some drugs and took them in an attempt to commit suicide. She became extremely sick and Stephenson (D) offered to take her to a hospital, but she refused. While she was being driven back to her house, she screamed in pain for a doctor. Stephenson (D) did not stop or administer an antidote. She was left off at her house and her parents called a doctor, who gave her an antidote. Within ten days, all her wounds healed, except for one which was infected. She continued to grow worse, even after the infection had healed. Twenty-seven days after Stephenson (D) brought her back home, she died. The cause of death was a combination of shock, loss of food and rest, poison, infection, and lack of early treatment.

ISSUE: If an accused committed a felony such as rape or attempted rape and inflicted on the victim both mental and physical injuries as a result of which the victim was rendered mentally irresponsible and suicide followed, would the accused be guilty of murder?

HOLDING AND DECISION: (Per curiam) Yes. If an accused committed a felony such as rape or attempted rape and inflicted on the victim both mental and physical injuries as a result of which the victim was rendered mentally irresponsible and suicide followed, the accused would be guilty of murder. An attempted suicide was a normal and foreseeable result of the treatment inflicted upon the victim by Stephenson (D). He had complete dominion and control over the woman from the time she was abducted. She had attempted to escape several times but was thwarted on each occasion. She did not know when Stephenson (D) would again attempt to rape her as he had done on the train. The same forces were working on her when she took the drug as when the defendant attempted to rape her. The whole ordeal was a single, interrelated transaction. Stephenson (D), by his acts, rendered the victim distracted and mentally irresponsible. This mental state was a natural and probable consequence of the defendant's unlawful acts. The suicide was an intervening cause which was a foreseeable result of Stephenson's (D) acts. The fact that other causes may have also contributed to the death will not relieve Stephenson (D) from liability. His acts were working on the mental process of the victim and generated the taking of the drug. Affirmed.

▶ ANALYSIS

To determine causation there are two steps. First, the defendant's act must have been the actual cause of the death. That is, the act must be a substantial factor in bringing about the resulting harm. Second, the act must be direct. That is to say, it is an actual cause in itself still operative at the moment of death. This is opposed to an indirect cause, where it is some other cause which results in the death.

■=■

Quicknotes

FORESEEABILITY A reasonable expectation that an act or omission would result in injury.

INTERVENING CAUSE A cause, not anticipated by the initial actor, which is sufficient to break the chain of causation and relieve him of liability.

SECOND-DEGREE MURDER The unlawful killing of another person, without premeditation, and characterized by either an intent to kill or by a reckless disregard for human life.

■=■

Commonwealth v. Root

State (P) v. Drag racer (D)

Pa. Sup. Ct., 403 Pa. 571, 170 A.2d 310 (1961).

NATURE OF CASE: Appeal from conviction for involuntary manslaughter.

FACT SUMMARY: Root (D) was engaged in a drag race in which the other driver was killed when he ran into a truck.

🏛 RULE OF LAW
For a charge of criminal homicide, it must be found that the defendant's act was the direct cause of the death and not just the proximate cause as that term is defined in tort law.

FACTS: Root (D) and the deceased engaged in a drag race. The race took place on a rural, three-lane highway. The traffic was light and the night was clear and dry. The speed limit was fifty miles per hour. The drivers were doing seventy to ninety immediately prior to the accident. When the two cars approached a bridge, the highway narrowed to two lanes. Root (D) was in front and the deceased was immediately behind him. The deceased attempted to pass Root (D). When he entered the other lane, he ran head on into an oncoming truck and was killed.

ISSUE: Does the tort law concept of proximate cause apply in determining criminal responsibility for homicide?

HOLDING AND DECISION: (Jones, C.J.) No. There is no rational basis for the use of the tort law concept of proximate cause in the field of criminal homicide. Proximate cause has undergone a continuing extension in favor of broadening the scope of civil liability. Prior to that extension, the concept was equally applicable to tort and criminal law. To use the concept as it has evolved in the field of criminal law would be to extend possible criminal liability to persons charged with reckless or unlawful conduct in circumstances not generally considered to present the likelihood of a resultant death. In the present case, it was the deceased who was the direct cause of his own death. The direct cause was his acts alone. Direct causation is a criminal law concept. Even under the tort law concept of proximate cause, the defendant's acts were not the proximate cause of the death, as a matter of law. The deceased was aware of the risk created by Root (D), and thereafter the deceased caused the death by an independent act of recklessness. Root's (D) reckless conduct was not a sufficiently direct cause of the death to make him criminally liable. Reversed.

DISSENT: (Eagen, J.) Root (D) caused the situation by his acts. The act of the deceased was a normal response to the race and that act was foreseeable by Root (D).

▶ ANALYSIS

Proximate cause simply denotes a causative factor which the criminal law will notice as sufficient for liability. It is a label used to express, rather than to reach, results obtained by the application of the criminal law's rules of causation. A cause is direct when it is still operative at the moment of the result. A cause is indirect when, although it is in the chain of events culminating in the result, the direct cause is some intervening act. If the intervening act was generated by the indirect cause, then liability will still attach.

Quicknotes

DIRECT CAUSE A cause that brings about an event without the happening of an intervening cause.

FORESEEABILITY A reasonable expectation that an act or omission would result in injury.

INVOLUNTARY MANSLAUGHTER The killing of another person without premeditation or deliberation or with the intent to kill or to commit a felony, which may be reasonably expected to result in death or serious bodily injury; involuntary manslaughter is characterized by reckless conduct in the commission of a lawful act, or by the commission of an unlawful act that is not a felony, but which leads to the killing of another.

PROXIMATE CAUSE The natural sequence of events without which an injury would not have been sustained.

RECKLESSNESS State of mind accompanying an action that shows indifference to or disregard of its consequences.

State v. McFadden

State (P) v. Convicted murderer (D)

Iowa Sup. Ct., 320 N.W.2d 608 (1982).

NATURE OF CASE: Appeal from conviction of two counts of involuntary manslaughter.

FACT SUMMARY: McFadden (D) was convicted of two counts of involuntary manslaughter following a drag race that McFadden (D) participated in, in which his competitor collided with another car, resulting in the competitor's death and the death of a passenger in the other car.

▥ RULE OF LAW
(1) The acts and omissions of two or more persons may work concurrently as the efficient cause of an injury.
(2) The tort concept of proximate cause is applicable in criminal cases.

FACTS: McFadden (D) entered into a drag race with another driver, Sulgrove. During the race, Sulgrove lost control of his automobile and struck another vehicle. As a result of this collision, both Sulgrove and a six-year-old passenger of the other vehicle were killed. McFadden's (D) vehicle did not physically contact either of the two colliding vehicles. He was convicted of two counts of involuntary manslaughter and appealed on the grounds that Sulgrove assumed the risk of his own death and in any event, a more stringent direct causal connection was required for conviction.

ISSUE:
(1) May the acts or omissions of two or more persons work concurrently as the efficient cause of an injury?
(2) Is the tort concept of proximate cause applicable in a criminal case?

HOLDING AND DECISION: (Allbee, J.)
(1) Yes. The acts or omissions of two or more persons may work concurrently as the efficient cause of an injury. Aiding and abetting and joint criminal conduct are theories of vicarious liability. These vicarious liability theories may be sufficient to convict McFadden (D) for the death of the child. Additionally, Sulgrove's own unlawful conduct does not absolve McFadden (D) from his guilt. McFadden's (D) acts were contributing and substantial factors in bringing about the deaths of Sulgrove and the child. Sulgrove's voluntary and reckless participation in the drag race does not of itself bar McFadden (D) from being convicted of involuntary manslaughter for Sulgrove's death.
(2) Yes. The tort concept of proximate cause is applicable in a criminal case. One reason for this is the similar functions that the requirement of proximate cause

plays in both sorts of trials. In both criminal prosecutions and civil suits, the element of proximate cause serves as an element that requires there to be sufficient causal relationship between the defendant's conduct and the harm caused. Affirmed.

▶ ANALYSIS

The *McFadden* court explicitly rejected the conclusion reached in *Commonwealth v. Root*, 170 A.2d 310 (1961), which held that a more direct causal connection was required to hold a fellow drag racer criminally liable for his competitor's death. Both cases involved the death of a willing participant in a dangerous and foolhardy game. The disparate outcomes of the two cases reflect the conflicting views held by jurisdictions as to the effect this factor should have on manslaughter liability.

■■■

Quicknotes

AIDING AND ABETTING Assistance given in order to facilitate the commission of a criminal act.

INVOLUNTARY MANSLAUGHTER The killing of another person without premeditation or deliberation or with the intent to kill or to commit a felony, which may be reasonably expected to result in death or serious bodily injury; involuntary manslaughter is characterized by reckless conduct in the commission of a lawful act, or by the commission of an unlawful act that is not a felony, but which leads to the killing of another.

OMISSION The failure to perform an act or obligation that one is required to perform by law.

PROXIMATE CAUSE The natural sequence of events without which an injury would not have been sustained.

VICARIOUS LIABILITY The imputed liability of one party for the unlawful acts of another.

■■■

Commonwealth v. Atencio

State (P) v. Russian roulette participants (D)

Mass. Sup. Jud. Ct., 345 Mass. 627, 189 N.E.2d 323 (1963).

NATURE OF CASE: Appeal from conviction for manslaughter.

FACT SUMMARY: Atencio (D) and Marshall (D) played Russian roulette with the deceased, who was killed when the gun discharged.

🏛 **RULE OF LAW**
Direct causation may be established by wanton and reckless conduct found in a joint enterprise.

FACTS: The deceased and two friends, Atencio (D) and Marshall (D), were drinking wine all day in the deceased's room. Marshall (D) had gone out and returned with a gun. Early in the evening, after the deceased's brother had left, they started talking about Russian roulette. The three decided to play the game. Marshall (D) examined the gun and saw that it contained one bullet. Marshall (D) went first and there was no discharge. Atencio (D) spun the barrel and then put the gun to his head but there was no discharge. The deceased spun the barrel, put the gun to his head, pulled the trigger, and was killed.

ISSUE: Is causation established where participants engage in a reckless and wanton joint enterprise which leads to an unintended death?

HOLDING AND DECISION: (Wilkins, C.J.) Yes. Atencio (D) and Marshall (D) were not under a duty to prevent the deceased from playing Russian roulette, but they were under a duty not to participate in reckless conduct which could lead to a death of one of the participants. It is not required that the defendants have forced the deceased to participate. There were not three independent acts that had no relationship to each other. This was not something only one person could do at a time. It was a joint enterprise. There is a distinction between Russian roulette and the highway drag race. In the race, it is mostly a question of skill which each driver possessed and used, independently of the other; in Russian roulette, it is solely a matter of chance and luck. All the participants were bound together by mutual encouragement, without any chance of controlling the outcome. Affirmed.

▌ ANALYSIS

The court is saying that the direct cause of the death was the mutual encouragement and cooperation. This joint enterprise state of mind was in existence when each person pulled the trigger. There were not three separate acts. Each pulling of the trigger was not an intervening act superseding the original agreement to play the game.

The distinction from the highway drag race in *Commonwealth v. Root*, 170 A.2d 310 (Pa. 1961), was not persuasive. In the race, there was mutual encouragement and joint enterprise. The issue of luck or skill is irrelevant. Had *Root* come before this case, criminal responsibility might very well have been found to exist.

Quicknotes

DIRECT CAUSE A cause that brings about an event without the happening of an intervening cause.

JOINT ENTERPRISE Venture undertaken based on an express or implied agreement between the members, common purpose and interest, and an equal power of control.

MANSLAUGHTER The killing of another person without premeditation, deliberation or with the intent to kill or to commit a felony, which may be reasonably expected to result in death or serious bodily injury; manslaughter is characterized by reckless conduct or by some adequate provocation on the part of the actor, as determined by a subjective standard.

Smallwood v. State

Rapist (D) v. State (P)

Md. Ct. App., 343 Md. 97, 680 A.2d 512 (1996).

NATURE OF CASE: Assault with intent to murder.

FACT SUMMARY: Smallwood (D) was convicted of three counts of assault with intent to murder his rape victims based on the awareness that despite the fact that he knew he was HIV positive he did not use a condom in any of his attacks.

🏛 **RULE OF LAW**
Before an intent to kill may be inferred based solely on the defendant's exposure of a victim to a risk of death, it must be shown that the victim's death would have been a natural and probable result of the defendant's conduct.

FACTS: Smallwood (D) was convicted of three counts of assault with intent to murder his rape victims based on the awareness that despite the fact that he knew he was HIV positive he did not use a condom in any of his attacks. Smallwood (D) appealed, contending that such fact was insufficient to infer an intent to kill.

ISSUE: Before an intent to kill may be inferred based solely on the defendant's exposure of a victim to a risk of death, must it be shown that the victim's death would have been a natural and probable result of the defendant's conduct?

HOLDING AND DECISION: (Murphy, C.J.) Yes. Before an intent to kill may be inferred based solely on the defendant's exposure of a victim to a risk of death, it must be shown that the victim's death would have been a natural and probable result of the defendant's conduct. The State (P) has presented no evidence from which it can be reasonably concluded that death by AIDS is a probable result from Smallwood's (D) actions to the same extent that death is the probable result of firing a deadly weapon at a vital part of someone's body. Reversed.

▶ **ANALYSIS**

In *State v. Raines*, 326 Md. 582 (1992), this court held that "an intent to kill may be inferred from the use of a deadly weapon directed at a vital part of the human body." The State's (P) argument here was based on the theory that HIV is analogous to a deadly weapon.

Quicknotes

INTENT TO KILL The desire to take the life of another.

RAPE Unlawful sexual intercourse by means of fear or force and without consent.

People v. Rizzo

State (P) v. Attempted robber (D)

N.Y. Ct. App., 246 N.Y. 334, 158 N.E. 888 (1927).

NATURE OF CASE: Appeal from conviction of attempted robbery.

FACT SUMMARY: Rizzo (D) and three others were arrested while they were driving around New York City looking for a payroll messenger they intended to rob.

🏛 RULE OF LAW
An attempt is committed when an act is performed which is so physically close to the contemplated victim or scene of the crime that completion of the offense is very likely but for timely interference.

FACTS: Rizzo (D) and three companions intended to rob a payroll messenger. They drove to several buildings looking for the messenger but were unable to find him. Finally, at one building, the four men were arrested by police who had become suspicious of their behavior. Rizzo (D) and the others were convicted of attempted robbery although they had never been anywhere near the payroll messenger.

ISSUE: Is there an attempt when the defendant's actions are far away from the completion of the intended crime because they have not even brought him near the intended victim or scene of the crime?

HOLDING AND DECISION: (Crane, J.) No. The existence of an attempt depends on actions which make the completion of the crime highly probable, but for timely interference. Such a probability of completion can only occur when the defendant's actions bring him in close proximity to the victim or place of the crime. In this case, Rizzo (D) intended to commit a crime, but his actions never brought him close to completing it because he never found, or came near, the payroll messenger he intended to rob. Reversed.

▶ ANALYSIS

Unlike other cases which use a dangerous proximity test, this decision was based on what is called the physical proximity test. To determine when an act becomes an attempt, this test focuses on what remains to be done and makes the defendant's relationship to the time and place of the crime very important. If the defendant's actions have not yet brought him near to the scene of the crime, there is no attempt. This is because so much remains to be done that it cannot be said that completion of the crime would occur as a natural and probable consequence of the defendant's actions.

Quicknotes

ATTEMPT An intent combined with an act falling short of the thing intended.

ROBBERY The unlawful taking of property from the person of another through the use of force or fear.

McQuirter v. State

Alleged attempted rapist (D) v. State (P)

Ala. Ct. App., 36 Ala. App. 707, 63 So. 2d 388 (1953).

NATURE OF CASE: Appeal from conviction for attempt to commit an assault with intent to commit rape.

FACT SUMMARY: McQuirter (D), a black man, followed a white woman down the street and then up the street.

RULE OF LAW
Since assault is, by definition, the attempt (i.e., intent plus some act in furtherance) to commit battery, attempted assault must be attempted battery by an act in furtherance of assault, which does not qualify as being in furtherance of battery.

FACTS: Mrs. Allen, a white woman, and her two children, walked down the street at 8 P.M. on a summer evening. McQuirter (D) was sitting in a truck as they walked by. He said something unintelligible as they walked past and then got out of the truck and followed her down the street. Allen turned into a friend's house when McQuirter (D) was two or three feet behind her. She waited ten minutes for McQuirter (D) to pass and then she proceeded on her way. She then observed McQuirter (D) walking toward her from behind a telephone pole. Allen sent the children to get another friend. When the friend appeared, McQuirter (D) went across the street and waited there thirty minutes. He then left and Allen went home. McQuirter (D) testified that he had just been walking up the street to go to another part of town and that Mrs. Allen just happened to be in front of him. When he got to the telephone pole, he waited, trying to decide whether to go on or not. After a few minutes thinking, he went on to the other part of town. He came back after thirty minutes. He denied saying anything or making any gestures toward Allen. A police chief testified that McQuirter (D) told him that he was sitting in the truck, and that he wanted a woman, and that he was going to have the first woman that came by whether he had to rape her or not. McQuirter (D) was found guilty of an attempt to commit an assault with intent to commit rape.

ISSUE: Since assault is merely the attempt to commit some battery (e.g., rape), may a person be held criminally liable for committing an attempted assault?

HOLDING AND DECISION: (Price, J.) Yes. An attempt to commit an assault with intent to commit rape is merely an attempt to commit rape which has not proceeded far enough to constitute an assault. The jury need only be satisfied that the accused actually intended to rape Mrs. Allen. In determining intent, the jury may look at all the circumstances, including social conditions and customs founded upon racial differences. Here, Mrs. Allen was a white woman and McQuirter (D) was a black man, and the jury may take this into account when deciding whether McQuirter's (D) actions indicated an intent to rape. Conviction affirmed.

ANALYSIS

Attempt to commit rape is a recognized offense which requires only that apparent ability to do so, and intent, be proved. As such, proof of conduct, which a jury believes to manifest the intent to commit a crime, is sufficient to convict. By hornbook law, assault is the attempted battery (e.g., rape) of another with the apparent ability to succeed. Where no act in furtherance of a battery occurs, however, no assault will arise. However, acts in furtherance of the object of the contemplated assault (e.g., rape) may be sufficient to establish an attempt to accomplish that object (e.g., following Mrs. Allen). Hence, an attempted assault arises. Note, however, that since such a rule permits criminal liability merely for manifesting an intent in one's actions, this case borders on a violation of the universal criminal law requirement of actus reus.

Quicknotes

ACTUS REUS The unlawful act that gives rise to criminal liability, as distinguished from the required mental state.

ASSAULT The intentional placing of another in fear of immediate bodily injury.

BATTERY Unlawful contact with the body of another person.

IMPOSSIBILITY A doctrine relieving the parties to a contract from liability for nonperformance of their duties thereunder, if the subject matter of the contract ceases to exist, a person essential to the performance of the contract is deceased, or the service or goods contracted for has become illegal.

United States v. Jackson

Federal government (P) v. Conspirator (D)

560 F.2d 112 (2d Cir. 1977).

NATURE OF CASE: Appeal from a conviction for conspiracy to rob and attempted robbery.

FACT SUMMARY: Jackson (D) claimed that, as a matter of law, the conduct he and his partners engaged in never crossed the line from "mere preparation" to an attempted robbery.

🏛 RULE OF LAW
An "attempt" requires that the defendant have acted with criminal purpose and that he engaged in conduct constituting a substantial step toward commission of the target crime.

FACTS: Having been convicted of conspiracy to rob and of attempting to rob a bank, Jackson (D) contended on appeal that, as a matter of law, the line between "mere preparation" and an "attempt" had not been crossed. The evidence indicated that he and other parties got together and discussed plans to rob the bank, that they went once but arrived too late to go through with their plan; that they then changed their plans to another day, and that one of their group was arrested in the meantime. That party informed the police of the plan, so they were keeping the bank under surveillance on the day the robbery was supposed to occur. Although the arrested friend had been told that the robbery was off, the rest of the gang appeared in a car and drove around the bank, canvassing it. When they saw the police, they took off in the car. When captured, the guns to be used in the robbery were in the car, and the license plates had been altered to prevent detection.

ISSUE: To prove an "attempt," must it be shown that the defendant acted with criminal purpose and that his conduct constituted a substantial step toward commission of the target crime?

HOLDING AND DECISION: (Bryan, J.) Yes. In order to find that one has perpetrated an "attempt," it must be proven that he was acting with the kind of culpability otherwise required from commission of the target crime (criminal purpose) and that he engaged in conduct constituting a substantial step toward commission of the crime. This is precisely the standard which was used in this case. The conduct must be strongly corroborative of criminal purpose in order for it to constitute a substantial step. It cannot be said that the steps taken in this case were "insubstantial" as a matter of law, so the finding that they constituted a substantial step toward commission of the target crime will not be overturned. Affirmed.

▶ ANALYSIS

Judge Learned Hand once noted that the original test for "attempt" was whether or not the person had done all that was within his power to do, but was prevented by intervention from outside. *United States v. Coplon*, 185 F.2d 629 (2d Cir. 1950). This test is no longer valid.

Quicknotes

ATTEMPT An intent combined with an act falling short of the thing intended.

CONSPIRACY Concerted action by two or more persons to accomplish some unlawful purpose.

SUBSTANTIAL STEP In reference to the crime of attempt, the undertaking of an action or omission that constitutes a substantial step in a general scheme to commit a crime.

State v. Davis

State (P) v. Alleged attempted murderer (D)

Mo. Sup. Ct., 319 Mo. 1222, 6 S.W.2d 609 (1928).

NATURE OF CASE: Appeal from conviction for attempted murder in the first degree.

FACT SUMMARY: Davis (D) paid an undercover police officer to kill the husband of his lover.

RULE OF LAW
Mere solicitation, unaccompanied by an act moving directly toward the commission of the intended crime, is not an overt act constituting an element of attempt.

FACTS: Davis (D) made a plan with a woman to kill her husband, collect the husband's life insurance, and then live together. Davis (D) approached a person to gain help in finding a hired killer. That person informed a police officer of Davis's (D) plan. The officer posed as the hired killer. Davis (D) paid the officer $600 to kill the husband, with more to be paid later. After several conferences and one aborted plan, the officer and Davis (D) decided on a course of action. The officer was to go to the husband's house, kill the husband, and cover the killing by making it look like it was done in the course of a robbery. Davis (D) gave the officer various maps and photographs of the house and its occupants. The officer went to the house, revealed his true identity, and later arrested Davis (D).

ISSUE: Did the solicitation of a planned murder, clearly indicating criminal intent, amount to a perpetration of an overt act in a criminal attempt?

HOLDING AND DECISION: (Davis, J.) No. Solicitation is a separate crime, and therefore more needs to be shown than mere solicitation in order to establish an overt act. Attempt requires an act moving toward the commission of a crime and not a mere solicitation. The verbal agreement, delivery of the maps and photographs, and the payment of part of the consideration were mere acts of preparation, failing to lead directly or proximately to attempted murder. The officer never had the intent to carry out the crime, and he performed no act amounting to perpetration. He merely listened to the plans, agreed to them, and then went to the husband's house. There was no overt act. The court does not decide whether an actual assault is necessary before the crime of attempt is established. Reversed.

ANALYSIS

Courts have come to different conclusions as to whether mere solicitation of the crime constitutes an attempt. In the present case, the *Davis* court found that the defendant did not commit an overt act which directly furthered the commission of the intended crime. Thus he was found not guilty of attempted murder. Many states hold that "no matter what acts the solicitor commits, he cannot be guilty of an attempt because it is not his purpose to commit the offense personally." (Model Penal Code, comment to § 5.02 at 369) However, a minority of courts have held that if a solicitation constitutes a "substantial step" to commit the offense, then the defendant can be charged with attempt of that offense.

Quicknotes

ATTEMPT An intent combined with an act falling short of the thing intended.

OVERT ACT An open act evidencing an intention to commit a crime.

SOLICITATION Contact initiated by an attorney for the purpose of obtaining employment.

People v. Jaffe

State (P) v. Buyer of goods (D)

N.Y. Ct. App., 78 N.E. 169 (1906).

NATURE OF CASE: Appeal from conviction for attempt to receive stolen property knowing it to be stolen.

FACT SUMMARY: A man offered to buy goods that he thought were stolen, but the goods in fact had been previously returned to their rightful owner so that they were no longer stolen property.

🏛 RULE OF LAW
A defendant cannot be convicted of an attempt to receive stolen property knowing it to be stolen if the goods he sought to buy were not, in fact, stolen property.

FACTS: Jaffe (D) received 20 yards of cloth believing the cloth to have been stolen. However, before Jaffe (D) made the purchase, the police had arrested the thief and returned the cloth to its rightful owner, and the cloth was offered to Jaffe (D) with the true owner's consent. Therefore, the goods Jaffe (D) tried to buy were not stolen goods. Jaffe (D) was convicted of an attempt to receive stolen property knowing it to be stolen, and he appealed. The intermediate appellate court affirmed, and Jaffe (D) sought further review in New York's highest court.

ISSUE: Can a defendant be convicted of an attempt to receive stolen goods knowing them to be stolen if the goods were not, in fact, stolen goods?

HOLDING AND DECISION: (Bartlett, J.) No. A defendant cannot be convicted of an attempt to receive stolen goods knowing them to be stolen if the goods were not, in fact, stolen goods. Jaffe (D) was convicted on the authority of cases holding that a defendant may be convicted of attempt to commit a crime despite facts unknown to the defendant that would make perpetration of the crime impossible. Here, Jaffe (D) made an offer to buy cloth that he mistakenly believed to be stolen. But if the sale had been completed, he could not have been convicted for receiving stolen property knowing it to be stolen because he could not know a fact that did not exist. The difference between this case and the factual-impossibility cases lies in the fact that the act intended by Jaffe (D) would not have been a crime if completed because the fact that the goods were, in fact, stolen is an essential element of the offense; a mere belief that goods are stolen is not sufficient because the statute requires knowledge of the stolen character. In true factual-impossibility cases, the act the defendant intended would have been a crime if completed. The rule is, then, if all the defendant intended would not have been a crime if completed, he cannot be convicted of an offense. Reversed.

▶ ANALYSIS

Jaffe turns on the elements of the offense required by statute. Since the goods were not stolen, the act was not criminal; any act done by the defendant thus was not a criminal attempt because it was not an act in furtherance of a criminal offense.

Quicknotes

ATTEMPT An intent combined with an act falling short of the thing intended.

FACTUAL IMPOSSIBILITY Refers to a circumstance in which a person commits an act that would otherwise constitute a criminal offense, however, the attendant facts and circumstances unknown to the actor make it impossible to commit the crime; factual impossibility does not constitute a defense to criminal liability.

People v. Dlugash

State (P) v. Convicted murderer (D)

N.Y. Ct. App., 41 N.Y.2d 725, 363 N.E.2d 1155 (1977).

NATURE OF CASE: Appeal from a murder conviction.

FACT SUMMARY: Dlugash (D) claimed that Michael Geller was already dead when he shot him.

> 🏛 **RULE OF LAW**
> While a defendant may not be convicted of murdering someone already dead, he can be convicted of attempted murder if he believed the person to be alive at the time.

FACTS: Two to five minutes after Bush shot Geller three times for pressing a demand for some rent money, Dlugash (D) shot Geller in the head and face five times. The expert testimony could not clearly establish precisely when Geller had died. Dlugash (D) asserted he was certain Geller was dead when he shot him and that he had only done so as he feared for his own life because Bush was holding a gun on him and telling him to shoot Geller or be killed. Dlugash (D) was convicted of murder, but the court set aside the indictment for the state's failure to prove beyond a reasonable doubt that Geller was alive when Dlugash (D) shot him. It also refused to modify the judgment to reflect a conviction for attempted murder and an appeal was taken.

ISSUE: Even though the victim may not actually have been alive at the time, can there be a conviction for attempted murder where the assailant believed the victim to be alive?

HOLDING AND DECISION: (Jasen, J.) Yes. Although a murder conviction is impossible if the state does not prove beyond a reasonable doubt that the victim was alive at the time of the assault, a conviction for attempted murder is possible upon proof only that the defendant believed his victim to be alive at the time. The New York Penal Code has followed the lead of the Model Penal Code in dispensing with the traditional rule that legal impossibility is a good defense to crimes of attempt, but factual impossibility is not. Instead, the focus is on the actor's own mind, which is the best standard for determining his dangerousness to society and, hence, his liability for attempted criminal conduct. A person is guilty of an attempt when, with intent to commit a crime, he engaged in conduct tending to effect the commission of such crime. Liability exists "if such crime could have been committed had the attendant circumstances been as such person believed them to be." In this case, his contrary statements notwithstanding, Dlugash (D) believed Geller was alive when he shot him. So the judgment should have been modified to reflect a conviction for the lesser included crime of attempted murder.

▶ ANALYSIS

Under the more traditional view, factual impossibility is not a defense to an attempted crime. It exists when the criminal law prohibits what the defendant intends to do, but he is prevented from completing his plan by unanticipated outside factors. Legal impossibility, which is a defense, exists if the defendant undertook to complete an activity which, even if completed, is not prohibited by the criminal law.

■═■

Quicknotes

ATTEMPT An intent combined with an act falling short of the thing intended.

BEYOND A REASONABLE DOUBT Standard of proof necessary to convict a defendant, requiring the absence of evidence that would cause a reasonable person to hesitate in making an important decision in his personal affairs.

FACTUAL IMPOSSIBILITY Refers to a circumstance in which a person commits an act that would otherwise constitute a criminal offense, however, the attendant facts and circumstances unknown to the actor make it impossible to commit the crime; factual impossibility does not constitute a defense to criminal liability.

LEGAL IMPOSSIBILITY An activity which the defendant believes to be unlawful, but which does not constitute a crime; legal impossibility is a defense to criminal liability.

■═■

Group Criminality

Quick Reference Rules of Law

Hicks v. United States

Aider and abettor (D) v. Federal government (P)

150 U.S. 442 (1893).

NATURE OF CASE: Action for aiding and abetting another in the commission of a murder.

FACT SUMMARY: Hicks (D) was convicted of verbally encouraging Rowe to kill the deceased.

🏛 RULE OF LAW
Before a person can be convicted of verbally aiding and encouraging another person in the commission of a crime, it must be shown that the words were intended to encourage and aid the perpetrator of the crime.

FACTS: Hicks (D) was charged with murder because he verbally and with gestures encouraged Rowe to kill the deceased. Hicks (D) claimed that he was trying to dissuade Rowe from shooting the deceased instead of encouraging him. The jury was instructed that if they found that the effect of the words uttered by Hicks (D) was to encourage Rowe to kill the deceased, they could find Hicks (D) guilty. They were further instructed that if Hicks (D) was present in order to aid and abet Rowe, but circumstances made it unnecessary for him to do anything, he is still guilty because he was there with the intent to help if required. Hicks (D) was found guilty of murder and appealed the conviction on the ground the requisite intent was not present.

ISSUE: When a person is convicted of encouraging another to commit a crime, must it be shown that the person actually intended the words used to help encourage the perpetrator of the crime?

HOLDING AND DECISION: (Shiras, J.) Yes. The court erred in instructing the jury because it must be shown that Hicks (D) intended the words he used to encourage Rowe. It isn't enough to show that Hicks (D) intended to use the words that he did, without showing that he intended that the words encourage Rowe to murder the deceased. The court also made a mistake in telling the jury that if Hicks (D) was present in order to help Rowe that he is guilty even if no help was needed. This is improper unless it is shown that Hicks (D) and Rowe had previously conspired to kill the deceased and there was no such evidence presented at the trial. Reversed and remanded.

▶ ANALYSIS

There has been an attempt in some states to hold persons present at the commission of a crime responsible if it is shown that they could have done something to prevent the commission of the crime. Some statutes require that there be a duty to act and this is the majority approach, but a few states have found liability if it is shown that the person could have prevented the crime. Under that view, Hicks (D) could have been convicted if it could be shown that it was within Hicks's (D) power to prevent the crime, unless he could have shown that he really was trying to stop Rowe.

Quicknotes

AIDING AND ABETTING Assistance given in order to facilitate the commission of a criminal act.

MURDER Unlawful killing of another person either with deliberation and premeditation or by conduct demonstrating a reckless disregard for human life.

SOLICITATION Contact initiated by an attorney for the purpose of obtaining employment.

State v. Gladstone

State (P) v. Drug dealer (D)

Wash. Sup. Ct., 78 Wash. 2d. 306, 474 P.2d 274 (1970).

NATURE OF CASE: Appeal from conviction for aiding and abetting in the unlawful sale of marijuana.

FACT SUMMARY: When approached by Thompson, Gladstone (D) told him he did not have enough marijuana to sell him any but gave him the address of another who eventually did sell some to Thompson.

RULE OF LAW

Mere communications to the effect that another might or probably would commit a criminal offense does not amount to aiding and abetting of the offense should it ultimately be committed.

FACTS: The Tacoma Police Department hired Thompson to purchase marijuana from Gladstone (D). He went to Gladstone's (D) home and asked to buy some marijuana, but Gladstone (D) said he did not have enough to sell any. He did, however, suggest that Kent might have enough to sell him and gave him Kent's address and a map he drew directing him there. Thompson did buy marijuana from Kent, and Gladstone (D) was convicted of aiding and abetting Kent in the unlawful sale of marijuana. He appealed.

ISSUE: Can one be convicted of aiding and abetting an offense for merely communicating the fact that another might or probably would commit the criminal offense that is ultimately committed?

HOLDING AND DECISION: (Hale, J.) No. It would be a dangerous precedent to hold that mere communications to the effect that another might or probably would commit a criminal offense amount to an aiding and abetting of the offense should it ultimately be committed. It is true that an aider and abettor need not be physically present at the commission of the crime to be held guilty. However, it is necessary that he "in some sort associate himself with the venture, that he participate in it as in something that he wishes to bring about, that he seek by his action to make it succeed," as Learned Hand wrote. There is no evidence that Gladstone (D) did anything more than describe Kent to Thompson as an individual who might sell some marijuana. This is not enough to convict him of aiding and abetting its sale. Reversed and remanded for dismissal.

DISSENT: (Hamilton, J.) The jury was warranted in concluding that when Gladstone (D) affirmatively recommended Kent as a source and purveyor of marijuana, he entertained the requisite conscious design and intent that his action would instigate, induce, procure, or encourage the perpetration of Kent's subsequent crime of selling marijuana to Thompson.

▶ ANALYSIS

New York is among the few jurisdictions which have established a new statutory crime called "criminal facilitation" covering one who "believing it probable he is rendering aid to a person who intends to commit a crime . . . engages in conduct which provides such person with means or opportunity for the commission thereof and which, in fact, aids such person to commit a felony." *People v. Gordon*, 32 N.Y. 62 (1973), held that a *Gladstone*-type defendant would not be guilty of criminal facilitation.

■=■

Quicknotes

ACCOMPLICE LIABILITY Liability of an individual who knowingly, purposefully or voluntarily combines with the main actor in the commission or attempted commission of a criminal offense.

AIDING AND ABETTING Assistance given in order to facilitate the commission of a criminal act.

■=■

State v. McVay

State (P) v. Captain (D)

R.I. Sup. Ct., 47 R.I. 292, 132 A. 436 (1926).

NATURE OF CASE: Question of law before criminal trial for manslaughter.

FACT SUMMARY: After Kelley hired McVay (D) to captain his steamer, the ship's boiler exploded resulting in the loss of many lives.

🏛 RULE OF LAW
A defendant may be indicted and convicted of being an accessory before the fact to the crime of manslaughter arising through criminal negligence.

FACTS: The steamer Mackinac's boiler exploded resulting in the loss of many lives. The steamer's captain McVay (D) was indicted for criminal manslaughter. Also, Kelley, the person who hired McVay (D), was indicted as an accessory to the manslaughter was. Kelley's indictment stated that Kelley did "before said manslaughter was committed feloniously and maliciously aid, assist, abet, counsel, hire, command and procure . . . McVay." Kelley argued that he couldn't be indicted legally as an accessory before the fact since, manslaughter being inadvertent and unintentional, cannot be maliciously incited before the crime is committed.

ISSUE: May a defendant be indicted and convicted of being an accessory before the fact to the crime of manslaughter arising through criminal negligence?

HOLDING AND DECISION: (Barrows, J.) Yes. A defendant may be indicted and convicted of being an accessory before the fact to the crime of manslaughter arising through criminal negligence. Although there can be no accessory before the fact of a killing resulting from a sudden and unpremeditated blow, premeditation is not consistent with every manslaughter. Here, it was not contradictory to charge Kelley as an accessory before the fact. He allegedly intentionally directed and counseled the grossly negligent act, i.e., in maintaining an unsafe boiler, which the indictment charges resulted in the crime. The facts set forth in the indictment allege that Kelley with the full knowledge of the possible danger to human life, recklessly and willfully advised, counseled, and commanded McVay (D) to take the chance by negligent action or failure to act. Question answered in the affirmative.

▌ ANALYSIS

In *People v. Marshall*, 362 Mich. 170, 106 N.W.2d 842 (1961), the defendant gave his car keys to McCleary who the defendant knew was intoxicated. McCleary was involved in a head-on collision that killed both McCleary and the driver of the other car. The defendant was convicted of involuntary manslaughter as an accessory to McCleary's crime.

■═■

Quicknotes

ACCESSORY BEFORE THE FACT An individual who combines with the main actor in the commission, or attempted commission, of a criminal offense before its performance; an accessory before the fact is not present when the offense is committed.

CRIMINAL NEGLIGENCE The degree of negligence necessary to render a person criminally liable and characterized by a reckless disregard for the consequences of one's actions or indifference to the safety of others.

MANSLAUGHTER The killing of another person without premeditation, deliberation or with the intent to kill or to commit a felony, which may be reasonably expected to result in death or serious bodily injury; manslaughter is characterized by reckless conduct or by some adequate provocation on the part of the actor, as determined by a subjective standard.

PREMEDITATION The contemplation of undertaking an activity prior to action; any length of time is sufficient.

■═■

Commonwealth v. Roebuck

State of Pennsylvania (P) v. Individual (D)

Pa. Sup. Ct., 32 A.3d 613 (2011).

NATURE OF CASE: Appeal from a verdict finding defendant guilty of third-degree murder as an accomplice.

FACT SUMMARY: Roebuck (D) participated in the death of an individual by assisting in luring the victim to an apartment complex where the victim was shot and killed by another person.

🏛 RULE OF LAW
When causing a particular result is an element of an offense, one is an accomplice if the one acts with the level of culpability that equals the level required to support criminal liability by the principal actor.

FACTS: The victim in this case was lured to an apartment complex and then shot and killed. Roebuck (D) assisted in luring the victim to the apartment, but did not shoot the victim. The State (P) charged Roebuck (D) as an accomplice to third-degree murder. The lower court found Roebuck (D) guilty and Roebuck (D) appealed. Roebuck's (D's) appellate argument was that accomplice liability required an intent element, and because third-degree murder by definition was an unintentional killing, accomplice liability could not attach to that crime.

ISSUE: When causing a particular result is an element of an offense, is one an accomplice if the one acts with the level of culpability that equals the level required to support criminal liability by the principal actor?

HOLDING AND DECISION: (Saylor, J.) Yes. When causing a particular result is an element of an offense, one is an accomplice if the one acts with the level of culpability that equals the level required to support criminal liability by the principal actor. The Model Penal Code 2.06(3) first defines an accomplice as follows: a person is an accomplice if, with the purpose of promoting or facilitating the commission of the offense by the principal actor, the accomplice aids or attempts to aid the principal actor in planning or committing the offence. Section 2.06(4) then discusses the level of culpability required: when causing a result is an element of the offense, the level of culpability of the accomplice need only equal that required for criminal liability on the part of the principal actor. Here, the level of culpability for third-degree murder is recklessness. A court need only find that Roebuck (D) also acted with the same recklessness as he participated in the events leading to the victim's death. The lower court found sufficient evidence to support the verdict. Affirmed.

CONCURRENCE: (Eakin, J.) Roebuck's (D) argument is wrong. An accomplice to third-degree murder does not intend to aid an unintentional killing, but he does intend to aid in a malicious act that results in a killing. The same logic that enables a murder charge against the principal applies to the accomplice as well.

▶ ANALYSIS

The significance of this holding is that an accomplice may be found guilty of murder when he acts recklessly as opposed to intentionally.

■■■

Quicknotes

ACCOMPLICE LIABILITY Liability of an individual who knowingly, purposefully or voluntarily combines with the main actor in the commission, or attempted commission, of a criminal offense.

■■■

People v. Russell

State (P) v. Defendant (D)

N.Y. Ct. App., 91 N.Y.2d 280, 693 N.E.2d 193 (1998).

NATURE OF CASE: Appeal of second-degree, depraved indifference murder conviction.

FACT SUMMARY: Three defendants engaged in a gun battle (D) were charged with second-degree murder for the killing of a bystander during a shootout.

🏛 RULE OF LAW

A depraved indifference murder conviction requires proof that the defendant, under circumstances evidencing a depraved indifference to human life, recklessly engaged in conduct creating a grave risk of death to another person, and thereby caused the death of another person.

FACTS: Three defendants engaged in a gun battle during which Daly, a public school principal, was fatally wounded. All three were charged with second-degree murder on the basis that each acted with the mental culpability required of the crime and that each "intentionally aided" the defendant who fired the fatal shot. On appeal, each defendant challenged the sufficiency of the evidence.

ISSUE: Does a depraved indifference murder conviction require proof that the defendant, under circumstances evidencing a depraved indifference to human life, recklessly engaged in conduct creating a grave risk of death to another person, and thereby caused the death of another person?

HOLDING AND DECISION: (Kaye, C.J.) Yes. A depraved indifference murder conviction requires proof that the defendant, under circumstances evidencing a depraved indifference to human life, recklessly engaged in conduct creating a grave risk of death to another person, and thereby caused the death of another person. There was adequate proof to sustain the finding that the three defendants tacitly agreed to engage in the gun battle that placed an innocent life at risk and killed Daly, supporting a finding of sufficient mental culpability for depraved indifference murder, and that they intentionally aided and encouraged each other to create the crossfire that killed Daly. Affirmed.

▶ ANALYSIS

The court here relies on *People v. Abbott*, 445 N.Y.S.2d 344 (1981), in which two defendants engaged in a drag race and one smashed into another car, killing the driver and two passengers. On appeal the court rejected the argument of the other defendant that his conviction should be set aside, since his conduct in participating in the race made the race possible.

■■■

Quicknotes

RECKLESSNESS The conscious disregard of substantial and justifiable risk.

SECOND-DEGREE MURDER The unlawful killing of another person, without premeditation, and characterized by either an intent to kill or by a reckless disregard for human life.

■■■

People v. Luparello

State (P) v. Convicted murderer (D)

Cal. Ct. App., 187 Cal. App. 3d 410, 231 Cal. Rptr. 832 (1987).

NATURE OF CASE: Appeal from conviction of first-degree murder.

FACT SUMMARY: Luparello (D) asked his friends to elicit information from Martin. They ended up killing him instead, resulting in a murder conviction for Luparello (D) based on aiding-and-abetting liability.

🏛 RULE OF LAW

A defendant may be found guilty not only of the offense he intended to facilitate or encourage, but also of any reasonably foreseeable offense committed by the person he aids and abets.

FACTS: Luparello (D) asked his friends to elicit information from Martin regarding his former girlfriend's whereabouts. He told them he wanted the information at any cost. Unable to get the information on their first try, the friends returned and shot Martin after luring him out of his house. Luparello (D) was charged with first-degree murder. The jury returned a guilty verdict based, in part, on an aiding-and-abetting theory. Luparello (D) appealed the verdict, contending that Martin's murder was an unplanned and unintended act of a coconspirator and thus not chargeable to him.

ISSUE: May a defendant be found guilty not only of the offense he intended to facilitate or encourage but also of any reasonably foreseeable offense committed by the person he aids and abets?

HOLDING AND DECISION: (Kremer, J.) Yes. A defendant may be found guilty not only of the offense he intended to facilitate or encourage but also of any reasonably foreseeable offense committed by the person he aids and abets. The accomplice and the perpetrator need not share an identical intent to be found criminally responsible for the same crime. Liability extends to reach the actual crime rather than the planned or intended crime on the policy that aiders and abettors should be responsible for the criminal harms they have naturally and foreseeably put in motion. In this case, the aiding and abetting theory provides a sound basis from which to derive Luparello's (D) criminal responsibility for first-degree murder. Affirmed.

CONCURRENCE: (Wiener, J.) Although courts are required to follow the reasonable foreseeability test as set forth by the Supreme Court, that does not mean that the test is theoretically sound. Artificially imputing some form of stepped-up intent to an accomplice is inconsistent with the notion that criminal punishment must be proportional to a defendant's culpable mental state.

▌ ANALYSIS

The reasonable foreseeability doctrine expressed in the above case represents the established majority view. In some states, the doctrine has even been expressly codified in accomplice liability statutes. The Model Penal Code, however, has rejected the doctrine in favor of a liability standard that requires that the aider and abettor encourage the identical crime committed by the principal.

■=■

Quicknotes

AIDING AND ABETTING Assistance given in order to facilitate the commission of a criminal act.

FIRST-DEGREE MURDER The willful killing of another person with deliberation and premeditation; first-degree murder also encompasses those situations in which a person is killed within the perpetration of, or attempt to perpetrate, specified felonies.

REASONABLE FORESEEABILITY A reasonable expectation that an act or omission would result in injury.

■=■

Wilcox v. Jeffery

Concert goer (D) v. State (P)

King's Bench Div., 1 All E.R. 464 (1951).

NATURE OF CASE: Action for aiding and abetting another in violating the Aliens Order of 1921.

FACT SUMMARY: Wilcox (D) bought a ticket and attended a concert by an American who was not legally permitted to perform in England.

🏛 RULE OF LAW
If a person is present at the commission of an illegal act, the fact that he was present may be used as evidence of aiding and abetting that crime, as long as the person intended to be there and was not there accidentally.

FACTS: Mr. Hawkins, an American, and four French musicians gave a concert in London in violation of Article 18(2) of the Aliens Order, 1920. Wilcox (D) knew that the musicians were violating the law, but purchased a ticket and attended the concert anyway. It was not shown that Wilcox (D) actually applauded the performance, but neither did he get up and protest the performance of the American. After attending the performance, Wilcox (D) wrote an article for the magazine which he worked for, in which he wrote a very laudatory description of the concert. On these facts, a magistrate found that he had aided and abetted in the violation of the Aliens Order. Wilcox (D) appealed the decision, asserting that mere presence at an illegal act is not evidence of aiding and abetting that crime.

ISSUE: Is the mere presence at the commission of an illegal act evidence of aiding and abetting that crime?

HOLDING AND DECISION: (Lord Goddard, C.J.) Yes. The fact that a person is present at the commission of an illegal act is evidence of the crime of aiding and abetting. However, the presence must be intended and, if it is only accidental, it cannot be used as evidence of aiding and abetting. Presence at the commission of an illegal act is only evidence to be used by the jury in determining if the person actually did aid and abet someone in committing a crime. It isn't, however, irrebuttable proof that the person actually committed the crime. It was shown that Wilcox (D) was present and his actions indicated that he supported the persons violating the law. He further took advantage of the act to write an article for his magazine. There was sufficient evidence for the magistrate to find that the crime of aiding and abetting had been committed. Affirmed.

▶ ANALYSIS

This case illustrates the generally held view, but some courts have gone even further and imposed a duty on those persons present at the commission of a crime to prevent the crime if it is within their power and to hold them liable if they fail to do so. Most courts still require that there be some preexisting duty to act before finding liability, however.

■━■

Quicknotes

ACCOMPLICE LIABILITY Liability of an individual who knowingly, purposefully or voluntarily combines with the main actor in the commission or attempted commission of a criminal offense.

AIDING AND ABETTING Assistance given in order to facilitate the commission of a criminal act.

DUTY An obligation owed by one individual to another.

■━■

State v. Hayes

State (P) v. Convicted burglar (D)

Mo. Sup. Ct., 105 Mo. 76, 16 S.W. 514 (1891).

NATURE OF CASE: Appeal of a conviction for burglary and larceny.

FACT SUMMARY: Hayes (D) was convicted of burglary even though he didn't actually enter the building.

🏛 RULE OF LAW
When some act essential to the crime charged is done by a party who does not have the same felonious intent as the other parties, that act cannot be imputed to the other parties.

FACTS: Hayes (D) approached Hill about helping him burglarize a general store. Hill played along but was actually a relative of the store owners and advised the store owners of the plan in order to obtain the arrest of Hayes (D). In carrying out their plan, Hayes (D) raised the window to the store and helped Hill in. Hill handed out a side of bacon and then they were arrested. The jury was instructed that if Hayes (D) with a felonious intent assisted and aided Hill to enter the building, regardless of the fact that Hill had no felonious intent in entering the building, Hayes was guilty of burglary. Hayes (D) appealed his conviction asserting that the entering of the building by Hill could not be imputed to him because Hill lacked intent.

ISSUE: Can an essential act of the crime committed by one coconspirator lacking a felonious intent be imputed to other coconspirators who have the requisite intent?

HOLDING AND DECISION: (Thomas, J.) No. In order to convict Hayes (D), it must be shown that he committed all of the elements of the crime. Since Hayes (D) did not enter the building, that act had to be imputed to him in order to find him guilty. The act of entering the building was not done with the requisite intent and therefore cannot be imputed to Hayes (D) in order to satisfy all of the elements of the crime. If Hill had entered the building with a felonious intent, that act could have been imputed to Hayes (D) and the conviction would have been proper. Hayes (D) may have been found guilty of petty larceny in taking the bacon, but the conviction for burglary is reversed and the cause remanded.

▶ ANALYSIS

The court in this case is apparently holding that Hayes (D) cannot be convicted because Hill could not be convicted of doing the very act being imputed to Hayes (D). Other courts have been willing to convict a person for helping and encouraging another to do an act which is not a crime as to the person actually committing the act but is to the person who encourages the act. One particular case involved a person who, for a felonious reason, encouraged another to claim the privilege against self-incrimination in a grand jury investigation. It is not a crime to claim the privilege, but it is a crime to encourage the use of the privilege for a felonious purpose. It is possible that a court using this case as a precedent would have ruled differently in this case.

■═■

Quicknotes

BURGLARY Unlawful entry of a building at night with the intent to commit a felony therein.

LARCENY The illegal taking of another's property with the intent to deprive the owner thereof.

■═■

Interstate Circuit, Inc. v. United States

Movie theater chain (D) v. Federal government (P)

306 U.S. 208 (1939).

NATURE OF CASE: Antitrust suit.

FACT SUMMARY: Interstate Circuit, Inc. (D) entered into contractual agreements with distributors specifying the conditions under which their movies could be played.

🏛 **RULE OF LAW**
An unlawful conspiracy may be formed without simultaneous action or agreement on the part of the conspirators.

FACTS: Interstate Circuit, Inc. (Interstate) and Texas Consolidated Theatres (Consolidated) (D), two related movie theater chains, dominated the geographic area in which they were located. Interstate and Consolidated (D) entered into contractual arrangements with eight independent distributors, under certain conditions. The district court restrained the theaters and distributors (D) from continuing such practices in violation of Section 1 of the Sherman Anti-trust Act. Interstate (D) appealed.

ISSUE: May an unlawful conspiracy be formed without simultaneous action or agreement on the part of the conspirators?

HOLDING AND DECISION: (Stone, J.) Yes. An unlawful conspiracy may be formed without simultaneous action or agreement on the part of the conspirators. Here a finding of an agreement of the distributors among themselves is supported by the evidence. It was enough that, knowing concerted action was intended and invited, the distributors adhered to the scheme and participated in it, knowing that the end result would be a restraint of commerce. Affirmed.

▌ *ANALYSIS*

The Court here notes that it is often that case that there is no direct evidence of an agreement among conspirators to enter into a conspiracy; thus, the finding of a conspiracy for antitrust analysis purposes may be inferred from the parties' conduct.

■══■

Quicknotes

ANTITRUST Body of federal law prohibiting business conduct that constitutes a restraint on trade.

CONSPIRACY Concerted action by two or more persons to accomplish some unlawful purpose.

SECTION 1 OF THE SHERMAN ACT Prohibits all contracts in restraint of trade.

■══■

People v. Lauria

State (P) v. Answering service proprietor (D)

Cal. Ct. App., 251 Cal. App. 2d 471 (1967).

NATURE OF CASE: Action for conspiracy to further prostitution.

FACT SUMMARY: Lauria (D) knew that some of his answering service customers were prostitutes who used his service for business purposes.

RULE OF LAW
The intent of a supplier (who knows of the criminal use to which his goods are put) to participate in the criminal activity may be inferred from circumstances showing that he has a stake in the criminal venture or by the aggravated nature of the crime itself.

FACTS: Lauria (D) and three people who used his answering service were arrested for prostitution. Lauria (D) knew that one of the people was a prostitute. He said he did not arbitrarily tell the police about prostitutes who used his service for business purposes.

ISSUE: Does a supplier necessarily become a part of a conspiracy to further an illegal venture by furnishing goods or services which he knows are to be used for criminal purposes, where the crime involved is a misdemeanor?

HOLDING AND DECISION: (Fleming, J.) No. Both the knowledge of the illegal use of the goods or services and the intent to further that use are necessary to support a conviction for conspiracy. Intent may be inferred from circumstances of the sale which show that the supplier had acquired a special interest in the activity. Or a supplier may be liable on the basis of knowledge alone where he furnishes goods which he knows will be used to commit a serious crime. However, this does not apply to misdemeanors. Here, Lauria (D) was not shown to have a stake in the venture and he is charged with a misdemeanor. Hence, he could not be charged with conspiracy to further prostitution. Affirmed.

ANALYSIS

In *U.S. v. Falcone*, 311 U.S. 205 (1940), the sellers of large quantities of sugar, yeast, and cans were absolved from participation in a moonlighting conspiracy. In *Direct Sales Co. v. U.S.*, 319 U.S. 703 (1943), a wholesale drug company was convicted of conspiracy to violate the narcotic laws by selling large quantities of drugs to a physician who was supplying them to addicts. The court distinguished these two leading cases on the basis of the character of the goods. The restricted character of the goods in *Direct Sales* showed that the defendant knew of their illegal use and had taken the step from knowledge to intent and agreement.

■=■

Quicknotes

CONSPIRACY Concerted action by two or more persons to accomplish some unlawful purpose.

MISDEMEANOR Any offense that does not constitute a felony, which is generally less severe and for which a lesser punishment is imposed.

■=■

Pinkerton v. United States

Tax evaders (D) v. Federal government (P)

328 U.S. 640 (1946).

NATURE OF CASE: Appeal from conviction for conspiracy to violate the Internal Revenue Code.

FACT SUMMARY: Walter (D) and Daniel Pinkerton (D), brothers who live a short distance apart, were convicted of various substantive violations of the Internal Revenue Code and conspiracy to violate the same.

RULE OF LAW
As long as a conspiracy continues, the overt act of one partner may be the act of all without any new agreement specifically directed to that act.

FACTS: Walter (D) and his brother, Daniel Pinkerton (D), were convicted of various substantive violations of the Internal Revenue Code and conspiracy to violate the same. They lived a short distance apart on Daniel's (D) farm and were apparently involved in unlawful dealings in whiskey. Daniel (D) contended that as only Walter (D) committed the substantive offenses, he could not be held to the conspiracy even though the substantive offenses were committed in furtherance of the conspiracy.

ISSUE: In addition to evidence that the offense was, in fact, committed in furtherance of the conspiracy, is evidence of direct participation in commission of the substantive offense or other evidence from which participation might fairly be inferred necessary?

HOLDING AND DECISION: (Douglas, J.) No. Here there was a continuous conspiracy with no evidence that Daniel (D) had withdrawn from it. As long as a conspiracy continues, the conspirators act for each other in carrying it forward. An overt act of one partner may be the act of all without any new agreement specifically directed to that act. Criminal intent to do the act is found in the formation of the conspiracy. The conspiracy contemplated the very act committed. If an overt act can be supplied by the act of one conspirator, "we fail to see why the same or other acts in furtherance of the conspiracy are likewise not attributable to the others for the purpose of holding them responsible for the substantive offense." Affirmed.

DISSENT IN PART: (Rutledge, J.) There was no evidence that Daniel (D) counseled, advised, or had knowledge of the particular acts or offenses. Simply finding them to be general partners in a crime is a dangerous precedent.

ANALYSIS

It is possible that the approach taken here had in mind the development of modern organized crime. Anyone who professed his allegiance to the criminal acts of another might be held to conspiracy. Questions also arise as to punishment of one who has withdrawn from the conspiracy. The test for abandonment of a conspiracy is generally whether the abandoning conspirator has brought home to his fellow conspirators that he is quitting. Even if not a defense, a withdrawal may start the statute of limitations to run at that point, prevent his being held for crimes committed after his withdrawal, or prevent admission of evidence against him of acts or declarations his former coconspirators did or said after his withdrawal.

Quicknotes

ABANDONMENT The voluntary relinquishment of a right without the intent of reclaiming it.

CONSPIRACY Concerted action by two or more persons to accomplish some unlawful purpose.

OVERT ACT An open act evidencing an intention to commit a crime.

STATUTE OF LIMITATIONS A law prescribing the period in which a legal action may be commenced.

Kotteakos v. United States

Loan applicant (D) v. Federal government (P)

328 U.S. 750 (1946).

NATURE OF CASE: Action for conspiracy to violate the National Housing Act.

FACT SUMMARY: Brown (D) made fraudulent applications for loans under the Housing Act for Kotteakos (D) and several other persons, who had no connection with each other.

🏛 RULE OF LAW
Where one person is dealing with two or more persons who have no connection with each other, although each deals individually with the same person, they cannot all necessarily be convicted of a single conspiracy.

FACTS: Brown (D) made fraudulent application for loans under the National Housing Act for Kotteakos (D) and several other persons. No connection was shown between Kotteakos (D) and the other loan applicants, other than that Brown (D) had acted as each person's broker for obtaining the loans. Kotteakos (D) contends there was no evidence of a single conspiracy.

ISSUE: Where one person deals with two or more persons who have no connection with each other, are they all necessarily guilty of a single conspiracy?

HOLDING AND DECISION: (Rutledge, J.) No. Thieves who dispose of their loot to a single fence do not, by that fact alone, become confederates. They may, but it takes more than knowledge that the fence is a fence to make them such. Here, the jury could not possibly have found that there was only one conspiracy, since many of the alleged conspirators had no connection with one another; and there was no proof that all were parties to a single common plan, scheme, or design. The evidence proved existence of not one, but of several, conspiracies. Reversed.

▶ ANALYSIS

"Wheel" conspiracies are those in which a single person or group (the hub) deals individually with two or more other persons or groups. "Chain" conspiracies are those in which there is successive communication and cooperation, analogous to the relationships between manufacturer and wholesaler, wholesaler and retailer, and retailer and consumer. A wheel arrangement is less likely to support the conclusion that the parties had a community of interest, as *Kotteakos* demonstrates. However, some wheel arrangements may be found to be conspiracies. For example, where the feasibility of an illegal horse racing service depends upon there being several customers paying high rates, subscribers aware of this situation are considered coconspirators.

Quicknotes

"CHAIN" CONSPIRACY A conspiracy in which the activities conducted involve multiple layers of persons similar to a chain, each performing specialized functions toward the accomplishment of the final goal.

CONSPIRACY Concerted action by two or more persons to accomplish some unlawful purpose.

"WHEEL" CONSPIRACY A conspiracy in which the activities conducted involve multiple layers of persons similar to a wheel, each performing specialized functions toward the accomplishment of the final goal.

United States v. Bruno

Federal government (P) v. Drug peddlers (D)

105 F.2d 921 (2d Cir. 1939); *rev'd on other grounds*, 308 U.S. 287 (1939).

NATURE OF CASE: Appeal from conviction of conspiracy to import, sell, and possess narcotics.

FACT SUMMARY: Smugglers, middle people, and retailers were involved in distributing narcotics to addicts. There was no evidence of communication between the smugglers and retailers.

RULE OF LAW
There is a single conspiracy where each member knows that the success of that part with which she was immediately concerned was dependent upon the success of the whole.

FACTS: Smugglers imported narcotics for which they were paid by middle persons who distributed them to two groups of retailers. There was no evidence of communication or cooperation between the smugglers and the retailers or between the two groups of retailers. Eighty-eight people from all four groups were indicted for a single conspiracy to import, sell, and possess narcotics.

ISSUE: Can a single conspiracy exist among people who neither cooperate nor communicate with each other?

HOLDING AND DECISION: (Per curiam) Yes. There is a single conspiracy where each member knows that the success of that part with which she was immediately concerned was dependent upon the success of the whole. Here, the smugglers knew that the middle people must sell to retailers and the retailers knew that the middle people must buy from importers. Thus, the conspirator at one end knew that the unlawful business would not stop with their buyers, and those at the other end knew that it had not begun with their sellers. Likewise, the retailers were as much a part of a single undertaking as sales people in the same shop. There was, therefore, only one conspiracy.

ANALYSIS

Bruno is an example of the chain conspiracy. *U.S. v. Peoni*, 100 F.2d 401 (1938), also involved a chain. There, Peoni sold counterfeit money to Regno, who sold it to Dorsey, who passed it onto innocent persons. Peoni was held not to be a coconspirator with Dorsey since there was no evidence that Peoni planned sales beyond Regno or that it made any difference to him whether Regno passed the bills himself or sold them to a second passer. *Peoni* is thus different from the usual chain conspiracy involving an ongoing scheme from which it may be concluded that the defendants had knowledge of and were dependent upon each other whether they ever actually communicated or not.

Quicknotes

CONSPIRACY Concerted action by two or more persons to accomplish some unlawful purpose.

United States v. McDermott

Federal government (P) v. Bank president (D)

245 F.3d 133 (2d Cir. 2001).

NATURE OF CASE: Appeal from a conviction for conspiracy to commit insider trading.

FACT SUMMARY: The mistress of an investment-bank president passed the president's stock recommendations on to another man with whom she was having another affair.

🏛 RULE OF LAW
An agreement to pass insider information to all members of a conspiracy is an essential element of the conspiracy.

FACTS: James J. McDermott (D), who was president of a New York investment bank, had an extramarital affair with an adult film star, Kathryn Gannon. McDermott (D) commonly recommended stocks to Gannon while they were involved. Unknown to McDermott (D), Gannon passed the stock recommendations on to another man with whom she was having also having an affair, Anthony Pomponio. Gannon and Pomponio earned about $170,000 during the period relevant to this case, though neither of them was trained or experienced in securities. The Government (D) charged McDermott (D), Gannon, and Pomponio with conspiracy to commit insider trading. The evidence at McDermott's (D) trial, however, failed to show that he had agreed for Gannon to pass his stock recommendations on to anyone. McDermott (D) was convicted on the conspiracy count, and he appealed, challenging the sufficiency of the evidence on the conspiracy count.

ISSUE: Is an agreement to pass insider information to all members of a conspiracy an essential element of the conspiracy?

HOLDING AND DECISION: (Oakes, J.) Yes. An agreement to pass insider information to all members of a conspiracy is an essential element of the conspiracy. The Government (P) argued that McDermott (D) conspired with Gannon and Pomponio even if he did not agree to make insider recommendations to both Gannon and Pomponio. The Government's (P) position is not well taken, though, because this Circuit has already held that a conspiracy cannot be extended as against a particular defendant to include alleged co-conspirators about whom the charged person had no knowledge. None of this Circuit's three exceptions applies to this case, either: the alleged conspiracy was not broader, Gannon's conveyance of information to Pomponio was not reasonably foreseeable, and McDermott (D) did not know of any relationship between Gannon and Pomponio. Accordingly, the Government's (P) evidence is insufficient as a matter of law on the essential element of an agreement to communicate information to Gannon and at least one other person. [Reversed.]

▶ ANALYSIS

Trial Practice 101: The party with the burden of proof must introduce evidence supporting a reasonable inference that each element of its claim did in fact occur. Based on the casebook's excerpt in *McDermott*, the trial judge should have granted a timely motion for directed verdict in McDermott's (D) favor on the conspiracy count after the Government (P) closed its case in chief.

■==■

Quicknotes

CONSPIRACY Concerted action by two or more persons to accomplish some unlawful purpose.

INSIDER Any person within a corporation who has access to information not available to the public.

INSIDER INFORMATION Information regarding a corporation that is available only to insiders.

■==■

Gebardi v. United States

Transporter (D) v. Federal government (P)

287 U.S. 112 (1932).

NATURE OF CASE: Appeal of conviction for conspiracy to violate the Mann Act.

FACT SUMMARY: Gebardi (D), not then married, transported a woman across state lines and engaged in illicit sexual relations with her.

🏛 RULE OF LAW
When a woman acquiesces to being transported across state lines for the purpose of engaging in illicit sexual relations, thus not being herself in violation of the Mann Act, she and the man involved may not be convicted of a conspiracy to violate the Mann Act.

FACTS: Gebardi (D) purchased railway tickets, and a woman (D), not then his wife, consented to travel with him across state lines for the purpose of engaging in illicit sexual relations. No other person conspired and no evidence showed that the woman took an active role in conceiving or carrying out the transportation. The two were found guilty of conspiring to violate the Mann Act.

ISSUE: Where a woman has not violated the Mann Act, may she be convicted of a conspiracy with the man to violate it?

HOLDING AND DECISION: (Stone, J.) No. Under the Mann Act, mere acquiescence by the woman transported in violation of the Mann Act is not, in itself, a violation by the woman of the Mann Act. However, incapacity of one to commit the substantive offense does not necessarily imply that he may, without fear of punishment, conspire with others who are able to commit it. Here, the criminal object of the conspiracy involved the agreement of the woman to her transportation by the man, the very conspiracy charged. The failure of the Mann Act to condemn the woman's consent is evidence of an affirmative legislative policy to leave unpunished her acquiescence. If she cannot commit the substantive offense, and only one other person, the man, is involved, she cannot conspire to commit the offense. And as a conspiracy necessarily requires at least two persons, there could be no conspiracy here. Reversed.

▶ *ANALYSIS*

It is proper to convict a person of conspiracy only if he will be guilty of participation in the crime that was committed. In a comment to the Model Penal Code, Tent. Draft No. 10 (1960), it was said, "The doctrine is clear upon principle, for an agreement to aid another to commit a crime is not rendered less dangerous than any other conspiracy by

virtue of the fact that one party cannot commit it so long as the other party can." But here the woman could not be punished for conspiring to commit a legal act, and the man alone could not be a conspiracy of one.

Quicknotes

CONSPIRACY Concerted action by two or more persons to accomplish some unlawful purpose.

SUBSTANTIVE OFFENSE An offense that is capable of being committed without also committing another offense.

Garcia v. State

Wife (D) v. State (P)

Ind. Sup. Ct., 271 Ind. 510, 394 N.E.2d 106 (1979).

NATURE OF CASE: Appeal from a conviction of conspiracy to commit murder.

FACT SUMMARY: The only party with whom Garcia (D) conspired in her effort to have her husband murdered was a police informant who only feigned his acquiescence in the scheme.

🏛 RULE OF LAW
Under a penal code that adopts a "unilateral" concept of conspiracy, as opposed to the common-law's traditional "bilateral" concept, a person can be convicted of conspiracy even if the only party with whom he "conspired" feigned acquiescence in the plan.

FACTS: Garcia (D) contacted Young to solicit the murder of her husband, whom she claimed constantly beat her and her children. The subsequent interactions culminated in her arrest and conviction of conspiracy to commit murder. Young, the only one with whom she allegedly "conspired," was a police informant who claimed he had only feigned his acquiescence in the scheme. Garcia (D) appealed her conviction on the ground that no conspiracy existed because there was thus no "conspiratorial agreement."

ISSUE: Does a penal code that adopts a "unilateral" concept of conspiracy permit one to be convicted of conspiracy even though the only party with whom one "conspired" feigned acquiescence in the plan?

HOLDING AND DECISION: (Prentice, J.) Yes. Where, as in this case, a penal code has abandoned the traditional common-law "bilateral" concept of conspiracy in favor of a "unilateral" concept, it is entirely possible for a person to be convicted of conspiracy even though the only party with whom he "conspired" feigned acquiescence in the scheme. The Model Penal Code, which takes the "unilateral" approach, explains rather well that "the major basis of conspiratorial liability—the unequivocal evidence of a firm purpose to commit a crime—remains the same" despite the fact that the person with whom the defendant conspired secretly intended not to go through with the plan. Thus, the traditional viewpoint that conspiracy necessitates actual mutual agreement on the part of two or more parties is not valid under the concept of conspiracy that Indiana's penal code now embraces, as do at least 26 states. Affirmed.

▶ ANALYSIS

The "unilateral" concept of conspiracy "creates" liability in a number of other situations where it would not traditionally exist. As the Model Penal Code states (in its comments after § 5.03), liability is intended to attach even in those cases where "the person with whom the defendant conspired has not been apprehended or tried, or his case has been disposed of in a manner that would raise questions of consistency about a conviction of the defendant."

Quicknotes

CONSPIRACY Concerted action by two or more persons to accomplish some unlawful purpose.

UNILATERAL One-sided; involving only one person.

United States v. Elliott

Federal government (P) v. Conspirators (D)

571 F.2d 880 (5th Cir. 1978).

NATURE OF CASE: Appeal from convictions for criminal conspiracy.

FACT SUMMARY: Elliott (D) and others were involved in a criminal organization which engaged in various criminal activities, the details and specifics of which were not known to every member thereof.

🏛 RULE OF LAW
When the charge is not conspiracy to engage in a crime but conspiracy to engage in criminal enterprise, it is proper to try jointly defendants accused of specific crimes committed in furtherance of the conspiracy but not within the knowledge of all the defendants and to introduce evidence of those crimes.

FACTS: Several defendants, including Elliott (D), were tried and convicted of violating the Racketeer Influenced and Corrupt Organizations Act of 1970 (RICO) by being involved in a conspiracy to engage in criminal enterprise. Some of the defendants allegedly furthered this enterprise by committing specific crimes of which the other defendants were unaware. On this basis, Elliott (D) and the others appealed their convictions, arguing that proof of multiple conspiracies was improper when the charge was that a single conspiracy existed. In essence, the argument was that defendants could not be tried en masse for the conglomeration of distinct and separate offenses committed by others.

ISSUE: If defendants are charged with conspiracy to engage in criminal enterprise rather than conspiracy to commit a crime, is it proper to try them jointly and introduce evidence of the specific crimes each participated in to further the conspiracy despite the fact that some of the defendants might not have had knowledge of or participated in those particular crimes?

HOLDING AND DECISION: (Simpson, J.) Yes. When the charge is not conspiracy to engage in a crime but conspiracy to engage in criminal enterprise, it is proper to try the defendants jointly and introduce evidence of the specific crimes each participated in to further the conspiratorial enterprise despite the fact that some of the defendants might not have had knowledge of or participated in those particular crimes. Elliott (D) and the others agreed to engage in organized criminal enterprise to produce profit, and where this type of "enterprise conspiracy" is alleged, there is no impropriety in introducing proof of the individual crimes committed by various defendants in furtherance of their collective goal. It is of no consequence that the particular crimes were not known to or participated in by all the defendants. The congressional intent in creating this new type of conspiracy law was to reach those bastions of organized crime unreachable under general conspiracy principles by redefining the nature of certain conspiracies so as to authorize effective new remedies, such as this type of joint trial.

▶ ANALYSIS

The first concept of conspiracy envisioned a spoke-like organization where each defendant radiated outward from a central "hub," necessitating at least one common illegal object. Then came recognition of chain conspiracies, each defendant being bound to the conspiracy by the realization that he was a cog in a chain which resulted in illegal activity. With the sophistication of organized crime, these former theories of conspiracy proved outdated and ineffective in coping with large-scale crime, so Congress passed the act addressed in this case.

■══■

Quicknotes

CONSPIRACY Concerted action by two or more persons to accomplish some unlawful purpose.

CRIMINAL ENTERPRISE Unlawful activities of a general character that represent broad criminal conduct in the aggregate.

RACKETEER INFLUENCED AND CORRUPT ORGANIZATIONS (RICO) ACT Federal and state statutes enacted for the purpose of prosecuting organized crime.

■══■

New York Central & Hudson River Railroad Co. v. United States

Railroad (D) v. Federal government (P)

212 U.S. 481 (1909).

NATURE OF CASE: Appeal from a criminal conviction.

FACT SUMMARY: New York Central (D) and its assistant traffic manager were convicted for the payment of rebates to certain companies shipping sugar from New York to Detroit on its trains.

🏛 RULE OF LAW
Although some crimes by their nature cannot be committed by a corporation, the modern authority is that a corporation can commit a crime.

FACTS: It was established that certain companies were given rebates upon shipments of sugar from New York to Detroit on New York Central's (D) trains. New York Central (D) and its assistant traffic manager were convicted for the payment of these rebates. In challenging its conviction, New York Central (D) maintained that a corporation cannot commit a crime and challenged the constitutionality of the Elkins Act. The Act provided that anything done or committed to be done by a corporation common carrier that would constitute a misdemeanor if done by one of its officers, agents, etc., would be held to be a misdemeanor committed by the corporation. It further provided that the act, omission, or failure of any officer, agent, or other person acting for or employed by the corporation would, in enforcing the aforementioned provision, be deemed to be the act, omission, or failure of the corporation common carrier.

ISSUE: Can a corporation commit a crime?

HOLDING AND DECISION: (Day, J.) Yes. While the earlier writers on common law held the law to be that a corporation could not commit a crime, the modern authority, universally, is the other way. It is true that there are some crimes which, by their nature, cannot be committed by corporations. But there is a large class of offenses, of which rebating under the federal statutes is one, wherein the crime consists in purposely doing the things prohibited by statute. In that class of crimes, there is no good reason why corporations may not be held responsible for and charged with the knowledge and purposes of their agents, acting within the authority conferred upon them. Statutes against rebates could not be effectually enforced as long as individuals only were subject to punishment for violation of the law, when the giving of rebates of concessions inures to the benefit of the corporations of which the individuals were but the instruments.

▶ ANALYSIS

The Model Penal Code does not adopt so simple an approach. It actually sets up three distinct systems of corporate criminal liability. One applies to crimes of intent where no "legislative purpose to impose liability on corporations plainly appears," another to crimes of intent for which the legislature did plainly intend to impose liability on corporations, and the third to strict liability crimes.

■=■

Quicknotes

AGENT An individual who has the authority to act on behalf of another.

OMISSION The failure to perform an act or obligation that one is required to perform by law.

STRICT LIABILITY Liability for all injuries proximately caused by a party's conducting of certain inherently dangerous activities without regard to negligence or fault.

■=■

United States v. Hilton Hotels Corp.

Federal government (P) v. Hotel company (D)

467 F.2d 1000 (9th Cir. 1972).

NATURE OF CASE: Appeal from a conviction for violation of the Sherman Act.

FACT SUMMARY: Hilton Hotels Corp. (D) was convicted for violating the Sherman Act after the judge charged the jury that a corporation is responsible for the acts and statements of agents, done or made within the scope of their employment, even if contrary to their actual instructions or to the corporation's stated policies.

🏛 RULE OF LAW
As a general rule, a corporation is liable under the Sherman Act for the acts of its agents in the scope of their employment, even though the acts are contrary to general corporate policy and/or express instructions to the agents.

FACTS: Although it was against the corporate policies of Hilton Hotels Corp. (D) and constituted a violation of instructions that he take no part in the boycott, the purchasing agent for its hotel in Portland, Oregon, had threatened a supplier with loss of the hotel's business unless the supplier paid an assessment to an association which the local businesses had organized to attract convention business to Portland. The agreement among the members of the association was that those suppliers who would not pay their assessment would be "boycotted" (i.e., no purchases would be made from them). Hilton Hotels (D) was convicted for violating the Sherman Act, the judge charging the jury that a corporation is responsible for the acts and statements of its agents, done or made within the scope of their employment, even if contrary to their actual instructions or to the corporation's stated policies. On appeal, Hilton Hotels (D) cited this as error.

ISSUE: Is a corporation liable under the Sherman Act for acts its agents commit in the scope of their employment, even if the acts are against corporate policies or express instructions to the agents?

HOLDING AND DECISION: (Browning, J.) Yes. Congress may constitutionally impose criminal liability upon a business entity for acts or omissions of its agent within the scope of the agent's employment, even without proof that the conduct was within the agent's actual authority and even though the conduct may have been contrary to express instructions to the agent or the policies of the corporation. While the Sherman Act does not expressly impose such liability, the construction of the act

that best achieves its purpose is that a corporation is liable for acts of its agents within the scope of their authority even when done against company orders. Affirmed.

▶ *ANALYSIS*

In "Note, Developments in the Law—Corporate Crime: Regulating Corporate Behavior through Criminal Sanctions," 92 *Harv. L. Rev.* 1227 (1979), one is reminded that "Corporations have been convicted of crimes requiring knowledge on the basis of the 'collective knowledge' of the employees as a group, even though no single employee possessed sufficient information to know that the crime was being committed."

■=■

Quicknotes

AGENT An individual who has the authority to act on behalf of another.

BOYCOTT A concerted effort to refrain from doing business with a particular person or entity.

SHERMAN ACT Makes every contract or conspiracy in unreasonable restraint of commerce illegal.

■=■

Commonwealth v. Beneficial Finance Co.

State (P) v. Corporation (D)

Mass. Sup. Jud. Ct., 360 Mass. 188, 275 N.E.2d 33 (1971).

NATURE OF CASE: Appeal from corporate convictions for bribery and conspiracy to engage in bribery.

FACT SUMMARY: Natural and corporate persons were convicted for bribery schemes intended to obtain favorable treatment from the Massachusetts Small Loan Regulatory Board.

🏛 RULE OF LAW

If a corporation has placed its agent in a position where he has the authority to act for and on behalf of the corporation in handling the particular corporate business, operation, or project in which he was engaged at the time he committed a criminal act, the corporation, as principal, is criminally liable.

FACTS: Beneficial Finance Co. (Beneficial) (D), two of its wholly-owned subsidiaries, and two employees, Farrell (D) and Glynn (D), were involved in a conspiracy to bribe, and in fact did bribe, members of the Small Loans Regulatory Board. Glynn (D) was the direct contact with the bribed officials, and Farrell (D) supervised Glynn's (D) conspiratorial activities and chaired the intercorporate meeting at which the bribery plan was eventually adopted. Beneficial (D) appealed, alleging error in the jury instructions, claiming that the parent corporation could not be held liable for the acts of Glynn (D) and Farrell (D).

ISSUE: If a corporation has placed its agent in a position where he has the authority to act for and on behalf of the corporation in handling the particular corporate business, operation, or project in which he was engaged at the time he committed a criminal act, is the corporation, as principal, criminally liable?

HOLDING AND DECISION: (Spiegel, J.) Yes. If a corporation has placed its agent in a position where he has the authority to act for and on behalf of the corporation in handling the particular corporate business, operation, or project in which he was engaged at the time he committed a criminal act, the corporation, as principal, is criminally liable. The jury may infer a corporate policy by the corporation's placing its agent in a certain position, commissioning him to handle the particular corporate affairs in which he was engaged at the time of committing the criminal act in question. Thus, the acts and intent of natural persons (officers, directors, and employees) can be treated as the acts and intent of the corporation itself. Combining the criminal standard of guilt—guilt beyond a reasonable doubt—with the rule of respondeat superior justifies the standard applied by the trial court to a criminal prosecution of a corporation for a specific-intent crime.

The size and complexity of large corporations, which necessitates the delegation of more authority to lesser corporate employees, allows lesser employees in several instances more authority and broader power in certain areas than a higher-ranking corporate officer. [Affirmed.]

▶ ANALYSIS

This case contains some basic concepts of corporation law. The doctrine of respondeat superior, which generally applies to employer-employee relationships, naturally arises here. Under that doctrine, the employer is liable for the conduct of his employee performed within the scope of his employment. A second concept concerns conduct of the corporation itself and its wholly-owned subsidiary, a second corporation. The two corporations being publicly represented as part of one system led the court to look through the corporate form in order to prevent the general availability of corporate insulation from protecting the parent corporation from punishment for wrongdoing by the other corporation with which it is basically one and the same. That is to say, where one corporation exercises management and control over the other, the acts of the subsidiary become the acts of the parent corporation.

Quicknotes

AGENT An individual who has the authority to act on behalf of another.

BRIBERY The unlawful offering or accepting of something of value with the intent of influencing the judgment or actions of a public official in the discharge of his official duties.

PRINCIPAL A person or entity who authorizes another (the agent) to act on its behalf and subject to its authority to the extent that the principal may be held liable for the actions of the agent.

RESPONDEAT SUPERIOR Rule that the principal is responsible for tortious acts committed by its agents in the scope of their agency or authority.

United States v. Guidant LLC

Federal government (P) v. Corporation (D)

708 F. Supp. 2d 903 (D. Minn. 2010).

NATURE OF CASE: Federal district court's decision whether to accept or reject a plea agreement.

FACT SUMMARY: Guidant LLC (D) manufactured implantable defibrillators for people suffering from fast heart rhythms. Two of the models had defects that could result in sudden cardiac arrest.

🏛 RULE OF LAW
A term of probation for a corporation may be appropriate to serve the public interest and to ensure accountability by the corporation by forcing it to implement internal compliance and ethics programs.

FACTS: Guidant LLC (D) manufactured implantable defibrillators for people suffering from fast heart rhythms. Two of the models had defects that could result in sudden cardiac arrest. Guidant discovered the defects, but failed to notify the Food and Drug Administration (FDA) as required by law. Guidant (D) plead guilty to two misdemeanor counts of making material false statements on reports to the FDA and failing to notify the FDA promptly about the problems. The Government (P) and Guidant (D) agreed to a plea agreement in which Guidant (D) would pay a criminal fine of $253,962,251 and a separate criminal forfeiture of $42,079,685. A term of probation was not part of the agreement. The federal trial court considered the agreement and issued this decision.

ISSUE: May a term of probation for a corporation be appropriate to serve the public interest and to ensure accountability by the corporation by forcing it to implement internal compliance and ethics programs?

HOLDING AND DECISION: (Frank, J.) Yes. A term of probation for a corporation may be appropriate to serve the public interest and to ensure accountability by the corporation by forcing it to implement internal compliance and ethics programs. Via a probation order, Guidant (D) could be ordered to perform community service to help restore and build the public's confidence in the FDA approval process and in the medical device industry's quality control process. Significantly, Guidant (D) could also be required to establish internal compliance and ethics programs. Such programs could appoint employees who would work directly with the FDA in reporting such progress. Accordingly, the court hereby declines to accept the plea agreement.

▌ ANALYSIS

The court's rationale for recommending a term of probation is to try and prevent the corporation from committing the same offense again. A fine alone, no matter how steep, often does not act as a deterrent particularly where such fines end up being paid by the innocent shareholders of the company.

■═■

Quicknotes

PROBATION A method of imposing sentence whereby the individual is not imprisoned but is under the supervision of a parole officer, subject to specified conditions.

■═■

Gordon v. United States

Partners (D) v. Federal government (P)

203 F.2d 248 (10th Cir. 1953); *rev'd*, 347 U.S. 909 (1954).

NATURE OF CASE: Appeal from conviction for violation of the Defense Production Act.

FACT SUMMARY: Gordon (D) and his partners (D) in an appliance business were convicted of violating the Defense Production Act by their salesmen's making sales of sewing machines without collecting the required down payment.

🏛 RULE OF LAW
Employers may be held liable criminally for the knowledge and acts of their agents and employees in cases involving "public welfare" offenses.

FACTS: Gordon (D) and his partners (D), also charged, ran a sewing machine and appliance business. Their salesmen, in violation of the Defense Production Act, sold sewing machines without collecting the down payment required by law. The salesmen were acting in the course of their employment at the time. Gordon (D) and his partners (D) lacked knowledge of the fact that their salesmen were violating the Act.

ISSUE: May the guilty acts of the employee be imputed, in cases involving public welfare offenses, to the innocent employer where the employee was acting within the course and scope of his employment?

HOLDING AND DECISION: (Murrah, J.) Yes. While it is deeply rooted in English and American criminal jurisprudence that criminal guilt is personal to the accused, and that one cannot intend an act which he did not consciously participate in, agree to, or have guilty knowledge of, in public welfare cases involving police regulation of food, drink, and drugs, the standard of proof for willful intent has been relaxed. Willfulness or guilty knowledge is not dispensed with. Rather, the employer is charged with knowledge of records which he is required to keep. Connoted is a course of conduct which may be construed by the trier of fact as deliberate and voluntary, and hence, intentional. Affirmed.

DISSENT: (Huxman, J.) A person cannot be held criminally responsible for the acts of his employee, even when committed within the scope of his employment, if he lacks personal knowledge of those criminal acts. The majority is confusing criminal law as applied to corporate employers. As a corporation is a legal fiction lacking a mind, it can only be held responsible through the knowledge of its agents. The Defense Production Act requires a willful violation which has not been shown.

ON APPEAL TO THE U.S. SUPREME COURT: (Per curiam) Reversed for new trial. On appeal, the government admitted it was error not to require a finding of willful violation of the Act.

▶ ANALYSIS

The student is reminded to ignore the opinion of the majority above as it is erroneous. The majority mistakenly applied corporate criminal law to a case involving a partnership. While a corporation is a legal fiction, a partnership exists because of at least two real persons who lack the corporate insulation from personal responsibility. Note that the majority discusses public welfare offenses involving food, drink, and drugs. Does the sale of sewing machines appear to come under such a heading? Even if it does, note further that all cases arising in the area dealt only with laws whose violation did not require willfulness.

Quicknotes

AGENT An individual who has the authority to act on behalf of another.

CORPORATION A distinct legal entity characterized by continuous existence; free alienability of interests held therein; centralized management; and limited liability on the part of the shareholders of the corporation.

PARTNERSHIP A voluntary agreement entered into by two or more parties to engage in business and to share any attendant profits and losses.

United States v. Park

Federal government (P) v. Corporate officer (D)

421 U.S. 658 (1975).

NATURE OF CASE: Appeal of conviction for violation of the federal Food, Drug and Cosmetic Act.

FACT SUMMARY: Park (D), president of Acme Markets, Inc. (D), was prosecuted for violations of the Food, Drug and Cosmetic Act.

🏛 RULE OF LAW
The manager of a corporate defendant may be prosecuted under the Federal Food, Drug and Cosmetic Act absent affirmative wrongdoing.

FACTS: Park (D) was president of Acme Markets, Inc. (Acme) (D). FDA inspectors found substantial quantities of food warehoused by Acme (D) to be rodent-infested. Following several subsequent inspections, which demonstrated the problem to be unresolved, Acme (D) and Park (D) were charged with violations of the Federal Food, Drug and Cosmetic Act. Acme (D) pleaded guilty and Park (D) was convicted. The court of appeals reversed, holding that a strict liability offense such as a violation of the Act required some affirmative wrongdoing. The Government (P) petitioned for certiorari.

ISSUE: May the manager of a corporate defendant be prosecuted under the Federal Food, Drug and Cosmetic Act absent affirmative wrongdoing?

HOLDING AND DECISION: (Burger, C.J.) Yes. The manager of a corporate defendant may be prosecuted under the Federal Food, Drug and Cosmetic Act absent affirmative wrongdoing. It must be remembered that a corporation can act only through the individuals acting on its behalf. The Act imposes an affirmative duty on one providing a product within its ambit to seek out and implement measures to prevent violations of the Act. In the case of corporations, the only effective way to ensure that this occurs is to hold those responsible for a corporation's violations to the same standard as the corporation itself. This being so, the affirmative wrongdoing requirement grafted on by the court of appeals was improper. Reversed.

DISSENT: (Stewart, J.) The instructions given by the district court did not comport with the rule fashioned by the Court today. The Court's rule would impose liability only if the defendant had a position of responsibility in the corporation related to the violation. The district court's instruction would impose liability on an individual with responsibilities in the corporation not so related.

▌ANALYSIS

The federal Food, Drug and Cosmetic Act is a "strict liability" offense. No proof of mental state is required. This type of offense is at odds with the traditional view of criminal culpability. Nonetheless, a good portion of "general welfare" laws impose strict liability.

■≡■

Quicknotes

AFFIRMATIVE DUTY An obligation to undertake an affirmative action for the benefit of another.

FEDERAL FOOD, DRUG, AND COSMETIC ACT Consumer-protection statute authorizing promulgation of rules governing food and drugs.

STRICT LIABILITY Liability for all injuries proximately caused by a party's conducting of certain inherently dangerous activities without regard to negligence or fault.

■≡■

United States v. MacDonald & Watson Waste Oil Co.

Federal government (P) v. Oil company (D)

933 F.2d 35 (1st Cir. 1991).

NATURE OF CASE: Appeal from conviction of knowingly transporting hazardous waste to a facility that had no permit.

FACT SUMMARY: D'Allesandro (D) contended that his conviction under the Resource Conservation and Recovery Act had been improper because the jury had been allowed to infer knowledge of the illegal activities based on D'Allesandro's (D) position as a responsible corporate officer.

RULE OF LAW
In a crime having knowledge as an express element, a mere showing of official responsibility is not an adequate substitute for direct or circumstantial proof of knowledge.

FACTS: MacDonald & Watson Waste Oil Company (MacDonald) (D) was found guilty of violating the Resource Conservation and Recovery Act (RCRA) after disposing solid toxic waste at a facility lacking the proper permits. D'Allesandro (D), the president of MacDonald (D), was also charged with knowingly transporting hazardous waste to a facility that did not have a permit. The court instructed the jury that RCRA's scienter element could be satisfied, in effect, by showing that D'Allesandro (D) was a responsible corporate officer who knew or believed that the same type of illegal activity had occurred before. D'Allesandro (D) was convicted and appealed, contending that the responsible corporate officer doctrine did not apply to felony statutes.

ISSUE: In a crime having knowledge as an express element, is a mere showing of official responsibility an adequate substitute for direct or circumstantial proof of knowledge?

HOLDING AND DECISION: (Campbell, C.J.) No. In a crime having knowledge as an express element, a mere showing of official responsibility is not an adequate substitute for direct or circumstantial proof of knowledge. Scienter, as an element in a criminal statute, cannot be inferred from a person's position of authority in an organization. The requisite scienter may, of course, be proven indirectly in a manner such that inference must be utilized. However, a mental state cannot be inferred merely from the position a person occupies. Simply because D'Allesandro (D) believed that on a prior occasion illegal transportation occurred, he did not necessarily possess knowledge of the violation charged in this case. Conviction vacated and remanded.

ANALYSIS

In the decisions above, Justice Campbell distinguished the seminal cases regarding the responsible corporate officer doctrine, *United State v. Dotterweich*, 320 U.S. 277 (1943) and *United States v. Park*, 421 U.S. 658 (1975). The *Dotterweich* court held a corporate officer criminally liable for commission of a public welfare—i.e., strict liability—offense, although he had no personal connection to the crime. The dissent argued that guilt is personal and should not be lightly imputed to someone who lacks evil intention or consciousness of wrongdoing. In *Park*, similarly, the president and CEO of the offending corporation was found to have "had a responsible relation to the situation" and was therefore held liable for the violation.

Quicknotes

SCIENTER Knowledge of certain facts; often refers to "guilty knowledge," which implicates liability.

STRICT LIABILITY Liability for all injuries proximately caused by a party's conducting of certain inherently dangerous activities without regard to negligence or fault.

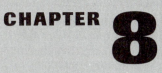

CHAPTER 8

Exculpation

United States v. Peterson

Federal government (P) v. Convicted murderer (D)

483 F.2d 1222 (D.C. Cir. 1973).

NATURE OF CASE: Appeal from a manslaughter conviction.

FACT SUMMARY: Peterson (D) appealed a manslaughter conviction after a trial in which he advanced the theory that he had acted in self-defense.

🏛 RULE OF LAW
In order for one to have the legal right to maim or kill in self-defense, there must have been an unlawful and immediate threat either actual or apparent, of the use of deadly force against the defender; he must have believed he was in imminent peril of death or serious bodily injury, and that the force he used was necessary to save himself therefrom.

FACTS: The issue of self-defense was at hand in Peterson's (D) appeal of his conviction for manslaughter.

ISSUE: Does one's right to maim or kill in self-defense depend on there having been an unlawful and immediate threat (either actual or apparent) of the use of deadly force against him so that he believed he was in imminent peril of death or serious bodily injury, and that the force he used was necessary to save himself therefrom?

HOLDING AND DECISION: (Robinson, J.) Yes. The doctrine of homicidal self-defense emerges from the body of the criminal law as a limited exception to legal outlawry of the arena of self-help in the settlement of potentially fatal personal conflicts. It remains as viable now as it was in Blackstone's time; it also remains a law of necessity. The right of self-defense arises only when the necessity begins, and equally ends with the necessity. Thus, to have the legal right to maim or kill in self-defense, there must have been an unlawful and immediate threat (actual or apparent) of the use of deadly force against the defender. The defender must have believed he was in imminent peril of death or serious bodily harm, and that his response was necessary to save himself therefrom. These beliefs must not only have been honestly entertained, but also objectively reasonable in light of the surrounding circumstances. Nothing less than a concurrence of these elements will suffice.

▶ ANALYSIS

Most modern statutes maintain the traditional requirement that the defender's honest belief that the defensive force he used was necessary to save himself from death or serious bodily harm be objectively reasonable. English commentators, the Criminal Law Revision Committee, and Professor Glanville Williams have supported the notion that

a wholly subjective test should be used instead, i.e., one which concerns itself only with whether the defender honestly believed he needed to use the force he did to save himself from death or serious bodily injury.

■═■

Quicknotes

MANSLAUGHTER The killing of another person without premeditation, deliberation or with the intent to kill or to commit a felony, which may be reasonably expected to result in death or serious bodily injury; manslaughter is characterized by reckless conduct or by some adequate provocation on the part of the actor, as determined by a subjective standard.

SELF-DEFENSE The right to protect an individual's person, family or property against attempted injury by another.

■═■

People v. Goetz

State (P) v. Subway passenger (D)

N.Y. Ct. App., 68 N.Y.2d 96, 497 N.E.2d 41 (1986).

NATURE OF CASE: Appeal from dismissal of attempted murder charges.

FACT SUMMARY: Goetz (D) contended that he was justified in shooting his assailants if he alone reasonably believed he was in danger, and not if a reasonable man believed so.

RULE OF LAW
A person is justified in the use of deadly force if, objectively, a reasonable man would, in his position, believe he was in danger of life or physical being.

FACTS: Goetz (D) was approached on a subway by several youths who asked him for money. Goetz (D), who had been attacked years before, subjectively believed he was being robbed and pulled a gun. He shot at the youths several times, even though they ran away. In one case, Goetz (D) approached an unarmed youth and shot him. Goetz (D) admitted he wanted to kill the youths. The prosecution instructed the Grand Jury that self-defense could be found only if Goetz (D) objectively, as a reasonable man, could have concluded his life was in danger. Indictments were handed down, yet the trial court dismissed them because it held the prosecution erroneously instructed that an objective rather than a subjective standard applied. The State (P) appealed.

ISSUE: Does an objective test apply to the determination of the availability of self-defense?

HOLDING AND DECISION: (Wachtler, C.J.) Yes. A person is justified in the use of self-defense by deadly force if, objectively, a reasonable man would believe he was in danger of life. Subjective basis for the use of such force cannot be the standard a civilized society uses. It is too easy to fabricate a justification for the use of force. The situation must objectively require the use of such force, and the factors must be identifiable by the trier of fact. Dismissed counts reinstated.

ANALYSIS

A common thread that runs through the defense of self-defense and the defense of insanity is the objective test. As seen above in *Goetz*, an objective reasonable person test was applied to determine whether the defendant was justified in taking the action he did to protect his own life. In insanity defense cases, the preferred approach is similar. If objectively viewed the defendant cannot appreciate the illegality of his conduct, the insanity defense can be assessed.

■=■

Quicknotes

MODEL PENAL CODE INSANITY DEFENSE A person is not liable for his criminal offenses if at the time of committing the crime(s) he suffered from a mental disease or defect and thereby lacked the substantial capacity to appreciate the wrongfulness of his actions or to conform his actions to the requirements of law.

OBJECTIVE STANDARD A standard that is not personal to an individual but is dependent on some external source.

REASONABLE PERSON STANDARD The standard of care exercised by a hypothetical person who possesses the intelligence, education, knowledge, attention, and judgment required by society of its members when governing behavior; the standard applies to a person's judgment when determining breach of a duty under the theory of negligence.

SELF-DEFENSE The right to protect an individual's person, family or property against attempted injury by another.

■=■

State v. Kelly

State (P) v. Convicted murderer (D)

N.J. Sup. Ct., 97 N.J. 178, 478 A.2d 364 (1984).

NATURE OF CASE: Appeal from conviction for reckless manslaughter.

FACT SUMMARY: Kelly (D) appealed from a decision affirming her conviction of reckless manslaughter, contending that the trial court erred in ruling that expert testimony concerning the "battered-woman's syndrome" was inadmissible on the issue of self-defense.

🏛 RULE OF LAW
The battered-woman's syndrome is an appropriate subject for expert testimony, and such testimony is admissible on the issue of self-defense.

FACTS: On May 24, 1980, Kelly (D) stabbed her husband to death with a pair of scissors. The facts surrounding the actual stabbing were in dispute. Kelly (D) claimed that she stabbed him in self-defense, while the State (P) contended that she was the aggressor in the attack. Evidence presented during the trial indicated that the marriage between Kelly (D) and her husband was a rocky one, with Kelly (D) being subjected to frequent, periodic beatings at the hand of her husband. Evidence was also presented that Kelly (D) had been threatened with death by Mr. Kelly on more than one occasion. Kelly (D) attempted to introduce expert testimony on the battered-woman's syndrome to help establish her claim of self-defense. The trial court, apparently believing that the purpose of the testimony was to explain and justify Kelly's (D) perception of being in fear of her life, ruled the testimony inadmissible, and Kelly (D) was convicted of reckless manslaughter. The appellate court affirmed the conviction, and from this decision, Kelly (D) appealed.

ISSUE: Is the battered-woman's syndrome an appropriate subject for expert testimony, and is such testimony admissible on the issue of self-defense?

HOLDING AND DECISION: (Wilentz, C.J.) Yes. The battered-woman's syndrome is an appropriate subject for expert testimony, and such testimony is admissible on the issue of self-defense. The battered-woman's syndrome is what some sociologists and psychologists call the effects of a sustained pattern of physical and psychological abuse that undeniably a substantial number of women suffer from. Among the effects of such abuse, and which the battered-woman's syndrome attempts to explain, is the demoralizing and degrading situation in which these women often exist and are often trapped by their own fear. Kelly's (D) credibility is a key issue in this case, since in order to find for her, the jury must believe that she acted in self-defense. The expert testimony excluded was clearly relevant to her state of mind, namely that it was admissible to show she honestly believed that she was in imminent danger of death, by showing that Kelly's (D) experience was common with other women in similar abusive relationships. The testimony would be relevant solely for this purpose, but not as to the objective reasonableness of Kelly's (D) belief. The battered-woman's syndrome is an area where the trier of fact's common perceptions may be mistaken. [After determining the testimony admissible, the court went on to rule that the testimony satisfied state Evidence Rule requirements for admissibility, in that the area was not one within lay knowledge, and that the testimony was sufficiently reliable.] Reversed; remanded for new trial.

▶ ANALYSIS

The battered-woman's syndrome creates problems for prosecutors, because the syndrome can help explain the actions of a battered woman who may act not in the face of an immediate threat, but in the face of an imminent threat, since the actions manifest over a period of time as a result of frequent and persistent abuse. Courts, in evaluating this type of case on appeal, are often called to rule based on perceptions of the battered-woman situation which do not comport with the opinions of sociologists and psychologists who have studied this situation extensively.

■═■

Quicknotes

BATTERED-WOMAN'S SYNDROME An affirmative defense to a charge of homicide, asserted by a wife who has been physically abused by her husband for many years and who kills her abuser while not under imminent circumstances.

RECKLESS MANSLAUGHTER The killing of another person without premeditation or deliberation or with the intent to kill or to commit a felony, which may be reasonably expected to result in death or serious bodily injury; reckless manslaughter is characterized by reckless conduct in the commission of a lawful act, or by the commission of an unlawful act that is not a felony, but which leads to the killing of another.

SELF-DEFENSE The right to protect an individual's person, family or property against attempted injury by another.

■═■

State v. Norman

State (P) v. Wife (D)

N.C. Sup. Ct., 324 N.C. 253, 378 S.E.2d 8 (1989).

NATURE OF CASE: Review of reversal of manslaughter conviction.

FACT SUMMARY: Norman (D), who had killed her sleeping husband, raised his longstanding abuse of her as a basis for self-defense.

🏛 RULE OF LAW
Absent imminent peril, a history of spousal abuse will not constitute a defense in a homicide prosecution.

FACTS: During the course of her 20-year marriage, Norman (D) had been subjected to severe abuse by her husband. Examples included battery, burning with cigarettes, forced prostitution, and being forced to eat dog food off the floor. One day, Norman (D) was beaten so badly she called the police. She declined out of fear to press charges, however, and they refused to arrest her husband. Norman (D) then attempted suicide. The next day, Norman (D) went to a social service agency; husband followed her there, dragged her out, and beat her. He later got drunk and passed out. Norman (D) went to a relative's house to get a gun, came home and shot her husband to death. Charged with murder, she raised the defense of self-defense. The trial court refused to allow the jury to consider acquittal. She was convicted of voluntary manslaughter and appealed. The court of appeals reversed, accepting that Norman (D) exhibited battered-wife syndrome and that the jury could have found her conduct justified as an act of perfect self-defense. The North Carolina Supreme Court granted review.

ISSUE: Absent imminent peril, will a history of spousal abuse constitute a defense in a homicide prosecution?

HOLDING AND DECISION: (Mitchell, J.) No. Absent imminent peril, a history of spousal abuse will not constitute a defense in a homicide prosecution. Self-defense may be raised in a criminal prosecution only when a defendant reasonably believes herself to be in imminent danger of death or such serious bodily harm that recourse to legal authority would not have been practicable. The killing of another human being is the most extreme recourse to a person's right of self-preservation and, therefore, can only be justified by real or apparent necessity. To accept the now in-vogue "battered wife syndrome" would remove such justification and open the floodgates to legal homicide based on a defendant's conjecture about possible future events. This would make homicidal self-help an accepted norm. Here, Norman (D) had ample time and opportunity to resort to other means of preventing further abuse by her husband. Reversed.

DISSENT: (Martin, J.) No sweeping revision of the law is necessary to sustain the court of appeals' judgment here. The facts of the case are such that Norman (D) could reasonably have believed herself to be in imminent peril.

▌ ANALYSIS

It has become a cliché that hard cases make bad law, but the court here declined to do so. If ever a fact situation called for acceptance of the defense, this was it. However, as experience in other states has shown, adoption of the battered-person syndrome as a defense has led to hung juries in some cases where self-defense was clearly an inappropriate defense.

■▬■

Quicknotes

BATTERED-WOMAN'S SYNDROME An affirmative defense to a charge of homicide, asserted by a wife who has been physically abused by her husband for many years and who kills her abuser while not under imminent circumstances.

MANSLAUGHTER The killing of another person without premeditation, deliberation or with the intent to kill or to commit a felony, which may be reasonably expected to result in death or serious bodily injury; manslaughter is characterized by reckless conduct or by some adequate provocation on the part of the actor, as determined by a subjective standard.

SELF-DEFENSE The right to protect an individual's person, family or property against attempted injury by another.

■▬■

State v. Abbott

State (P) v. Assailant (D)

N.J. Sup. Ct., 36 N.J. 63, 174 A.2d 881 (1961).

NATURE OF CASE: Appeal from conviction of assault and battery.

FACT SUMMARY: Abbott (D) and Michael, Mary, and Nicholas Scarano were in a fight during which Abbott (D) hurt Nicholas with a hatchet.

🏛 RULE OF LAW
A person has a duty to retreat before using deadly force to defend himself, but he need only retreat where he knows that he can do so with complete safety.

FACTS: There was a fight between Nicholas Scarano and Abbott (D). A jury could find Nicholas was the aggressor. Michael Scarano joined the fight armed with a hatchet, and Mary Scarano joined, armed with a knife. All of the Scaranos were hit with the hatchet. Abbott (D) claimed that they were hit while struggling for the hatchet. A jury could find, however, that Abbott (D) intentionally inflicted the blows.

ISSUE: Does a person have a duty to retreat before using deadly force to defend himself?

HOLDING AND DECISION: (Weintraub, C.J.) Yes. A person has a duty to retreat before using deadly force to defend himself. Deadly force may not be used in self-defense when there is an opportunity to retreat. However, the actor must know of the opportunity and must be able to escape with complete safety. The burden is on the defendant to produce evidence to support the defense. But the state has the burden of proving, beyond a reasonable doubt, that the defense is not true. In a case involving the issue of retreat, the state must prove beyond a reasonable doubt that the defendant knew that he could retreat in complete safety. While the retreat issue only arises when deadly force was used, it is relevant where deadly force results in injury, rather than death. In this case, if Abbott's (D) version of the story, which is that all of the Scaranos came after him, is believed, it may be that the retreat issue should be resolved in his favor. Reversed.

▶ ANALYSIS

It is agreed that one need not retreat before using non-deadly force. The majority of U.S. jurisdictions hold that the defender need not retreat, even though he knows he can do so safely, before using deadly force upon an assailant whom he reasonably believes will kill him. While there is a strong policy against the unnecessary taking of human life, there seems to be a stronger policy against making one act in a "cowardly" and "humiliating" manner. Advocates of "no retreat" say that "The manly thing is to hold one's ground and society should not demand what smacks of cowardice." A strong minority of jurisdictions, in which "courageous" men have not prevailed, do not reward such male foolishness, and hold that one must retreat before using deadly force, if the defendant knows he can retreat in safety.

■▬■

Quicknotes

ASSAULT AND BATTERY Any unlawful touching of another person without justification or excuse.

DUTY TO RETREAT The duty to retreat from an encounter before utilizing deadly force in self-defense or in defense of others.

PROOF BEYOND A REASONABLE DOUBT Standard of proof necessary to convict a defendant, requiring the absence of evidence that would cause a reasonable person to hesitate in making an important decision in his personal affairs.

SELF-DEFENSE The right to protect an individual's person, family or property against attempted injury by another.

■▬■

United States v. Peterson

Federal government (P) v. Convicted murderer (D)

483 F.2d 1222 (D.C. Cir. 1973).

NATURE OF CASE: Appeal from conviction of manslaughter.

FACT SUMMARY: Peterson (D) shot and killed Keitt while Keitt was attempting to steal windshield wipers from Peterson's (D) car.

🏛 RULE OF LAW
One cannot support a self-defense claim by a self-generated necessity to kill.

FACTS: While Keitt was attempting to steal windshield wipers from Peterson's (D) car, Peterson (D) went into his house and retrieved a pistol. After warning him that he would shoot if Keitt took another step, Keitt continued to advance toward Peterson (D) and Peterson (D) shot him in the face. Peterson (D) was convicted of manslaughter and appealed, complaining that the judged erred in the jury instruction given with respect to his self-defense claim.

ISSUE: Can one support a self-defense claim by a self-generated necessity to kill?

HOLDING AND DECISION: (Robinson, J.) No. One cannot support a self-defense claim by a self-generated necessity to kill. One who is an aggressor in a conflict culminating in death cannot invoke the necessities of self-preservation. Only if he communicates a good-faith attempt to withdraw may the right of self-defense be reinstated. The trial judge's charge was in compliance with these principles. Affirmed.

▶ ANALYSIS

Here though Keitt may have initially been the aggressor, Peterson's (D) act of retrieving the pistol reversed their roles. The court gleans the general rule from the body of case law on the subject of self-defense "that an affirmative unlawful act reasonably calculated to produce an affray foreboding injurious or fatal consequences is an aggression which, unless renounced, nullifies the right of homicidal self-defense."

■══■

Quicknotes

MANSLAUGHTER The killing of another person without premeditation, deliberation or with the intent to kill or to commit a felony, which may be reasonably expected to result in death or serious bodily injury; manslaughter is characterized by reckless conduct or by some adequate provocation on the part of the actor, as determined by a subjective standard.

SELF-DEFENSE The right to protect an individual's person, family or property against attempted injury by another.

■══■

People v. Ceballos

State (P) v. Trap gun setter (D)

Cal. Sup. Ct., 12 Cal. 3d 470, 526 P.2d 241 (1974).

NATURE OF CASE: Appeal from conviction for assault with a deadly weapon.

FACT SUMMARY: Ceballos (D) was convicted of assault with a deadly weapon when a trap gun he set up in his garage fired into the face of a teenage boy who broke open the garage door.

🏛 RULE OF LAW
A person may be held criminally or civilly liable if he sets upon his premises a deadly mechanical device and that device kills or injures another.

FACTS: Ceballos (D) lived in his apartment over his garage. One month some tools were stolen from his garage. Later, he noticed the lock had been bent and that there were pry marks on the door. Ceballos (D) then set up a trap gun which would fire when someone opened the garage. Two boys, Robert, 15, and Stephen, 16, both unarmed, pried off the lock. When Stephen opened the door, he was shot in the face by the trap gun.

ISSUE: Could Ceballos (D), who contends that the shooting would have been justified had he been present, do indirectly—use deadly force—what he could have done directly?

HOLDING AND DECISION: (Burke, J.) No. A person may be held criminally or civilly liable under statutes proscribing homicides with intent to injure if he sets upon his premises a deadly mechanical device and that device kills or injures another. An exception has been recognized where the intrusion is, in fact, such that the person, were he present, would be justified in taking life or inflicting the bodily harm with his own hands. But if the actor is present there is the possibility that he will realize that deadly force is not necessary, while a device lacks that discretion. Deadly devices should be discouraged because, even though the law of torts recognizes an exception as stated above, that exception is not appropriate to criminal law, for it does not prescribe a workable standard of conduct; liability depends on fortuitous results. While burglary is a dangerous crime at common law, by statute that crime has a much wider scope, so where the character and manner of a burglary would not create a fear of great bodily harm, there is no use of deadly force. Affirmed.

▌ *ANALYSIS*

Defense of property relies on the theory that a man's home is his castle. Deadly force may be used where it appears reasonable and necessary to prevent an unlawful trespass apparently committed to harm the occupants or commit a felony therein. A mere trespass without felonious intent or not creating a serious threat of danger to the occupants will not justify the use of deadly force. Notice that the exception being argued on appeal is a rule of tort law and that the court noted that its decision was against the position of the Restatement (Second) of Torts. The tort rule simply did not state a clear enough standard to be applicable to criminal situations.

∎≡∎

Quicknotes

ASSAULT The intentional placing of another in fear of immediate bodily injury.

BURGLARY Unlawful entry of a building at night with the intent to commit a felony therein.

DEFENSE OF PROPERTY An affirmative defense to criminal liability for the use of force in the protection of one's property.

TRESPASS Unlawful interference with, or damage to, the real or personal property of another.

∎≡∎

Durham v. State

Game warden (D) v. State (P)

Ind. Sup. Ct., 199 Ind. 567, 159 N.E. 145 (1927).

NATURE OF CASE: Appeal from conviction of assault and battery.

FACT SUMMARY: Durham (D), a game warden, arrested Long for illegal fishing. While Long was beating him with an oar, Durham (D) shot him.

🏛 RULE OF LAW
While a police officer is not justified in killing or inflicting great bodily harm in attempting to arrest one accused of a misdemeanor, where the accused resists arrest the officer may repel such resistance with such force as is necessary, short of taking life, and may seriously wound or kill the accused if necessary to prevent the accused from seriously wounding or killing him.

FACTS: Durham (D), a game warden, arrested Long for illegal fishing. Long attempted to escape in his boat. Durham (D) pursued him, and while Long was beating him with an oar, Durham (D) shot him in the arm.

ISSUE: Is an arresting officer ever justified in seriously wounding one whom he is attempting to arrest for a misdemeanor?

HOLDING AND DECISION: (Martin, J.) Yes. An officer may use all the force reasonably necessary to arrest one accused of a misdemeanor. However, he may not, merely for the purpose of effecting the arrest, kill or inflict great bodily harm. Hence, he may not kill a fleeing misdemeanant. If the accused resists, however, the officer may repel the resistance with such force, short of taking life, as is necessary to effect the arrest. Further, in repelling the resistance, the officer is justified in seriously wounding or killing the accused if that is necessary to prevent the accused from seriously wounding or killing the officer. Durham's (D) conviction is reversed.

▶ ANALYSIS

Generally, an officer may use deadly force if he reasonably believes it necessary to prevent the escape of a person fleeing from an arrest for a felony, although as stated in Durham, he may not use such force against one fleeing from an arrest for a misdemeanor. Thus, an officer is not justified in shooting at a speeding auto which does not heed his signal to stop. If he aims at and kills the driver, he is guilty of murder. If he aims at the tire, he is guilty of manslaughter if the driver's death results. According to Professor LaFave, while the felony portion of this rule may have made some sense when all felonies were punishable by death, it is too harsh in present times when many felonies do not carry such a penalty. He advocates that an officer's right to use deadly force to arrest an accused felon be limited to dangerous felonies generally involving a substantial risk of death or great bodily harm.

■▬■

Quicknotes

ASSAULT AND BATTERY Any unlawful touching of another person without justification or excuse.

MISDEMEANOR Any offense that does not constitute a felony, which is generally less severe and for which a lesser punishment is imposed.

■▬■

Tennessee v. Garner

State (P) v. Fleeing suspect (D)

471 U.S. 1 (1985).

NATURE OF CASE: Appeal from reversal of dismissal of civil rights action.

FACT SUMMARY: Garner's (P) decedent, an unarmed suspect, was shot and killed while fleeing from arrest.

🏛 RULE OF LAW
A police officer may not use deadly force to prevent the escape of an unarmed suspect unless it is necessary to prevent the escape and the officer has probable cause to believe the suspect poses a significant threat to others.

FACTS: Memphis police officers responded to a dispatch sent out regarding a prowler. When they arrived at the scene, Garner's (P) decedent was seen running across the backyard. One officer was able to see that he was unarmed. The decedent failed to stop when ordered to, and one of the officers fired at him, killing him. Tennessee law permitted the use of deadly force to stop a fleeing suspect in all circumstances. Garner (P) brought a civil rights action.

ISSUE: May a police officer use deadly force to prevent the escape of an unarmed suspect unless it is necessary to prevent the escape and the officer has probable cause to believe the suspect poses a significant threat to others?

HOLDING AND DECISION: (White, J.) No. A police officer may not use deadly force to prevent the escape of an unarmed suspect unless it is necessary to prevent the escape and the officer has probable cause to believe the suspect poses a significant threat to others. The rights of the individual must be balanced against the governmental interest. The suspect's interest in not being killed is obvious. The use of deadly force is a highly suspect procedure in effecting arrest, as a dead suspect cannot be arrested. Further, it dates from a time when almost all felonies were punishable by death so the suspect would merely receive his punishment a bit sooner. This is not so today. The fact that using deadly force against non-dangerous suspects is disfavored is demonstrated by the fact that less than 15 percent of all police departments allow it. For these reasons, such force is unconstitutional when applied to non-dangerous suspects, and the individual's interest outweighs those of the government. Here, the police had no cause to believe the decedent was dangerous, so the force was excessive. Affirmed.

DISSENT: (O'Connor, J.) To allow a suspect to escape is often to lose all hope of ever catching him. Society has an interest in being protected against suspects at large.

Further, an officer in the field cannot be expected to analyze the situation to the extent the Court's rule requires.

▌ ANALYSIS

The Court analyzed this case in terms of the Fourth Amendment. The use of deadly force was seen as a seizure of the person. The private interest-governmental interest balancing test the Court used has become the established method of determining the constitutional validity of a seizure.

━━

Quicknotes

FOURTH AMENDMENT Provides that persons be secure as to their person and private belongings against unreasonable searches and seizures.

PROBABLE CAUSE A reasonable basis for believing that a crime has been committed.

SEIZURE The removal of property from one's possession due to unlawful activity or in satisfaction of a judgment entered by the court.

━━

People v. Unger

State (P) v. Prison escapee (D)

Ill. Sup. Ct., 66 Ill. 2d 333, 362 N.E.2d 319 (1977).

NATURE OF CASE: Prosecution for escape from prison.

FACT SUMMARY: Unger (D) escaped from a minimum security honor farm allegedly to avoid homosexual assaults and threats of death.

🏛 RULE OF LAW
The defenses of necessity and compulsion are available in escape cases, and the jury should be so instructed where evidence adduced at trial is sufficient to raise the defense.

FACTS: Unger (D) was repeatedly assaulted sexually and threatened with death and physical injury at a minimum security honor farm. Unger (D) left the farm and was apprehended several days later. Unger (D) alleged that his escape was not voluntary and had been caused by compulsion (the acts of others) and necessity (outside forces, e.g., natural conditions). The court refused to instruct the jury that these facts were a defense to the charge. Rather, the court instructed the jury that Unger's (D) reasons for escaping were immaterial.

ISSUE: Are compulsion or necessity defenses to an escape charge?

HOLDING AND DECISION: (Ryan, J.) Yes. While escape situations do not fit within the traditional ambit of either compulsion or necessity defenses, they have been recognized by several jurisdictions in similar situations. Since compulsion requires an imminent threat of great bodily harm, many commentators suggest that the situation fits within the necessity defense. The prisoner is forced to choose between the lesser of two evils. We likewise find that compulsion and necessity are a defense to a charge of escape. Where the defendant raises sufficient evidence at trial, the jury should be instructed as to the availability of the defense. It is a limited defense and the jury may consider factors such as whether the defendant's fears were justified; whether the threat was imminent and sufficiently severe; whether there was time to resort to either the courts or prison officials and if this would be effective; and whether the prisoner immediately reported his escape to the police. These factors go to the weight of the defense. A jury might find the defense valid even if one or more of these factors are missing. Reversed.

DISSENT: (Underwood, J.) An unconditional recognition of these defenses could lead to future problems. I would allow the defenses only where the prisoner exactly complies with the requirements stated by the majority.

Failure to immediately report the escape should prevent their being pleaded as a defense.

▶ ANALYSIS

Duress was recognized as a defense to escape in a situation similar to *Unger* in *People v. Harmon*, 53 Mich. App. 482 (1974). The traditional response by most jurisdictions is that the defense should not be available on public policy grounds. Other jurisdictions would allow the defense on a limited basis, only if certain conditions existed, which were similar to those stated by the majority in *Unger*. *People v. Lovercamp*, 43 Cal. App. 3rd 823 (1974).

Quicknotes

COMPULSION DEFENSE Imminent threat of great bodily harm or death by one party so as to induce the other to commit a criminal offense.

NECESSITY DEFENSE A defense to liability for unlawful activity where the conduct is unavoidable and is justified by preventing the occurrence of a more serious harm.

United States v. Schoon

Federal government (P) v. Vandals (D)

971 F.2d 193 (9th Cir. 1992).

NATURE OF CASE: Appeal from trespass and vandalism convictions.

FACT SUMMARY: A group of individuals (D), who had entered and vandalized an Internal Revenue Service office to protest U.S. involvement in El Salvador, claimed the necessity defense when criminally charged for these acts.

🏛 RULE OF LAW
The necessity defense is unavailable as a matter of law to one committing indirect civil disobedience.

FACTS: Schoon (D) and other individuals (D) entered an Internal Revenue Service office in Tucson, Arizona. Their purpose was to protest U.S. involvement in El Salvador. They engaged in disorderly conduct and splashed simulated blood on the walls and countertops. When they refused to leave, they were arrested and charged with trespass and vandalism. At trial, they sought to raise the defense of necessity, contending that they were trying to save lives in El Salvador. The district court refused to allow them to raise the defense, and they were convicted. They appealed.

ISSUE: Is the necessity defense available to one committing indirect civil disobedience?

HOLDING AND DECISION: (Boochever, J.) No. The necessity defense is unavailable as a matter of law to one committing indirect civil disobedience. The necessity defense contains four conditions: (1) the defendant must have chosen the lesser of two evils; (2) he must have acted to prevent imminent harm; (3) there must have been a direct causal relationship between the defendant's acts and the harm to be averted; and (4) no legal alternatives to disobeying the law existed. The last three conditions can never be met in the case of indirect civil disobedience, which is disobedience of a law that is not, itself, the object of protest. The very purpose of indirect civil disobedience is to bring about a change in law or policy. In a democratic society, the proper avenue for such a goal is political participation. Legal alternatives to civil disobedience will always exist, such as legal protest, voting or some other form of political discourse. Furthermore, since the harm resulting from criminal action taken to secure the repeal of a law necessarily outweighs any benefit of the action, the district court properly refused to offer the necessity instruction. Affirmed.

⏵ *ANALYSIS*

The justification behind the necessity defense is not that the pressure of the situation causes the defendant to somehow lack the mens rea to commit the crime, but that it is a matter of public policy. In order to promote the achievement of higher values—that is, the greater good for the society—the society permits the defendant to violate the literal language of a law. Note that the same rationale underlies the defenses of duress, self-defense, and the defense of others.

Quicknotes

MENS REA Criminal intent.

NECESSITY DEFENSE A defense to liability for unlawful activity where the conduct is unavoidable and is justified by preventing the occurrence of a more serious harm.

TRESPASS Unlawful interference with, or damage to, the real or personal property of another.

VANDALISM Willful destruction of or damage to property.

Public Committee Against Torture v. State of Israel

Committee (P) v. Government (D)

Israel Sup. Ct., H.C. 5100/94 (1999).

NATURE OF CASE: Petition seeking an order prohibiting the use of physical means during interrogations.

FACT SUMMARY: Petitioners sought an order prohibiting the General Security Service from utilizing certain physical means against individuals suspected of committing crimes against Israel's (D) security during interrogations.

🏛 RULE OF LAW
Neither the government nor heads of security services possess the authority to authorize the use of liberty infringing physical means during interrogation of suspects.

FACTS: Israeli authorities issued "a directive" authorizing General Security Service (GSS) interrogators to utilize physical means against individuals suspected of committing crimes against Israel's (D) security under certain circumstances. The applicants, representatives of those arrested and interrogated by the GSS, petitioned the court for an order prohibiting the use of such means.

ISSUE: Does the Government or heads of security services possess the authority to authorize the use of liberty infringing physical means during interrogation of suspects?

HOLDING AND DECISION: (Barak, J.) No. Neither the Government (D) nor heads of security services possess the authority to authorize the use of liberty infringing physical means during interrogation of suspects. Thus the GSS does not have the authority to "shake" a man, hold him in the "Shabach" position, or deprive him of sleep in a manner that is other than inherently required for the interrogation. This decision does not negate the availability of the necessity defense to GSS investigators.

CONCURRENCE: (J'Kedmi, J.) It is difficult to accept that the State should be helpless in those extreme cases referred to as "ticking bombs." I suggest that the judgment be suspended from enforcement for one year in which the GSS could employ exceptional interrogational methods in those rare instances.

▶ ANALYSIS

The Government (D) here relied on the defense of necessity with respect to its interrogation methods. The Government (D) argued that such methods were necessary in order to combat terrorism, such as in the case of "ticking bombs" where such information is necessary to prevent imminent death or injury to many.

Quicknotes

NECESSITY DEFENSE A defense to liability for unlawful activity where the conduct is unavoidable and is justified by preventing the occurrence of a more serious harm.

Cruzan v. Director, Missouri Dept. of Health
Patient (P) v. State officials (D)

497 U.S. 261 (1989).

NATURE OF CASE: Review of order upholding refusal of state authorities to terminate life support on a comatose individual.

FACT SUMMARY: Missouri officials (D) refused to terminate life support on a comatose patient, Cruzan, because they contended that state law requiring clear and convincing evidence that such action would comport with the parents' wishes had not been satisfied.

🏛 RULE OF LAW
A state may require that a person not be denied life support unless a desire for such denial can be shown by clear and convincing evidence.

FACTS: As a result of an auto accident, Cruzan was left in a "permanent vegetative state," exhibiting motor reflexes but no perceptible cognitive function. Cruzan's parents (P), citing Cruzan's wishes as expressed prior to her accident, requested that life support be discontinued. The hospital staff refused. Cruzan's parents (P) filed an action to obtain an injunction mandating the cessation of Cruzan's life support. The trial court issued the injunction, but the Missouri Supreme Court reversed. The supreme court held that Missouri law required clear and convincing evidence that a person wished the cessation of life support, and the evidence that this had been Cruzan's wishes did not satisfy that burden. The United States Supreme Court granted review.

ISSUE: May a state require that a person not be denied life support unless a desire for such denial can be shown by clear and convincing evidence?

HOLDING AND DECISION: (Rehnquist, C.J.) Yes. A state may require that a person not be denied life support unless a desire for such denial can be shown by clear and convincing evidence. It can be assumed that a person enjoys a constitutionally protected liberty interest in declining to accept life-saving medical treatment. However, the state has countervailing interests as well. A state's most important role is to protect the lives of its citizens. This, plus the irrevocable nature of a decision to discontinue life support, justifies a state's decision to demand clear and convincing evidence of a patient's wishes. When the patient is lucid, this presents no problem. When, as here, the patient is unable to communicate her wishes, evidence of past expressions may suffice. Here, the Missouri Supreme Court found Cruzan's past expressions insufficient to constitute clear and convincing evidence, a finding it was entitled to make. Affirmed.

▶ ANALYSIS
This was a closely watched case because it was supposed to reveal the Supreme Court's long-awaited final word on the "right to die." As it often does, the Court disappointed its watchers here. The Court merely held that a state could set a high evidentiary standard before allowing a patient to die. A right to die was assumed for the sake of argument but not expressly decided upon.

Quicknotes
CLEAR AND CONVINCING An evidentiary standard requiring a demonstration that the fact sought to be proven is reasonably certain.

INJUNCTION A remedy imposed by the court ordering a party to cease the conduct of a specific activity.

Washington v. Glucksberg

State (D) v. Physician (P)

521 U.S. 702 (1997).

NATURE OF CASE: Review of an order holding that a state law banning assisted-suicide was unconstitutional.

FACT SUMMARY: Washington's (D) statute banning assisted-suicide was held to be unconstitutional on due process grounds.

🏛 RULE OF LAW
The asserted "right" to assistance in committing suicide is not a fundamental liberty interest protected by the Due Process Clause.

FACTS: Glucksberg (P) and other physicians and their terminally ill patients sued the State (D) seeking a declaratory judgment that the State (D) ban on assisted suicide violated the Due Process Clause. The district court agreed and the Ninth Circuit Court of Appeals affirmed.

ISSUE: Is the asserted "right" to assistance in committing suicide a fundamental liberty interest protected by the Due Process Clause?

HOLDING AND DECISION: (Rehnquist, C.J.) No. The asserted "right" to assistance in committing suicide is not a fundamental liberty interest protected by the Due Process Clause. Washington's (D) assisted-suicide ban is rationally related to legitimate government interests, since Washington (D) has an unqualified interest in the preservation of human life, in protecting the integrity and ethics of the medical profession, and in protecting vulnerable groups of people.

▶ ANALYSIS

In a companion case, the Court also rejected the argument that the Fourteenth Amendment Equal Protection Clause would be violated by laws prohibiting suicide. The law has long used actors' intent to distinguish between two acts that may have the same result. Thus, refusing life-sustaining treatment is to be distinguished from suicide.

■━■

Quicknotes

ASSISTED SUICIDE The aiding of another in terminating his own life.

EQUAL PROTECTION CLAUSE A constitutional guarantee that no person should be denied the same protection of the laws enjoyed by other persons in like circumstances.

FOURTEENTH AMENDMENT Declares all persons born or naturalized in the United States and of the state wherein they reside and prohibits states from abridging their privileges and immunities.

RATIONAL BASIS REVIEW A test employed by the court to determine the validity of a statute in equal protection actions, whereby the court determines whether the challenged statute is rationally related to the achievement of a legitimate state interest.

STRICT SCRUTINY The method by which courts determine the constitutionality of a law when a law affects a fundamental right. Under the test, the legislature must have a compelling interest to enact the law and measures prescribed by the law must be the least restrictive means possible to accomplish its goal.

SUBSTANTIVE DUE PROCESS A constitutional safeguard limiting the power of the state, irrespective of how fair its procedures may be; substantive limits placed on the power of the state.

UNDUE BURDEN Unlawfully oppressive or troublesome.

■━■

State v. Toscano

State (P) v. Chiropractor (D)

N.J. Sup. Ct., 74 N.J. 421, 378 A.2d 755 (1977).

NATURE OF CASE: Appeal from conviction for conspiracy to obtain money by false pretenses.

FACT SUMMARY: The trial judge decided that Toscano's (D) claims that he engaged in certain illegal acts because of fear that another party would harm himself or his wife in the future were, even if true, insufficient to constitute a defense of duress—and he so instructed the jury.

🏛 RULE OF LAW
Duress is a defense to a crime (other than murder) if the defendant engaged in conduct because he was coerced to do so by the use of, or threat to use, unlawful force against his person or the person of another, which a person of reasonable firmness in his situation would have been unable to resist.

FACTS: At his trial for conspiracy to obtain money by false pretenses, Toscano (D), a chiropractor, admitted that he had aided in the preparation of a fraudulent insurance claim by making out a false medical report. He maintained that he did so, however, because the architect of the conspiracy had implied that the future safety of himself and his wife depended on it. Because he found there was no evidence that Toscano (D) acted under a present, imminent, and impending threat of serious bodily injury to himself or another, the trial judge instructed the jury that "the circumstances described by Toscano (D) leading to his implication in whatever criminal activities in which you may find he participated are not sufficient to constitute the defense of duress." The appellate division affirmed his conviction.

ISSUE: Is the defense of duress available to one who was coerced into illegal conduct by the use of or threat to use unlawful force against his person or the person of another?

HOLDING AND DECISION: (Pashman, J.) Yes. At common law, the defense of duress applied only if the alleged coercion involved a use or threat of harm which is "present, imminent and pending" and "of such a nature as to induce a well-grounded apprehension of death or serious bodily harm if the act is not done." Not satisfied with this common-law standard, some commentators have advocated a flexible rule which would allow a jury to consider whether the accused actually lost his capacity to act in accordance with "his own desire, or motivation, or will," under the pressure of real or imagined forces. The focus, then, would be on the weaknesses and strengths of a particular defendant, and his subjective reaction to unlawful demands. In essence, this approach does away with the common law's "standard of heroism" (where one is expected to lay down his own life rather than be coerced by threats into taking another innocent life) in favor of a set of expectations based on the defendant's character and situation. The drafters of the Model Penal Code and this state's penal code sought to steer a middle course between these two extremes by focusing on whether the standard imposed upon the accused was one with which "normal members of the community will be able to comply." Thus, they proposed that a court limit its consideration of an accused's "situation" to stark, tangible factors which differentiate the actor from another, like his size or strength or age or health, excluding matters of temperament. They substantially departed from the existing statutory and common-law limitations requiring that the result threatened be death or serious bodily harm, that the threat be immediate and aimed at the accused, or that the crime be a noncapital offense. While these factors would be given evidentiary weight, the failure to satisfy one or more of these conditions would not justify the trial judge's withholding the defense from the jury. In this particular case, the jury may well have found that threats were made to Toscano (D) that induced a reasonable fear in him. It would then have been solely for the jury to determine whether a "person of reasonable firmness in his situation" would have failed to seek police assistance or refused to cooperate, or whether as a person Toscano (D) should reasonably have been expected to resist. Exercising our authority to revise the common law, this court has decided to adopt this approach as the law of New Jersey. Henceforth, duress shall be a defense to a crime other than murder if the defendant engaged in conduct because he was coerced to do so by the use of, or threat to use, unlawful force against his person or the person of another, which a person of reasonable firmness in his situation would have been unable to resist. Reversed and remanded.

▶ ANALYSIS

As the holding in this case implies, the New Jersey Penal Code does not permit duress as a defense to murder, although it can reduce murder to manslaughter. In contrast, the Model Penal Code treats duress as an affirmative defense to a murder charge. At common law, of course, duress served as a defense for an entire range of serious offenses, yet it would not excuse the killing of an innocent person.

Continued on next page.

Quicknotes

CONSPIRACY Concerted action by two or more persons to accomplish some unlawful purpose.

DURESS Unlawful threats or other coercive behavior by one person that causes another to commit acts that he would not otherwise do.

■══■

People v. Hood

State (P) v. Assailant (D)

Cal. Sup. Ct., 1 Cal. 3d 444, 462 P.2d 370 (1969).

NATURE OF CASE: Appeal from conviction for assault with a deadly weapon upon a peace officer and assault with intent to commit murder.

FACT SUMMARY: While intoxicated, Hood (D) resisted the efforts of a policeman to arrest and subdue him by grabbing the officer's gun and shooting him in the legs.

🏛 RULE OF LAW
In crimes of general intent evidence of the accused's intoxication shall not be considered in determining guilt or innocence.

FACTS: While a policeman attempted to subdue and arrest Hood (D) who was drunk, Hood (D), in the struggle, grabbed the officer's gun and shot him in the legs. Hood (D) was convicted on a count of assault with a deadly weapon upon a peace officer and on a count of assault with intent to commit murder. The conviction on the first count was reversed for failure to instruct on the lesser offense of simple assault, with the other count reversed because of the conflicting instructions given on the effect of intoxication.

ISSUE: In crimes of general intent, should evidence of the accused's intoxication be admitted?

HOLDING AND DECISION: (Traynor, C.J.) No. The difficulty in making this determination rests upon the confusion in defining the terms "general intent" and "specific intent." Usually, when the definition of a crime consists of only a description of the particular act without reference to intent to do a further act or achieve a future consequence, an intention to do a proscribed act is deemed to be general criminal intent. When the definition refers to doing some further act or some additional consequence, the crime is deemed to be specific intent. Under the California Criminal Code, there is ambiguity as to whether assault is to be defined as general or specific. In the context of assault with a deadly weapon and simple assault, the distinction between general and specific intent is minor. Whether or not to hear evidence of intoxication rests on different considerations, such as the effect of alcohol on human behavior. Alcohol distorts judgment and relaxes control on aggressive and antisocial behavior. While a drunken man may be able to form a simple intent, he is not as capable of exercising judgment on the social consequences of his act. A drunken man is more apt to act rashly and impulsively or in the heat of passion. Evidence of intoxication should not relieve one of blame for simple assault or assault with a deadly weapon, crimes which are frequently committed rashly or in anger. [A retrial was ordered.]

▶ ANALYSIS

In most jurisdictions, intoxication is a defense at least to negate specific intent. But note that intoxication of the accused itself at the time of commission of the crime does not constitute a defense apart from evidencing legal insanity or rebutting mens rea. A criminal act is no less criminal for having been committed in a state of voluntary intoxication.

Quicknotes

ASSAULT The intentional placing of another in fear of immediate bodily injury.

GENERAL INTENT The intention to conduct unlawful activity, as opposed to a particular unlawful act.

INTOXICATION DEFENSE A defense to criminal liability for an unlawful act committed when the defendant involuntarily consumed substances rendering him incapable of understanding the nature of his acts; voluntary intoxication is not a defense to criminal liability, but it is a factor that may be considered when determining whether the defendant possessed the requisite intent.

SPECIFIC INTENT The intent to commit a specific unlawful act which is a required element for criminal liability for certain crimes.

Regina v. Kingston
State (P) v. Child molester (D)

Ct. App., Criminal Div., 4 All E.R. 373 (1993); *rev'd*, House of Lords, 3 All E.R. 353 (1994).

NATURE OF CASE: Intermediate and final appeals from a conviction for indecent assault.

FACT SUMMARY: A man sexually assaulted a 15-year-old boy after the man was drugged by a third party.

RULE OF LAW
Involuntary intoxication does not negate the mens rea necessary for criminal liability.

FACTS: Penn, intending to blackmail Kingston (D), lured a 15-year-old boy into his apartment and invited Kingston (D) over to molest the boy. After administering a drug to Kingston (D), Penn photographed and video-taped the ensuing molestation. Kingston (D) was charged with indecent assault. At trial, he claimed that his involuntary intoxication negated the requisite mens rea for the crime, but the trial court rejected this argument. Kingston (D) was convicted, and he appealed.

ISSUE: Does involuntary intoxication negate the mens rea necessary for criminal liability?

HOLDING AND DECISION: (Lord Taylor, C.J. [for the Court of Appeal]) Yes. Involuntary intoxication negates the mens rea necessary for criminal liability. Criminal law exists to inhibit criminal inclinations, not to erase them. If a person acts on criminal impulses when the wall between restraint and action has been involuntarily abolished by a third party, the person did not have the requisite mens rea for criminal liability for any acts performed when his impulses were involuntarily unleashed. [Vacated.]

HOLDING AND DECISION: (Lord Mustill, J. [for the House of Lords]) No. Involuntary intoxication does not negate the mens rea necessary for criminal liability. When a drug removes a person's inhibitions, it may allow him to commit an act that he is otherwise inclined to do but that he normally possesses sufficient self-restraint to avoid. The essential evil mental state exists; the drug only allows it to be acted upon. To recognize this as a complete defense would make assessing guilt in any matter involving intoxication exceedingly complex and raise a host of evidentiary problems. The preferable approach to involuntary intoxication is to continue to use the concept of diminished capacity at sentencing, rather than to create a complete defense. [Reversed.]

ANALYSIS

The Model Penal Code permits intoxication as a defense only if it negates an element of the offense—with one exception. If an individual, by reason of involuntary intoxication, lacked substantial capacity to appreciate the criminality of his conduct or to conform to the requirements of the law, he may raise the defense of intoxication. The student should note that this is the same test that is used for legal insanity. However, intoxication does not in itself constitute mental disease under the Code.

Quicknotes

DIMINISHED CAPACITY A defense to criminal liability that the perpetrator suffered from a mental incapacity at the time the crime was committed so that he did not possess the requisite mental state.

INVOLUNTARY INTOXICATION A defense to criminal liability for an unlawful act committed when the defendant involuntarily consumed substances rendering him incapable of understanding the nature of his acts.

MENS REA Criminal intent.

M'Naghten's Case

State (P) v. Murderer (D)

House of Lords, 10 Cl. & F. 200, 8 Eng. Rep. 718 (1843).

NATURE OF CASE: Debate in House of Lords following finding of not guilty of murder by reason of insanity.

FACT SUMMARY: M'Naghten (D) was found not guilty of murder by reason of insanity.

🏛 RULE OF LAW
A defendant will be found not guilty by reason of insanity if, as a result of mental disease, he did not know the nature or quality of the criminal act he committed or did not know that what he was doing was wrong.

FACTS: M'Naghten (D) was indicted for murder. His defense was that at the time of the killing he was insane and obsessed with morbid delusions. The judge instructed the jury that M'Naghten (D) should be found not guilty if, at the time the act was committed, he did not know that the act he was doing was wrong and did not know that he was violating the laws of God and man. The jury found M'Naghten (D) not guilty by reason of insanity. The holding resulted in a debate on the defense of legal insanity in the House of Lords. The House invited Lord Chief Justice Tindal to answer certain questions as to legal insanity, and his answers resulted in the *M'Naghten* rule.

ISSUE: Should the defense of legal insanity be based on the defendant's ability to know if the nature or quality of the criminal act he committed or his act was right or wrong?

HOLDING AND DECISION: (Lord Tindal, C.J.) Yes. Every defendant will be presumed sane until the contrary is proved in defense. To establish the defense of legal insanity, it must be clearly proved that at the time of the commission of the act, the defendant had a mental disease so as not to know the nature and quality of the act he was doing or, if he did know the nature and quality of his act, he did not know that what he was doing was wrong. The basic question is whether, at the time of the act, he knew the difference between right and wrong. If the defendant did not know that his act was illegal but did realize that it was wrong, he will be held guilty. The question of legal insanity is a question of fact to be decided by the jury.

▶ *ANALYSIS*

The *M'Naghten* rule, also known as the "right-from-wrong" test, is the test for legal insanity in the majority of jurisdictions. This rule focuses solely on the cognitive ability of the defendant. Some courts supplement this test with the "irresistible impulse" test, which states that the defendant will also be found legally insane if, as a result of mental disease, he is unable to control his conduct. The third standard for legal insanity is the "substantial capacity" test which finds a defendant legally insane if, as a result of mental disease, he lacks the substantial capacity to apprehend the nature, quality, or wrongfulness of his conduct or to conform his conduct to the requirements of law. The final standard is the "product" test, which is discussed in the case of *Durham v. United States*, 214 F.2d 862, 875 (C.A.D.C. Cir. 1954).

Quicknotes

INSANITY (DEFENSE) An affirmative defense to a criminal prosecution that the defendant suffered from a mental illness, thereby relieving him of liability for his conduct.

M'NAGHTEN RULE A defense to a criminal prosecution that the defendant was not guilty due to a mental disease or defect that rendered him incapable of knowing the nature and quality of his conduct or that such conduct was wrong.

Blake v. United States

Bank robber (D) v. Federal government (P)

407 F.2d 908 (5th Cir. 1969).

NATURE OF CASE: Appeal from a conviction for bank robbery.

FACT SUMMARY: Blake (D) appealed his conviction for bank robbery on the basis that the definition of insanity given to the jury was outdated and prejudicial.

🏛 RULE OF LAW
A person is not responsible for criminal conduct if at the time of such conduct as a result of mental disease or defect he lacks substantial capacity either to appreciate the wrongfulness of his conduct or to conform his conduct to the requirements of law.

FACTS: Blake (D) was constantly in psychiatric care. He was arrested for shooting his second wife and placed in a state mental hospital. Blake (D) robbed a bank with which he had a quarrel regarding a trust. Blake (D) appealed his conviction on the basis that the definition of insanity given to the jury was outdated and prejudicial.

ISSUE: Is a person responsible for criminal conduct if at the time of such conduct as a result of mental disease or defect he lacks substantial capacity either to appreciate the wrongfulness of his conduct or to conform his conduct to the requirements of law?

HOLDING AND DECISION: (Bell, J.) No. A person is not responsible for criminal conduct if at the time of such conduct as a result of mental disease or defect he lacks substantial capacity either to appreciate the wrongfulness of his conduct or to conform his conduct to the requirements of law. Here, Blake's mental condition could have supported a reasonable inference that the condition absolved him from responsibility for the charged conduct; he thus could not prevail under a *Davis* instruction. Regardless of whether he was experiencing a psychiatric episode during the charged conduct, he was not unconscious, could still distinguish between right and wrong, and his will was not completely destroyed within the meaning of *Davis v. United States*, 165 U.S. 373, 378 (1897). The Model Penal Code's use of the adjective "substantial" to modify a defendant's lack of mental capacity still commits the final decision to the province of the jury and is therefore appropriate. Affirmed.

▶ ANALYSIS

The court here rejects the approach followed in *Davis*, which required that the defendant suffer from such a defect to render him incapable of distinguishing between right and wrong or otherwise unconscious at the time of the act so that the voluntariness of such actions is negated.

Quicknotes

MODEL PENAL CODE INSANITY DEFENSE A person is not liable for his criminal offenses if at the time of committing the crime he suffered from a mental disease or defect and thereby lacked the substantial capacity to appreciate the wrongfulness of his actions or to conform his actions to the requirements of law.

United States v. Lyons

Federal government (P) v. Drug addict (D)

731 F.2d 243, 739 F.2d 994 (5th Cir. 1984) (en banc).

NATURE OF CASE: Appeal from conviction for possession of narcotics.

FACT SUMMARY: Lyons (D) was convicted of narcotics possession, over his defense that his addiction prevented him from conforming his conduct to law.

🏛 RULE OF LAW
A person is not responsible for criminal conduct on the grounds of insanity only if at the time of the conduct, as a result of a mental disease or defect, the person is unable to appreciate the wrongfulness of that conduct.

FACTS: Lyons (D) was arrested and charged with possession of narcotics. His defense was that he was an addict, and that the drugs had affected his brain so that he had lost the capacity to conform his conduct according to the law. The district court did not allow Lyons (D) to introduce this defense, and he was convicted. Lyons (D) then appealed.

ISSUE: Is a person not responsible for criminal conduct on the grounds of insanity only if at the time of the conduct, as a result of a mental disease or defect, the person is unable to appreciate the wrongfulness of that conduct?

HOLDING AND DECISION: (Gee, J.) Yes. A person is not responsible for criminal conduct on the grounds of insanity only if at the time of the conduct, as a result of a mental disease or defect, the person is unable to appreciate the wrongfulness of that conduct. The advances in psychology earlier this century led to the "irresistible impulse" definition of insanity, which could exculpate a defendant if he lacked the ability to conform his conduct to the law. The adoption of this standard now appears premature. Most scientists agree that they do not possess a sufficient scientific basis for measuring a person's capacity for self-control. It simply is not within the state of the art in psychology to discern between an irresistible impulse and a choice to behave criminally. To use this standard is to base the defense on speculation, something this court will not do. Here, Lyons (D) could not show he lacked the ability to understand the wrongfulness of his act, so his conviction was proper. Affirmed.

DISSENT: (Rubin, J.) An adjudication of guilt requires moral blameworthiness, something that cannot exist when a defendant cannot conform to the law. Mere difficulty in applying a test in an area as crucial as this should not justify scuttling it.

▶ ANALYSIS

The insanity defense has come under sharp disfavor in the last several years. Deserved or not, there is a public perception that it allows the guilty to go scot-free. Since the highly-publicized acquittal of John Hinckley, the process of retreating from the "irresistible impulse" test to the one adopted by the court here has accelerated.

■=■

Quicknotes

INSANITY (DEFENSE) An affirmative defense to a criminal prosecution that the defendant suffered from a mental illness, thereby relieving him of liability for his conduct.

IRRESISTIBLE IMPULSE RULE A defense to a criminal prosecution that the defendant, due to some mental disease or defect, was unable to resist the impulse to commit the crime due to his inability to control his actions.

■=■

State v. Crenshaw

State (P) v. Convicted murderer (D)

Wash. Sup. Ct., 98 Wash. 2d 789, 659 P.2d 488 (1983).

NATURE OF CASE: Appeal of murder conviction.

FACT SUMMARY: Crenshaw (D), contending he killed his wife out of religious duty, argued that the insanity defense may apply to one not aware that his conduct is morally wrong.

🏛 RULE OF LAW
The insanity defense requires that a defendant be unable to differentiate right from wrong legally as opposed to morally.

FACTS: Crenshaw (D) suspected that his new wife had been unfaithful. He beat her unconscious, stabbed her to death, and dismembered her body, hiding the parts. The murder was discovered, and Crenshaw (D) was tried for murder. He argued in his defense that his religion compelled him to kill an unfaithful wife, and that therefore he had been unable to perceive, morally speaking, the wrongness of the act. He was convicted, and appealed.

ISSUE: Does the insanity defense require that a defendant be unable to differentiate right from wrong legally as opposed to morally?

HOLDING AND DECISION: (Brachtenbach, J.) Yes. The insanity defense requires that a defendant be unable to differentiate right from wrong legally as opposed to morally. It is society's morals, not the individual's, that are the standard for judging whether one can appreciate the wrongness of one's acts, for purposes of the insanity defense. If individual moral beliefs were the standard, the criminal law would be seriously undermined. This being so, only if a defendant was unable to appreciate the illegality of his conduct may the insanity defense be applied. Here, there was ample evidence that Crenshaw (D) understood the illegality of his conduct. Affirmed.

▶ ANALYSIS

The test used here was the classic *M'Naghten* rule, House of Lords, 10 Cl. & F. 200, 8 Eng. Rep. 718 (1843), which relied strictly on cognitive ability. At one point, this test began to be replaced by a test that permitted the insanity defense if the defendant suffered from an "irresistible impulse." In the last decade, however, this test has fallen out of favor.

■═■

Quicknotes

INSANITY (DEFENSE) An affirmative defense to a criminal prosecution that the defendant suffered from a mental illness, thereby relieving him of liability for his conduct.

IRRESISTIBLE IMPULSE RULE A defense to a criminal prosecution that the defendant, due to some mental disease or defect, was unable to resist the impulse to commit the crime due to his inability to control his actions.

M'NAGHTEN RULE A defense to a criminal prosecution that the defendant was not guilty due to a mental disease or defect that rendered him incapable of knowing the nature and quality of his conduct or that such conduct was wrong.

■═■

State v. Guido

State (P) v. Wife (D)

N.J. Sup. Ct., 40 N.J. 191, 191 A.2d 45 (1963).

NATURE OF CASE: Appeal from conviction for murder.

FACT SUMMARY: Guido (D) contended the prosecution unjustifiably told the jury she and her defense team had defrauded the court by changing a psychiatric report to include a more expansive legal test of insanity.

> ## 🏛 RULE OF LAW
> A person with a "disease of the mind" severe enough to preclude distinction between right and wrong is incapable of guilt.

FACTS: Guido (D) shot her husband who had physically abused her in the past. She claimed temporary insanity and was examined by doctors to determine her mental state. Believing the legal standard for insanity required a diagnosed psychosis, the doctors concluded she was legally sane. Guido's (D) defense attorney pointed out the correct standard based upon the ability to show a distinction between right and wrong, and the doctors changed their legal conclusion. The prosecutor pointed out this change to the jury and claimed it represented a fraud on the court. The jury convicted her, and she appealed.

ISSUE: Is a person with a diseased mind, who is unable to make a distinction between right and wrong, legally insane?

HOLDING AND DECISION: (Weintraub, C.J.) Yes. A person with a disease of the mind severe enough to preclude distinction between right and wrong is incapable of guilt. The change in the doctor's report was a change in the legal standard applied. The medical conclusions did not change. Thus, it was improper of the prosecution to charge such change was a fraud. The jury was thus misled, and the conviction must be overturned. Reversed.

▶ *ANALYSIS*

An ongoing problem exists concerning the classification of the issue of sanity as a legal or a medical concept. Medical experts can testify concerning their findings based upon examinations and tests. These results must then be used by the trier of fact in applying them to the legal standard of sanity.

■═■

Quicknotes

INSANITY An affirmative defense to a criminal prosecution that the defendant suffered from a mental illness, thereby relieving him of liability for his conduct.

MURDER Unlawful killing of another person either with deliberation and premeditation or by conduct demonstrating a reckless disregard for human life.

■═■

United States v. Brawner

Federal government (P) v. Convicted murderer (D)

471 F.2d 969 (D.C. Cir. 1972).

NATURE OF CASE: Appeal from conviction for second-degree murder and carrying a dangerous weapon.

FACT SUMMARY: In considering Brawner's (D) appeal from his convictions for carrying a dangerous weapon and second-degree murder, the court reconsidered the rule of *Fisher v. United States*, which limited the use of a diminished capacity defense on issues of premeditation and deliberation.

🏛 RULE OF LAW
Evidence of the condition of the mind of the accused at the time of the crime, together with the surrounding circumstances may be introduced, not for the purpose of establishing insanity, but to prove that the situation was such that a specific intent was not entertained, i.e., to show absence of any deliberate or premeditated design.

FACTS: Brawner (D) was convicted of second-degree murder and carrying a dangerous weapon. In this portion of its opinion adjudicating Brawner's (D) appeal, the court of appeals reconsidered the rule of *Fisher v. United States*, 149 F.2d 28 (1946), in which the court upheld the trial court's refusal to instruct the jury that on issues of pre-meditation and deliberation "it should consider the entire personality of the defendant, his mental, nervous, emotional and physical characteristics as developed by the evidence in the case."

ISSUE: May evidence of the condition of the mind of the accused at the time of the crime, together with the surrounding circumstances, be introduced to show absence of any deliberate or premeditated design?

HOLDING AND DECISION: (Leventhal, J.) Yes. Evidence of the condition of the mind of the accused at the time of the crime, together with the surrounding circumstances may be introduced, not for the purpose of establishing insanity, but to prove that the situation was such that a specific intent was not entertained, i.e., to show absence of any premeditated or deliberate design. On the other hand, a claim of insanity cannot be used for the purpose of reducing the degree of the crime of murder or reducing murder to manslaughter. If the defendant is responsible at all, he is responsible in the same degree as a sane man; if he is not responsible at all, he is entitled to acquittal no matter what the degree. In overruling the rule of *Fisher*, the court permitted the introduction of expert testimony as to abnormal condition, if it is relevant to negate, or to establish the specific mental condition that is an element of the crime.

▶ ANALYSIS

The rule of *Brawner* must be distinguished from what is generally termed "diminished" or "partial responsibility." Under the "partial responsibility" doctrine, a defendant who is mentally disturbed, although not to the degree necessary to prove the defense of insanity, is entitled to a reduction in severity of his sentence. *Brawner*, instead, goes to the question of intent. The court stated, "Neither logic nor justice can tolerate a jurisprudence that defines the elements of an offense as requiring a mental state such that one defendant who properly argues that his voluntary drunkenness removed his capacity to form the specific intent—but another defendant is inhibited from a submission of his contention that an abnormal mental condition for which he was in no way responsible—negated his capacity to form a particular specific intent, even though the condition did not exonerate him from all criminal responsibility."

Quicknotes

DELIBERATION Reflection; the pondering and weighing of the consequences of an action.

DIMINISHED CAPACITY A defense to criminal liability that the perpetrator suffered from a mental incapacity at the time the crime was committed so that he did not possess the requisite mental state.

PREMEDITATION The contemplation of undertaking an activity prior to action; any length of time is sufficient.

SECOND-DEGREE MURDER The unlawful killing of another person, without premeditation, and characterized by either an intent to kill or by a reckless disregard for human life.

SPECIFIC INTENT The intent to commit a specific unlawful act which is a required element for criminal liability for certain crimes.

Clark v. Arizona

Paranoid-schizophrenic murderer (D) v. State (P)

548 U.S. 735 (2006).

NATURE OF CASE: Appeal from a conviction for first-degree murder.

FACT SUMMARY: A man who was indisputably paranoid-schizophrenic shot and killed a police officer during a traffic stop.

RULE OF LAW

Due process does not require consideration of evidence of mental illness on the element of mens rea.

FACTS: A police officer pulled Clark (D) over for a traffic stop. Clark (D), an undisputed paranoid-schizophrenic whose behavior had become more and more erratic in the preceding year, shot and killed the officer during the stop. Clark (D) was charged under an Arizona (P) statute defining one form of first-degree as "knowingly or intentionally" killing a police officer who is on duty. At Clark's (D) bench trial, the judge ruled that Clark (D) could not introduce evidence of his mental illness on the element of mens rea; such evidence, the trial judge ruled, could be considered on Clark's (D) insanity defense. The trial court convicted Clark (D). Clark (D) appealed, challenging the exclusion of evidence on the element of mens rea as a violation of federal due process. Arizona's (P) intermediate appellate court and Supreme Court both affirmed, and Clark (D) sought further review in the United States Supreme Court.

ISSUE: Does due process require consideration of evidence of mental illness on the element of mens rea?

HOLDING AND DECISION: (Souter, J.) No. Due process does not require consideration of evidence of mental illness on the element of mens rea. This case involves the application of the rule announced in *State v. Mott*, 931 P.2d 1046 (Ariz. 1997), where the Arizona Supreme Court held that evidence of mental illness could be considered only on an insanity defense and not on the element of mens rea. Under *Mott*, three categories of evidence can come into play on a claim such as Clark's (D): "observation evidence," "mental-disease evidence," and "capacity evidence." *Mott* restricts evidence only in the latter two categories, each of which involves opinion testimony (as opposed to more descriptive observation testimony) that typically is offered by professional psychologists and psychiatrists. Such evidence is relevant on the element of mens rea and can help a defendant's defense, but even relevant evidence can properly be excluded. The well-established grounds for such exclusions of evidence are unfair prejudice, confusion of the issues, and potential to mislead the jury. The problems with evidence of mental illness include its unreliability, given the debate over

mental illness in the scientific community; the evidence's potential to mislead jurors; and the risk that the evidence would suggest a more authoritative judgment of the defendant's mental state than even the experts would claim for their own opinions. Accordingly, Arizona (P) has reasonable grounds for channeling mental-illness evidence away from mens rea and toward the insanity defense. Affirmed.

DISSENT: (Kennedy, J.) Arizona's (P) rule prevented Clark (D) from presenting evidence that was central to his defense that he was delusional at the time of the offense because of his schizophrenia. Like other states, Arizona (P) has procedural rules to ensure reliable expert testimony, and potential jury confusion does not justify the exclusion because juries can resolve differences on factual issues. These considerations should have particular force where the State's (P) own expert agreed that Clark (D) was psychotic when he killed the officer. Ultimately, the disagreement between the two sides' experts means only that Clark's (D) evidence was contested, not that it was irrelevant or misleading. Permitting mental-illness evidence on insanity does not compensate for excluding it on an element of the charged offense because the analyses have different purposes and standards of proof. Although other states do permit such exclusions of evidence on mens rea, automatically and conclusively excluding it, as Arizona (P) does, plainly violates due process by preventing the defendant from proving the straightforward defense that he did not commit the charged offense.

► ANALYSIS

Justice Kennedy's dissent focuses on perhaps the gravest weakness in the majority opinion in *Clark*: Under *Clark*, a state may totally prohibit a defendant from presenting evidence to contest the prosecution's evidence on the elements of the charged offense itself. The defendant may introduce mental-illness evidence to prove that he was insane at the time he committed the offense—but he may not introduce such evidence to prove that he simply did not commit the offense. As Justice Kennedy also suggests, any problems with potential jury confusion are the same problems that exist in any trial where jurors must resolve differences between competing evidence and theories of a case. Such problems are best resolved, not by prohibiting a defendant from creating doubts in jurors' minds in his own defense, but by trusting that jurors will be able to sort through the competing evidence and reach a reasonable conclusion.

Continued on next page.

Quicknotes

FIRST-DEGREE MURDER The willful killing of another person with deliberation and premeditation; first-degree murder also encompasses those situations in which a person is killed within the perpetration of, or attempt to perpetrate, specified felonies.

INSANITY DEFENSE An affirmative defense to a criminal prosecution that the defendant suffered from a mental illness, thereby relieving him of liability for his conduct.

MENS REA Criminal intent.

Robinson v. California

Alleged drug user (D) v. State (P)

370 U.S. 660 (1962).

NATURE OF CASE: Appeal from conviction for narcotic addiction.

FACT SUMMARY: A California (P) statute makes it a criminal offense for a person to be addicted to the use of narcotics.

🏛 RULE OF LAW
A state law that imprisons a person addicted to narcotics, even though he has never touched any drug within the state or been guilty of any irregular behavior there, inflicts a cruel and unusual punishment in violation of the Eighth and Fourteenth Amendments.

FACTS: A California (P) statute makes it a criminal offense for a person to be addicted to the use of narcotics. The evidence against Robinson (D) was a police officer's testimony that Robinson (D) had scar tissue, discoloration, and needle marks which indicated his frequent use of narcotics.

ISSUE: Is a law that makes narcotics addiction a criminal offense constitutional?

HOLDING AND DECISION: (Stewart, J.) No. Narcotics addiction is an illness that may be contracted innocently or involuntarily. Like mental illness, leprosy, or venereal disease, a state could establish a program of compulsory treatment, involving quarantine or confinement for narcotic addicts. However, a law that makes a criminal offense of narcotic addiction inflicts a cruel and unusual punishment in violation of the Eighth and Fourteenth Amendments. The California (P) statute imprisoning a person addicted to narcotics, even though he has never used any drug within the state, or been guilty of any irregular behavior there, is unconstitutional. Reversed.

CONCURRENCE: (Douglas, J.) Confinement for the purposes of punishing, rather than curing, drug addiction cannot be upheld.

CONCURRENCE: (Harlan, J.) Since addiction alone cannot reasonably amount to more than a propensity to use narcotics, the effect of the jury instruction was to authorize punishment for the mere desire to commit a criminal act.

DISSENT: (White, J.) The Court has removed the state's power to deal with the recurring case where there is ample evidence of use, but no evidence of the precise location of use.

▶ ANALYSIS

Following the *Robinson* case, the California Supreme Court upheld an involuntary five-year commitment of a person on a finding that he was a narcotic addict. After examining both the "civil" and "criminal" features of his commitment, the court decided that the "civil" overtones predominated and that it was, therefore, not unconstitutional under *Robinson* (*In re De La O*, 59 Cal. 2d 128 (1963)). "*Robinson* may have established the Eighth Amendment as a basis for invalidating legislation that is thought to inappropriately invoke criminal sanction, despite an entire lack of precedent for the idea that punishment may be cruel not because of its mode but because the conduct for which it is imposed should not be subjected to the criminal sanction." Packer, 77 *Harv. L. Rev.* 1071 (1964).

Quicknotes

EIGHTH AMENDMENT The Eighth Amendment to the federal Constitution prohibiting the imposition of excessive bail, fines and cruel and unusual punishment.

FOURTEENTH AMENDMENT Declares that no state shall make or enforce any law which shall abridge the privileges and immunities of citizens of the United States.

Powell v. Texas

Alcoholic (D) v. State (P)

392 U.S. 514 (1968).

NATURE OF CASE: Appeal from conviction for public drunkenness.

FACT SUMMARY: Powell (D), a chronic alcoholic, was found to have a condition beyond his control which resulted in his being intoxicated in public, an act for which he was arrested.

🏛 **RULE OF LAW**
In light of current medical knowledge, it appears that chronic alcoholics in general do not suffer from such an irresistible compulsion to drink and to get drunk in public, that they are utterly unable to control their performance of either or both of these acts, and thus cannot be deterred at all from public intoxication.

FACTS: Powell (D), a chronic alcoholic, was found guilty of being drunk in public. It was argued that his appearance in public was not of his own volition, and that to punish him for his illness would be cruel and unusual in violation of the Eighth Amendment as applied to the states by the Fourteenth Amendment. The medical profession has not firmly determined whether alcoholism is an illness, is physically addicting, or merely psychologically habituating.

ISSUE: Is alcoholism a condition of such an involuntary nature that to punish an appearance in public while intoxicated would be cruel and unusual?

HOLDING AND DECISION: (Marshall, J.) No. There is widespread argument in the medical profession over whether alcoholism is a disease. A disease is anything the medical profession determines it to be. Facilities for treating indigent alcoholics are woefully lacking. At least a short time in jail permits the alcoholic to sober up. Generally, commission to an institution is for the time it takes to cure, while time in jail for drunkenness is usually limited. Powell (D) was not convicted for being a chronic alcoholic, but for being drunk in public. He is not within the ambit of *Robinson [v. California]*, 370 U.S. 660 (1962), which holds that a conviction for being of the status of a drug addict alone is cruel and unusual. Here, the conviction protects public safety and health. *Robinson* says a person may be punished only for committing some act which society has an interest in preventing. Affirmed.

CONCURRENCE: (Black, J.) "The States should (not) be held constitutionally required to make the inquiry as to what part of a defendant's personality is responsible for his actions and to excuse anyone whose action was,

in some complex, psychological sense, the result of a 'compulsion.'"

CONCURRENCE: (White, J.) If it cannot be a crime to have an irresistible urge to use narcotics, it should not be a crime to yield to that compulsion. But here, there is nothing in the record to show that the chronic alcoholic has a compulsion to drink in public.

DISSENT: (Fortas, J.) "Alcoholism is caused and maintained by something other than the moral fault of the alcoholic, something that, to a greater or lesser extent . . . cannot be controlled by him." Thus, to punish the alcoholic would be cruel and unusual punishment.

▶ *ANALYSIS*

It would appear, at least according to J. White, that once one proves his compulsion, he cannot be protected from conviction for failing to take precautions against it. For example, an epileptic may not be punished for his illness, unless he drives a vehicle. Yet the dissent, while stipulating that the statute did not punish the mere status of alcoholism, feels that the accused was punished for a condition he was helpless to avoid. Is the majority then taking the pragmatic way out? Recognizing the lack of adequate care facilities for indigent chronic alcoholics, it would seem that the Court would rather have the public drunk spend a night in jail to dry out than be committed for an unspecified term to an inadequate institution until deemed "cured."

Quicknotes

CRUEL AND UNUSUAL PUNISHMENT Punishment that is excessive or disproportionate to the offense committed and which is prohibited by the Eighth Amendment to the United States Constitution.

IRRESISTIBLE IMPULSE RULE A defense to a criminal prosecution that the defendant, due to some mental disease or defect, was unable to resist the impulse to commit the crime due to his inability to control his actions.

United States v. Moore

Federal government (P) v. Heroin possessor (D)

486 F.2d 1139 (D.C. Cir. 1973).

NATURE OF CASE: Appeal from conviction for possession of heroin.

FACT SUMMARY: Moore (D) was convicted on two counts of possession of heroin.

🏛 RULE OF LAW
Evidence of long and intensive dependence on drugs resulting in substantial impairment of behavioral controls and self-control over the use of the drug in question is not admissible on the issue of criminal responsibility.

FACTS: Moore (D), a heroin addict and apparently a trafficker in the drug, was convicted on two counts of possession of heroin. He contended his conviction was improper because as an addict having an overpowering need for heroin, he should not be held responsible for its possession.

ISSUE: Is evidence of a drug user's long and intensive use and dependence on a drug resulting in substantial impairment of his behavioral controls and a loss of self-control over the use of the drug relevant to his criminal responsibility, in this case for unlawful possession?

HOLDING AND DECISION: (Wilkey, J.) No. Moore's (D) claim that he has lost the power of self-control with regard to his addiction cannot be a defense to the capacity to control behavior which is a prerequisite to criminal responsibility. To hold otherwise would carry over to all other illegal acts of any type having a purpose to obtain narcotics for personal use. Affirmed.

CONCURRENCE: (Leventhal, J.) It is illogical to claim that because there are different kinds of addicts, such as those who can limit their use of drugs to acquiring what they need for their habit and those who commit crimes other than possession to support their habit, punishment should be based upon the compulsion under which various addicts act. While Moore (D) claims he has lost self-control, he contends he does not commit crimes other than possession and acquisition. But it would appear that the addict who must commit crimes against others to support his habit has even less self-control. If lack of self-control could negate [mens rea], it would have to be a defense to all actions taken under compulsion of need to obtain the drug. Just because one condition, such as insanity, excuses a crime if it results in impaired behavioral control, it does not follow that any other condition resulting in similar impairment should be a defense. Rather than a broad principle of exculpation on grounds of lack of control, there is a series of particular defenses made clear in manageable areas calling for justice to the individual in ascertainable and verifiable conditions within the limitations of society's interests.

DISSENT: (Wright, J.) Two dominant value judgments have shaped the concept of criminal responsibility in Western society. First, punishment must be morally legitimate. Second, it must not unduly threaten the individual's liberties and dignity in his relationship to society. Thus, to be criminally responsible, a man's actions must result from his free will. While at some time in the past each addict voluntarily decided to use drugs, it is the present that must be considered in seeing that the addict lacks self-control. "The law looks to the immediate, and not to the remote cause."

CONCURRENCE AND DISSENT: (Bazelon, C.J.) Loss of self-control as a result of drug addiction should be a defense to armed robbery or trafficking in drugs in determining whether the defendant was acting under duress or compulsion because of which he could not conform his conduct to the law's requirements.

▶ ANALYSIS

This is another case raising the problem of what defenses are acceptable within established legal doctrine, in this case, mens rea. Criminal responsibility is a cloudy area. Courts generally attempt to allow in as much evidence as possible on that issue. But where a defense could wipe out a legal doctrine so basic, here to the criminal law, chances are it will be excluded.

Quicknotes

IRRESISTIBLE IMPULSE RULE A defense to a criminal prosecution that the defendant, due to some mental disease or defect, was unable to resist the impulse to commit the crime due to his inability to control his actions.

MENS REA Criminal intent.

Quick Reference Rules of Law

Commonwealth v. Tluchak

State (P) v. Seller (D)

Pa. Super. Ct., 166 Pa. Super. 16, 70 A.2d 657 (1950).

NATURE OF CASE: Appeal from conviction for larceny.

FACT SUMMARY: The Tluchaks (D) sold their house and certain personal property, but failed or refused to deliver the personal property to the buyer.

🏛 RULE OF LAW
Larceny is a crime against the lawful possession of personal property, and one who is in lawful possession, even though not the owner, is incapable of trespassing on his own lawful possession.

FACTS: The Tluchaks (D) agreed in a written instrument to sell their farm to the buyer. The agreement did not recite any personal property, but did include items such as lighting fixtures, shrubbery, and plants. When the purchasers took possession, they found certain items missing which had been on the premises when the sale was executed. These items included an unattached commode and washstand, some peach trees, a hay carriage, and an electric cord. The State (P) argued that these items, which were not covered by the written agreement, had been sold by an oral agreement between the parties. The court assumed for the decision that the Tluchaks (D) sold but failed or refused to deliver the goods to the purchasers under the terms of the oral contract.

ISSUE: Are sellers in lawful possession of goods who refuse or fail to deliver goods sold to their purchasers, capable of a trespassory taking of these goods, considered as the personal property of the purchasers?

HOLDING AND DECISION: (Reno, J.) No. Larceny is a crime against lawful possession. One who is in lawful possession of goods or money of another cannot commit larceny by feloniously converting them to his own use. The defendants had possession of the goods, and not mere custody. Even though lawful title passes to the purchasers upon payment of the purchase price, possession remained rightfully in the sellers. When the sellers converted those goods to their own use, it was not a trespass on the purchaser's lawful possession. The defendants were incapable of committing larceny. They had retained possession after the sale without trick or fraud and without any fraudulent intent to convert the goods to their own use. Because they were incapable of trespassing on their own lawful possession, the crime of larceny cannot be charged to them. Reversed.

▶ ANALYSIS

The court suggested that the defendants could have been charged and found guilty of fraudulent conversion of goods rightfully in possession but later converted to one's own use. Perhaps larceny by bailee would have been possible if the vendor retaining the goods sold can be charged as a constructive bailee until delivery. Larceny is solely a crime against lawful possession of personal property, regardless of who may have lawful title. Larceny is the trespassory taking and carrying away of the personal property of another with the specific intent to deprive the possessor of it permanently. In this case, there simply was no trespass against another's possession.

■■■

Quicknotes

BAILEE Person holding property in trust for another party.

CONVERSION The act of depriving an owner of his property without permission or justification.

LARCENY The illegal taking of another's property with the intent to deprive the owner thereof.

TRESPASS Unlawful interference with, or damage to, the real or personal property of another.

■■■

Topolewski v. State

Meat thief (D) v. State (P)

Wis. Sup. Ct., 130 Wis. 244, 109 N.W. 1037 (1906).

NATURE OF CASE: Appeal from conviction for larceny.

FACT SUMMARY: Topolewski (D) stole meat with the aid of a bogus accomplice who provided Topolewski (D) with the meat in order for the police to capture him.

🏛 RULE OF LAW
When the owner of property aids in the commission of the offense of larceny of such property, the accused is not guilty of that crime.

FACTS: Dolan, an employee of a meat packing company, owed Topolewski (D) some money. As payment, Topolewski (D) arranged for Dolan to place some meat on a company loading platform so that Topolewski (D) could put it on his wagon and drive away. Dolan informed the company of the plan. He was told to feign cooperation. The company instructed its loading platform manager, Klotz, not only to put the meat on the platform but also that a man would come and take it away. Klotz was not told about the impending theft. Klotz inferred that Topolewski (D) was that man and that it was proper to deliver the meat to him. Klotz did not assist Topolewski (D) in the loading of the meat, but he did allow the meat to be taken and did help arrange the wagon. Klotz also took an order from Topolewski (D) for the dispensation of a separate barrel of meat. From a conviction for larceny, Topolewski (D) appealed.

ISSUE: Does consent to a taking of property negate the element of trespassory taking in the crime of larceny?

HOLDING AND DECISION: (Marshall, J.) Yes. There can be no larceny without a trespass. Trespass is lacking where one allows his property to be taken or delivered to a person intending to commit larceny, regardless of the guilty purpose of the accused. Where the setting of a trap to catch a suspected thief goes no further than to afford an opportunity to carry out a criminal purpose, the deception so practiced is not sufficient in and of itself to excuse the would-be criminal. But the deception must not amount to consent in the taking. Here, Klotz, the agent of the company, actually permitted the accused to take the meat as per his instructions from the company. In effect, meat was given to the accused by the company. A mere guilty purpose is not sufficient for conviction when one of the essential elements of the crime of larceny is missing. Since taking of the meat here was not a trespassory taking, conviction is reversed and remanded.

▶ ANALYSIS

It would seem that under these facts there would be no way for the company to set a trap to catch the accused. Once the company was informed of the plan by Dolan, they could not allow anyone to place the meat on the platform for the accused to take it away. Any placing of the meat on the platform, knowing that the accused would steal it, would amount to a consent to the taking. Trespass means that the accused's action at the time he takes possession must be wrongful as against some other person's lawful possession. The company here consented to the accused taking possession and, therefore, the taking was not trespassory.

■=■

Quicknotes

ACCOMPLICE An individual who knowingly, purposefully or voluntarily combines with the main actor in the commission or attempted commission of a criminal offense.

LARCENY The illegal taking of another's property with the intent to deprive the owner thereof.

TRESPASS Unlawful interference with, or damage to, the real or personal property of another.

■=■

Nolan v. State

Employee (D) v. State (P)

Md. Ct. App., 213 Md. 298, 131 A.2d 851 (1957).

NATURE OF CASE: Appeal from conviction for embezzlement.

FACT SUMMARY: Nolan (D) appropriated money from his employer's cash drawer at the end of the work day.

> 🏛 **RULE OF LAW**
> Once property of the employer has passed from the rightful possession of the employee into the constructive possession of the employer, the employee is incapable of committing the crime of embezzling those funds.

FACTS: Nolan (D) was the office manager of the Federal Discount Corporation, a finance company which made loans and collections. As payments were received, they would be placed in the cash drawer. At the end of the day, an accomplice would prepare a report showing the daily cash receipts. Nolan (D) would then appropriate some of the cash from the drawer. The accomplice would then recompute the adding tapes to equal the remaining sum of cash.

ISSUE: Is property in the constructive possession of its owner where the employee has placed the property where the owner has directed with the intent to steal the property at a later time?

HOLDING AND DECISION: (Collins, J.) Yes. Where the property is taken from the owner's possession, the crime is larceny and not embezzlement. Embezzlement only covers the situation where the accused is in rightful possession of his employer's or master's property and wrongfully appropriates it to his own use before the owner has gained possession. Larceny is the crime against possession. This money had reached its destination, the crash drawer. Once there, the money is in the constructive possession of the owner, though not the actual possession. The cash drawer is the exact place where the employer had instructed his employees to put any cash belonging to the employer. Once in the cash drawer, the employee is incapable of embezzling it. Because of these technical differences between larceny and embezzlement, it is always prudent to join a count of larceny with that of embezzlement. The accused has committed larceny, but because he was charged with the wrong crime, the conviction is reversed and the case remanded.

CONCURRENCE: (Prescott, J.) The majority has made an overly fine distinction between larceny and embezzlement. Such refinements aid only the criminal. The legislature should pass a law allowing conviction for either crime under an indictment which charges only one of those crimes to the accused.

▶ ANALYSIS

One who fraudulently converts property of another rightfully entrusted to his possession is guilty of embezzlement. The issue in this case revolved around whether the accused converted the money already in his employer's constructive possession—larceny—or whether the conversion took place before the owner had possession—embezzlement. Such a refinement is a result of the fact that embezzlement was not a common-law crime and was therefore, strictly construed to be different from larceny in its essentials.

■══■

Quicknotes

CONSTRUCTIVE POSSESSION Exists if someone does not have actual, physical possession of property but has the power to exercise control over it.

EMBEZZLEMENT The fraudulent appropriation of property lawfully in one's possession.

LARCENY The illegal taking of another's property with the intent to deprive the owner thereof.

■══■

Burns v. State

Constable (D) v. State (P)

Wis. Sup. Ct., 145 Wis. 373, 128 N.W. 987 (1911).

NATURE OF CASE: Appeal of larceny conviction.

FACT SUMMARY: Burns (D), a constable, misappropriated funds taken off a person he arrested.

🏛 RULE OF LAW
Where a person who comes into possession of the property of another is under any duty to preserve or restore it he is bailee of that property and, as such, any later conversion of it is a constructive trespass sufficient to establish larceny.

FACTS: Burns (D), a constable, and others pursued a certain insane man, Adamsky. Upon catching him, Burns (D) was given money, which Adamsky had dropped, by a fellow pursuer. Burns (D) later misappropriated this money and was charged with larceny for doing so. At his trial, the trial court judge instructed the jury that Burns (D) was the bailee of the money he received—qualifying him as such as a "bailee breaking bulk" for larceny purposes (i.e., constituting a constructive trespass). This appeal followed.

ISSUE: May a bailment relationship for larceny purposes arise absent evidence of some contractual relationship between the parties involved?

HOLDING AND DECISION: (Marshall, J.) Yes. Where a person who comes into possession of the property of another is under any duty to preserve or restore it, he is a bailee of that property and, as such, any conversion of it later is a constructive trespass (i.e., bailee breaking bulk) for larceny purposes. It makes no difference who entrusts the property to the bailee—the owner, his agent, or even a finder may do so. Where a bailee converts property so entrusted to him, he is guilty of larceny (the old distinction between simple larceny and larceny by bailee was abolished long ago). Here, Burns (D) accepted the money of another as a constable. In such a capacity, he surely was to hold it for the owner. Conviction affirmed.

▶ ANALYSIS

This case points up the "bailee breaking rule" of constructive trespass for larceny. By Hornbook law, larceny is the trespassory taking and carrying away of the personal property of another with the intent to permanently deprive. The element of trespass often causes problems, however. At common law, for example, it was held that a common carrier was deemed to have possession only of the container of any goods shipped. The contents remained in the constructive possession of the owner of the goods. If the carrier opened the container before converting it in its entirety, he was trespassorily taking the contents out of the "constructive possession" of the owner, which was larceny. This was called the "breaking bulk doctrine" and was used to get around the fact that the carrier ostensibly had lawful possession and was immune to larceny. As this case illustrates, this rationale was later applied to bailees who originally had a lawful possession but later appropriated the goods to their own use.

■══■

Quicknotes

BAILEE Person holding property in trust for another party.

CONVERSION The act of depriving an owner of his property without permission or justification.

LARCENY The illegal taking of another's property with the intent to deprive the owner thereof.

■══■

State v. Riggins

State (P) v. Collection agency operator (D)

Ill. Sup. Ct., 8 Ill. 2d 78, 132 N.E.2d 519 (1956).

NATURE OF CASE: Appeal from a conviction for embezzlement.

FACT SUMMARY: Riggins (D), operator of a collection agency, commingled funds and did not report collection of accounts to the client whom he represented.

RULE OF LAW
A collection agent, who acts in the fiduciary capacity of agent to his principal, is within the purview of embezzlement statutes.

FACTS: Riggins (D), operator of a collection service, called on Tarrant and asked to collect her business's delinquent accounts. They reached an oral agreement whereby he need not account until the bill was paid in full, at which time he was to remit by check. It was not clear whether the amount remitted should be in full with commission to be deducted or in net amount with commission already deducted. Riggins (D) admittedly commingled funds collected for all clients in a personal bank account from which he drew for personal, business, and family expenses. Tarrant brought embezzlement charges when she found that Riggins (D) had collected accounts in full but had not remitted to her. Riggins (D) claimed he was not her agent but, rather, an independent business not within the ambit of embezzlement statutes.

ISSUE: Is a collection agent acting in such a fiduciary capacity within the purview of embezzlement statutes?

HOLDING AND DECISION: (Hershey, C.J.) Yes. While early decisions had held that a collection agent operating as an independent businessman and who had a right to commingle funds could not be convicted as an "agent" under general embezzlement statutes, a change in statutory language then held that embezzlement occurred irrespective of whether the agent claims any commission or interest in the collected debt. In accordance with the statute, Riggins (D) was an agent who received money in a fiduciary capacity. The relationship of principal and agent is a fiduciary one. Reversed on other grounds.

DISSENT: (Schaefer, J.) Riggins's (D) clients knew of the commingled account and could not be held vicariously liable for Riggins's (D) actions in collecting their accounts. The statute should be strictly construed with the word "agent" not being given a popular meaning.

▶ ANALYSIS

The dissent contends that the meaning of "agent" was improperly construed as meaning a person who transacts business for another by the latter's authority and who renders an account of such business in a popular sense. The majority felt that a fiduciary relationship arose whereby special confidence was reposed in Riggins (D), who was thereby bound in good conscience and in equity to act in good faith with due regard to the interest of the person reposing the confidence. The court appears to be plugging a loophole in the law of embezzlement, which was designed to plug a loophole in the law of larceny. Embezzlement filled a gap left when larceny laws did not cover personalty entrusted to one which was then misappropriated by the one to whom it was entrusted.

Quicknotes

AGENT An individual who has the authority to act on behalf of another.

EMBEZZLEMENT The fraudulent appropriation of property lawfully in one's possession.

FIDUCIARY Person holding a legal obligation to act for the benefit of another.

PERSONALTY Personal, movable property not attached to real estate.

PRINCIPAL A person or entity who authorizes another (the agent) to act on its behalf and subject to its authority to the extent that the principal may be held liable for the actions of the agent.

VICARIOUS LIABILITY The imputed liability of one party for the unlawful acts of another.

Hufstetler v. State

Driver (D) v. State (P)

Ala. Ct. App., 37 Ala. App. 71, 63 So.2d 730 (1953).

NATURE OF CASE: Appeal from conviction for petit larceny.

FACT SUMMARY: Hufstetler (D) had gasoline put in his car but failed to pay for it.

🏛 RULE OF LAW
If the possession of property is obtained by fraud or trick with the intent at that time to convert the property to one's own use, then larceny has been established as long as the owner intends merely to part with possession and not with title to the property.

FACTS: Hufstetler (D) drove his car into Wharton's gas station. There were two or three other men in the car. One man got out and went to look for a phone. Wharton informed him that there was not a phone on the premises. Wharton was then told to fill up the tank. Six and a half gallons were put into the car. Wharton was then told to get a quart of oil to put in the car. As Wharton went for the oil, Hufstetler (D) drove off without paying the $1.94 for the gasoline.

ISSUE: Can the element of trespass in the crime of larceny be established even though the owner of the goods voluntarily gave up possession of those goods?

HOLDING AND DECISION: (Carr, J.) Yes. If the possession is obtained by fraud or trick with the intent, at the time the goods are received, to convert them to one's own use, then larceny has been established so long as the owner intended merely to part with possession and not with title to the goods. The trick or fraud will vitiate the consent of the owner to part with possession. The owner will still be considered in constructive possession of his property. Larceny, a crime against lawful possession, can be proven without an actual trespass, where fraud or trick is present. In this case, the fraud is inferable from the factual background. Affirmed.

▌ *ANALYSIS*

This crime is more specifically known as a larceny by trick. The defendant's fraud or trick is deemed to vitiate the owner's consent to the defendant taking possession. The owner is still deemed to be in constructive possession and therefore the taking is a trespass. It can only be committed when the owner intends to part simply with possession, not with title to the goods. It is the owner's belief that controls, not the thief's intent. If the owner intended to give up both possession and title, then the crime of false pretenses would be the correct charge. In the above case, the court stated that Wharton only intended to give up possession of the gas. There was no intent to give up title until the gasoline had been paid for.

■■■

Quicknotes

FALSE PRETENSES The unlawful obtaining of money or property from another with an intent to defraud and with the utilization of false representations.

LARCENY BY TRICK The illegal taking of another's property with the intent to deprive the owner thereof and through the means of deception.

PETTY LARCENY The illegal taking of another's property with the intent to deprive the owner thereof the value of which is less than the statutory amount (usually $100).

TRESPASS Unlawful interference with, or damage to, the real or personal property of another.

■■■

Graham v. United States

Attorney (D) v. Federal government (P)

187 F.2d 87 (D.C. Cir. 1950).

NATURE OF CASE: Appeal from conviction for grand larceny.

FACT SUMMARY: Graham (D), an attorney, told his client, Gal, that he could prevent Gal's arrest from damaging his application for U.S. citizenship for $2,000 to be used to bribe police, which was never done.

🏛 RULE OF LAW
One, who obtains money from another upon the representation that he will perform certain services therewith for the latter, intending at the time to convert the money and actually converting it to his own use, is guilty of larceny.

FACTS: Francisco Gal, an immigrant, had been arrested for disorderly conduct. He went to Graham (D) in Graham's (D) professional capacity as a lawyer, fearing his arrest would impede his obtaining U.S. citizenship. Gal testified that Graham (D) said he required $200 for his fee and $2,000 to "talk" with the police. The police officer talked with Graham (D), said Gal was in no trouble, and testified that Graham (D) offered him no money for his help. Graham (D) kept the money, claiming Gal gave him full title to it.

ISSUE: Did Graham (D) commit larceny by trick?

HOLDING AND DECISION: (Washington, J.) Yes. There is a distinction between one who gives up possession of a chattel for a special purpose to another who, by converting it to his own use, is held to have committed a trespass and one, although induced by fraud or trick, who still actually intends that title shall pass to the wrongdoer. Here, Gal intended to give the money to Graham (D) for a special purpose. It was not intended to be a fee. Thus, a trespass was committed against Gal, for which Graham (D) is criminally liable. Affirmed.

▶ ANALYSIS

In larceny by trick, the use of fraud to procure possession of an item or money vitiates the consent with which it was given. If the recipient forms the fraudulent intent later on, there still is larceny but by a doctrine of continuing trespass. Do not confuse this with embezzlement, which concerns the fraudulent conversion of rightfully-possessed property.

Quicknotes

GRAND LARCENY The illegal taking of another's property with the intent to deprive the owner thereof, the value of which is greater than the statutory amount (usually $100).

LARCENY BY TRICK The illegal taking of another's property with the intent to deprive the owner thereof and through the means of deception.

TRESPASS Unlawful interference with, or damage to, the real or personal property of another.

People v. Ashley

State (P) v. Borrower (D)

Cal. Sup. Ct., 42 Cal. 2d 246, 267 P.2d 271 (1954).

NATURE OF CASE: Appeal from conviction for theft.

FACT SUMMARY: Ashley (D) procured "loans" from two elderly ladies upon false promises to repay.

🏛 RULE OF LAW
A promise made in exchange for something of value with no present intention to perform that promise is the obtaining of property by false pretenses where the fraudulent and deceitful acquisition includes both title and possession.

FACTS: Ashley (D) was convicted of grand theft. He obtained $7,200 from an elderly lady by promising that the loan would be secured by a first mortgage on certain improved property owned by his corporation. Ashley (D) gave her no more than a note for that amount and threatened to kill himself so she could collect on his life insurance. The corporation only leased the property in question. Ashley (D) obtained another loan of $13,590 from a second woman and did not provide her the promised security. He obtained another $4,470 from her after taking out a gun in front of her. Ashley (D) contends the evidence was insufficient to find guilt either for larceny by trick or obtaining property by false pretenses.

ISSUE: Is a false promise a false pretense for the purpose of satisfying the elements of obtaining property by false pretenses?

HOLDING AND DECISION: (Traynor, J.) Yes. Larceny by trick and device is the appropriation of property, possession of which is fraudulently obtained. Obtaining property by false pretenses differs in that it has the additional element of acquisition of possession and title. It must be shown that there was a false pretense or misrepresentation with intent to defraud the owner of his property, and that the owner was in fact defrauded. The majority rule has not held accountable future promises made without intention to perform because a promise of future conduct from which any injury might arise could be averted by common prudence and caution. This view was based on two erroneous English cases and a third case from Massachusetts. It has been supported by the argument that it protects debtors who might be found to have acted criminally in default on their obligations. But the problem of proving intent when the false pretense is a false promise is no more difficult than when the false pretense is a misrepresentation of existing fact. Thus, the intent not to perform a promise is regularly proved in civil actions for deceit. "If false promises were not false pretenses, the

legally sophisticated, without fear of punishment, could perpetrate on the unwary fraudulent schemes like that divulged by the record in this case." Affirmed.

CONCURRENCE: (Schauer, J.) The evidence establishes obtaining property by false pretenses as to existing facts, making it unnecessary for this case to go against the majority rule.

▶ ANALYSIS

In many modern jurisdictions, larcenous crimes are consolidated into the single crime of theft, but their elements have not changed as a result.

■■■

Quicknotes

FALSE PRETENSES The unlawful obtaining of money or property from another with an intent to defraud and with the utilization of false representations.

LARCENY BY TRICK The illegal taking of another's property with the intent to deprive the owner thereof and through the means of deception.

THEFT The illegal taking of another's property with the intent to deprive the owner thereof. Theft is a popular term for larceny, but is generally a broader term that includes swindling and embezzlement.

■■■

Nelson v. United States

Buyer (D) v. Federal government (P)

227 F.2d 21 (D.C. Cir. 1955).

NATURE OF CASE: Appeal from conviction for obtaining goods by false pretenses.

FACT SUMMARY: Nelson (D) purchased property on credit, giving as security a car that already had an outstanding lien on it.

🏛 **RULE OF LAW**
In a prosecution for false pretenses, intent to defraud may be presumed from unlawful acts.

FACTS: Nelson (D) purchased merchandise from a wholesaler, Potomac Distributors, for the purpose of resale. His account with the company was in arrears more than thirty days for in excess of $1,800. Nelson (D) then sought more merchandise from Potomac, asserting that he had already sold the merchandise (and even produced the sales contracts). He promised payment that night, offering as security for the merchandise a car worth $4,260—asserting total ownership of the car except for one $55 payment that was not yet due. In reliance on these representations, Potomac gave Nelson (D) merchandise worth $349 secured by a mortgage on the car and the merchandise. Nelson (D) was supposed to make payment on the total amount he owed Potomac within a few days, but he left town without paying. The car was involved in an accident that caused $1,000 worth of damage to it and was thereupon repossessed by the bank that had the prior chattel mortgage on it in the amount of $3,028. From a conviction for false pretenses, Nelson (D) appealed.

ISSUE: In a prosecution for false pretenses, may intent to defraud be presumed from unlawful acts?

HOLDING AND DECISION: (Danaher, J.) Yes. In a prosecution for false pretenses, intent to defraud may be presumed from unlawful acts. The intent to injure or defraud in false pretenses is presumed when an unlawful act, which results in loss or injury, is proved to have been knowingly committed. Intent is presumed from commission of the unlawful act. An accused's assertion of innocent-intent cannot justify misrepresentations known and intended to be false and to be relied upon. Here, the fact that $349 worth of merchandise was exchanged for a security interest in a car in which Nelson (D) had over $1,000 worth of equity is irrelevant. Potomac would not have exchanged the property if Nelson (D) had not misrepresented facts upon which he knew Potomac would rely. Affirmed.

DISSENT: (Miller, J.) Although Nelson (D) falsely inflated the value of the security he offered, he did not intend to defraud Potomac Distributors. At the time of the transaction, the security he pledged for the television sets had an actual value of not less than $1,172 to secure a debt of only $349.50 for the transaction with the television sets themselves. In the circumstances, it is completely illogical to infer that he intended to defraud the distributor. The evidence thus is not sufficient on the charge of obtaining goods by false pretenses, and that count should not have been submitted to the jury.

▶ **ANALYSIS**

It is not sufficient that an accused merely make an untrue representation; he must know it to be false before the crime of false pretenses occurs. An accused "knows something to be false" when he has personal knowledge of its falsity, or when he believes it to be false and it is in fact false, or when he knows that he does not know whether it is false or not and it is in fact false. The perpetrator of false pretenses also must possess the intent to defraud when he makes the misrepresentation (a specific intent). As this case illustrates, however, the prosecution does not have to come up with specific and direct proof of the accused's specific intent to defraud. Indeed, for most cases, that would be an impossible task; instead, the intent may be inferred.

■=■

Quicknotes

FALSE PRETENSES The unlawful obtaining of money or property from another with an intent to defraud and with the utilization of false representations.

■=■

State v. Harrington

State (P) v. Lawyer (D)

Vt. Sup. Ct., 128 Vt. 242, 260 A.2d 692 (1969).

NATURE OF CASE: Appeal from extortion conviction.

FACT SUMMARY: Harrington (D), a divorce lawyer for Ms. Morin, sent a letter to Mr. Morin threatening the release of incriminating evidence to authorities unless Mr. Morin submitted to a divorce settlement.

🏛 RULE OF LAW
The use of threats of criminal proceedings to obtain a favorable civil settlement constitutes extortion.

FACTS: Ms. Morin came to Harrington (D), an attorney, seeking a divorce. As Ms. Morin had no money, Harrington (D) agreed to a contingency fee arrangement. Harrington (D) "set up" Mr. Morin with the classic ruse of hiring a prostitute to solicit him, whereupon photos were taken of Mr. Morin in compromising circumstances. Harrington (D) then sent a letter to Mr. Morin threatening to circulate the photos unless he granted a divorce on Ms. Morin's terms. Harrington also made vague threats about reporting Mr. Morin's financial affairs to the Internal Revenue Service (IRS). Harrington (D) was later prosecuted for blackmail based on the letter. He was convicted and appealed.

ISSUE: Does the use of threats of criminal proceedings to obtain a favorable civil settlement constitute extortion?

HOLDING AND DECISION: (Holden, C.J.) Yes. The use of threats of criminal proceedings to obtain a favorable civil settlement constitutes extortion. Vermont law provides that one who threatens to accuse another of a crime with intent to extort money or gain a pecuniary advantage is guilty of blackmail. In this case, Harrington (D) threatened to initiate criminal proceedings against Mr. Morin with the express purpose of obtaining a favorable settlement. Because of the contingency fee arrangement, Harrington (D) had a pecuniary interest in the matter. Therefore, his acts were blackmail. Affirmed.

▶ ANALYSIS

States differ as to what sort of threats rise to the level of blackmail. Although threats of injury or criminal accusations suffice in every jurisdiction, ultimatums regarding exposure of defamatory information are not universally considered extortion. The Model Penal Code provides that a person is guilty of theft if he obtains property of another by, among other things, threatening to inflict bodily injury, making accusations of a criminal offense, exposing any secret subjecting the victim to hatred or ridicule, or "inflict[ing] any harm which would not benefit the actor."

■═■

Quicknotes

CONTINGENCY FEE AGREEMENT A fee agreement between an attorney and client that is contingent upon the ultimate disposition of the case and comprises a percentage of the party's recovery.

DEFAMATORY Subjecting to hatred, ridicule or injuring one in his occupation or business.

■═■

People v. Fichtner

State (P) v. Employees (D)

N.Y. Sup. Ct., App. Div., 281 A.D. 159, 118 N.Y.S.2d 392; *aff'd without opinion*, 305 N.Y. 864, 114 N.E.2d 212 (1953).

NATURE OF CASE: Appeal from conviction for extortion.

FACT SUMMARY: Smith stole some items from Hill Market. Fichtner (D) and McGuinness (D), Hill employees, induced Smith to pay $25 to the market by threatening to accuse him of larceny.

🏛 RULE OF LAW
One who uses threats to induce another to repay money is guilty of extortion even where the victim actually did steal some goods and the defendant honestly believed the victim was guilty of theft.

FACTS: Smith stole some items from Hill Market. Fichtner (D) and McGuinness (D) testified that they believed that over several months Smith had stolen $75 worth of merchandise from the market. They told Smith they would accuse him of larceny if he did not pay them $75. He agreed to pay and gave them $25. They did not keep any of the money, but it went into the Hill Market company funds.

ISSUE: Is a defendant who uses threats to induce another to repay money guilty of extortion where the victim actually did steal some goods and the defendant honestly believed the victim was guilty of theft?

HOLDING AND DECISION: (Johnston, J.) Yes. The extortion statutes are intended to prevent the collection of money by the means of threats to accuse the debtor of a crime, even where the victim is in fact guilty of the crime the defendant actually believes him to be. Here, Fichtner (D) and McGuinness (D) are guilty of extortion since they induced Smith to pay Hill Market $25 by threatening to accuse him of larceny. It is also irrelevant that they did not keep the money themselves. The convictions are affirmed.

DISSENT: (Wenzel, J.) If Fichtner (D) and McGuinness (D) were not acting on their own behalf and if they acted with good faith and without malice, they could not be guilty of extortion as there would be no criminal intent.

▶ ANALYSIS

It is, of course, no defense to extortion that the victim is guilty of the crime or exposes the defect which the defendant threatens to expose. There is a dispute concerning how far one who has been injured by another's crime can go in threatening to expose the wrongdoer's guilt unless the latter makes restitution. Some courts find that in these circumstances there is no intent to extort or to gain. Other courts dealing with statutes which do not specifically require an intent to gain have found the threatened guilty under these circumstances. The statute involved in *Fichtner* was of the latter type. It defined extortion as obtaining another's property through "a wrongful use of fear."

Quicknotes

EXTORTION The unlawful taking of property of another by threats of force.

GOOD FAITH An honest intention to abstain from any unconscientious advantage of another.

LARCENY The illegal taking of another's property with the intent to deprive the owner thereof.

MALICE The intention to commit an unlawful act without justification or excuse.

RESTITUTION The return or restoration of what the defendant has gained in a transaction to prevent the unjust enrichment of the defendant.

State v. Miller

State (P) v. Buyer (D)

Or. Sup. Ct., 192 Or. 188, 233 P.2d 786 (1951).

NATURE OF CASE: Appeal from conviction of obtaining property by false pretenses.

FACT SUMMARY: Miller (D) induced one company to guarantee his indebtedness to another upon the misrepresentation that he owned a tractor free and clear while it was actually purchased under a conditional sales contract.

🏛 **RULE OF LAW**
Property capable of being the subject of larceny must be something capable of being possessed and the title to which can be transferred.

FACTS: Miller (D) induced the Hub Lumber Company to agree to guarantee his indebtedness to another upon his false representation he owned a tractor free and clear and upon his executing a chattel mortgage thereto as security. Actually, Miller (D) was buying the tractor under a conditional sales contract. He was charged with obtaining property by false pretenses.

ISSUE: Can intangible property be the subject of larceny?

HOLDING AND DECISION: (Lusk, J.) No. The history of the crime of false pretenses generally holds that the thing obtained must be the subject of common-law larceny. By statute, the obtaining of a signature with intent to defraud or the making of a bill of sale has been added so as to be criminal and indicates that intangibles could not previously be the subject of larceny since they were not to be regarded as property. Here, the conduct was only oral and not the subject of any statute. No crime could thus have been committed. Reversed and action dismissed.

▶ *ANALYSIS*

Originally, property for the purposes of larceny had to be tangible and personal. Modern statutes are now more expansive in most jurisdictions and cover virtually all property, tangible or intangible, real or personal.

■■■

Quicknotes

CONDITIONAL SALES CONTRACT An agreement pursuant to which title to goods or land does not pass from seller to buyer until payment is tendered.

FALSE PRETENSES The unlawful obtaining of money or property from another with an intent to defraud and with the utilization of false representations.

LARCENY The illegal taking of another's property with the intent to deprive the owner thereof.

■■■

United States v. Girard

Federal government (P) v. Informant (D)

601 F.2d 69 (2d Cir. 1979).

NATURE OF CASE: Appeal from convictions for sale of government information.

FACT SUMMARY: Girard (D), who was convicted of selling government information, argued that the applicable federal statute covered only tangible property or documents.

🏛 RULE OF LAW
A statute which makes it a crime to sell any "thing of value" without authority to do so is not limited to covering the sale of tangible property and encompasses the sale of information.

FACTS: 18 U.S.C. § 641 makes it a crime to sell or knowingly receive any "record . . . or thing of value" of the United States without authority. Girard (D) was convicted under the statute for using an inside source at the Drug Enforcement Administration (DEA) to get information on whether or not certain parties were government informants. He used this information pursuant to his promise to one Bond that he could, for $500 per name, secure DEA reports that would show whether any participant in a proposed illegal drug venture was a government informant. Girard (D) appealed his conviction on the ground that the aforementioned statute covered only the sale of tangible property and did not encompass the sale of information.

ISSUE: If a statute makes the unauthorized sale of any "thing of value" a crime, does it cover the sale of information?

HOLDING AND DECISION: (Van Graafeiland, J.) Yes. The reach of a statute making it a crime to sell any "thing of value" without authority is not limited to the sale of tangible property, but extends its coverage to the sale of information. The phrase "thing of value" is found in many criminal statutes. These words have become, in a sense, words of art and the word "thing" is generally construed to cover intangibles as well as tangibles. The Government (P) has a property interest in certain of its private records which it may protect by statute as things of value. It has done so by enacting § 641, which is not simply a statutory codification of the common law of larceny. Indeed, theft is not a requisite element of the statutory offense, which is based upon unauthorized sale or conversion. Inasmuch as all the challenges to this conviction fail of their own accord, it must stand. Affirmed.

▶ ANALYSIS

That a "thing of value" includes intangibles is well documented in case law. For example, amusement was held a "thing of value" under gambling statutes and sexual intercourse or the promise thereof a thing of value under bribery statutes. A promise to reinstate an employee, an agreement not to run in a primary election, and the testimony of a witness, have also been held to be "things of value."

Quicknotes

CONVERSION The act of depriving an owner of his property without permission or justification.

LARCENY The illegal taking of another's property with the intent to deprive the owner thereof.

THEFT The illegal taking of another's property with the intent to deprive the owner thereof. Theft is a popular term for larceny, but is generally a broader term that includes swindling and embezzlement.

Regina v. Stewart

Government (P) v. Union informer (D)

Canada Sup. Ct., 50 D.L.R. 4th 1, 41 C.C.C.3d 481 (1988).

NATURE OF CASE: Review of conviction of attempted theft.

FACT SUMMARY: Stewart (D) attempted to obtain certain confidential information regarding union employees of a hotel by bribing a security guard.

RULE OF LAW
Confidential information is not property subject to laws against theft.

FACTS: A union sought to organize employees at a hotel in Toronto, Canada. Stewart (D) was hired by the union to obtain the names and addresses of the hotel's employees, which the hotel had refused to divulge. Stewart (D) offered a hotel employee money to provide the information. The employee informed the hotel, and the hotel informed the authorities. Stewart (D) was charged with attempted theft. The trial court ruled that confidential information alone was not property and not subject to theft laws. Stewart (D) was acquitted. The court of appeals, holding to the contrary, entered an order of conviction. The Canada Supreme Court granted review.

ISSUE: Is confidential information a form of property subject to laws against theft?

HOLDING AND DECISION: (Lamer, J.) No. Information is not property subject to laws against theft. While the taking of confidential information from another may certainly give rise to liability in the civil arena, the considerations in the criminal arena are somewhat broader. As opposed to the owner of confidential information, whose interests will almost always lie with keeping the information secret, society at large will often benefit from the release of information. Beyond this, to criminalize the "theft" of information alone would create serious practical problems, such as defining "confidential." What one person considers confidential information might not be viewed as such by another. Finally, the civil arena provides a sufficient mechanism for settling disputes in this area. For these reasons, theft of confidential information alone will not come within the meaning of "theft" in the criminal sense. Reversed.

► ANALYSIS

Had Stewart (D) obtained a list on paper, he would have been convicted here, as a list is something tangible. However, the court distinguished a list or any other tangible object actually containing information from the information itself—a pure intangible. The information Stewart (D) sought did not belong to anyone and thus could not be considered property until the legislature defined it as such.

Quicknotes

LARCENY The illegal taking of another's property with the intent to deprive the owner thereof.

THEFT The illegal taking of another's property with the intent to deprive the owner thereof. Theft is a popular term for larceny, but is generally a broader term that includes swindling and embezzlement.

Skilling v. United States

Individual convicted on multiple counts (D) v. Federal government (D)

130 S. Ct. 2896 (2010).

NATURE OF CASE: Appeal from jury verdict convicting defendant of an honest services fraud conspiracy charge.

FACT SUMMARY: Skilling (D) participated in an alleged conspiracy to prop up the energy company Enron's stock prices by exaggerating the company's financial well-being.

RULE OF LAW
The honest services doctrine, arising under the mail and wire fraud statutes outlawing use of the mails or wire to advance any scheme to defraud, shall apply only in those cases involving bribes or kickbacks, and not to the broader class of cases relating to undisclosed self-dealing by a public official or private employee.

FACTS: Skilling (D), Enron's chief executive officer, participated in an alleged conspiracy to prop up the energy company Enron's stock prices by exaggerating the company's financial well-being. After several years of investigations, the Government (P) charged Skilling (D) with multiple counts of securities fraud, wire fraud, making false representations, and insider trading. The jury convicted him of multiple counts, including an honest services fraud conspiracy charge. Skilling (D) appealed on the ground the honest services statute was constitutionally vague because Congress failed to define specifically what types of conduct was illegal under the statute.

ISSUE: Shall the honest services doctrine, arising under the mail and wire fraud statutes outlawing use of the mails or wire to advance any scheme to defraud, apply only in those cases involving bribes or kickbacks, and not to the broader class of cases relating to undisclosed self-dealing by a public official or private employee?

HOLDING AND DECISION: (Ginsburg, J.) Yes. The honest services doctrine, arising under the mail and wire fraud statutes outlawing use of the mails or wire to advance any scheme to defraud, shall apply only in those cases involving bribes or kickbacks, and not to the broader class of cases relating to undisclosed self-dealing by a public official or private employee. Since 1909, courts have interpreted the mail and wire fraud statute to include deprivation not just of property rights, but also intangible rights as well. This is known as the intangible rights theory or honest services doctrine. The doctrine allowed for use of the mail and wire fraud statutes when the public was denied the honest services of a corrupt public official who had used the mail to further a scheme to defraud the public. In 1987, in *McNally v. United States*, 483 U.S. 650 (1987), this Court effectively did away with the honest services doctrine by requiring that the victim prove a loss of property. In the next year, Congress amended the statutes to protect the public's right to honest services by removing the requirement of a showing of a loss of property. The question in this case is the extent of Congress's amendment. The Court holds that mail and wire fraud statutes shall cover fraud only in those cases involving bribery and kickback schemes. Those cases constituted the majority of pre-*McNally* cases, as opposed to those cases involving undisclosed self-dealing by private or public officials. There is simply no consensus on what conduct constitutes illegal activity in the context of self-dealing by private or public officials. To allow the statute to cover those cases would indeed open the statute up to a constitutional claim of vagueness. Limiting the statutes to cover only those cases involving bribes or kickbacks leaves the statutes on better constitutional footing. The conviction for the honest services fraud conspiracy charge is reversed.

CONCURRENCE: (Scalia, J.) Unfortunately, the pre-*McNally* cases failed to provide clear guidance as to what constituted the denial of the right to honest services. The Court's decision here does nothing to provide any additional guidance. There remains no consensus from the courts or Congress on the fundamental question: what is the criterion of guilt for mail and wire fraud cases?

▶ ANALYSIS

The text notes there is a pending piece of legislation in Congress that could broaden the scope of the honest services doctrine to include those cases involving undisclosed self-dealing. The difficult issue in all of these cases is the problem of proof. One reason for the Court's limiting of the doctrine is that federal criminal statutes have a better chance of surviving judicial scrutiny when they are limited in scope. Here, the Court sought to limit the statute's coverage to scenarios where there exists the possibility of concrete evidence to support the alleged crime, such as a bribe or a kickback.

Quicknotes

MAIL FRAUD A federal offense whereby an individual utilizes the mails with the intent to defraud.

People v. Brown

State (P) v. Bicycle thief (D)

Cal. Sup. Ct., 105 Cal. 66, 38 P. 518 (1894).

NATURE OF CASE: Prosecution for larceny.

FACT SUMMARY: Brown (D) took a boy's bicycle to "get even" with him for the boy's throwing oranges at him. Brown (D) intended to return the bicycle but was apprehended before he could do so.

🏛 RULE OF LAW
For there to be felonious intent for a larceny, the one who takes another's property must intend to permanently deprive the owner of it.

FACTS: Brown (D) took a boy's bicycle to "get even" with the boy who had been throwing oranges at him previously and did not stop when told to do so by Brown (D). Brown (D) tried to hide the bicycle but was apprehended before he was able to return it. He did not intend to keep it.

ISSUE: Can there be a larceny if the taker does not intend to deprive the owner of his property permanently?

HOLDING AND DECISION: (Garoute, J.) No. There must be felonious intent to deprive the owner of the property permanently. If there is no such intent, the taking is merely a trespass. The intent need not be to convert the property to the taker's own use, only to permanently deprive the owner of it. Reversed and remanded.

▶ ANALYSIS

Intent to steal, commonly appearing in the Latin, *animus furandi*, requires an intent to deprive the owner of his property permanently. It takes more than the unlawful and antisocial conduct of intentionally borrowing another's property temporarily for there to be a larceny. Intentional use for a short period of time usually will not imperil the owner's substantial rights in the property. If a person is caught before he can return the property, he runs the risk of conviction for larceny, as the jury might not believe the taker's intent as testified, but the instruction to the jury must clearly describe the intention requisite for conviction.

■=■

Quicknotes

LARCENY The illegal taking of another's property with the intent to deprive the owner thereof.

TRESPASS Unlawful interference with, or damage to, the real or personal property of another.

■=■

Regina v. Feely

State (P) v. Branch manager (D)

Q.B., Ct. of App., 2 W.L.R. 201 (1973).

NATURE OF CASE: Appeal from a conviction for theft.

FACT SUMMARY: Feely (D), branch manager for a firm of bookmakers, was convicted of theft of $30 which he had taken from the till, intending to repay it.

🏛 RULE OF LAW
A taking committed without evil intent is not within the concept of stealing at common law or under modern theft statutes.

FACTS: Feely (D) was the branch manager for a bookmaking firm. Circulars were sent to all branch managers instructing them that the practice of borrowing from the till must stop. Even so, Feely (D) took $30 from the branch safe and a few days later happened to be transferred to another branch. When his successor found a $40 shortage, Feely (D) gave him an IOU for that amount. Feely (D) explained to the security staff that $10 accounted for bets paid out, but that he took $30 because he was short of cash; that he was owed $70 by his employer, and intended to deduct the amount he took from that owed him. The trial judge said it was no defense to say he intended to repay the money. Feely (D) was convicted of theft.

ISSUE: May the accused defend himself by showing that he did not intend to keep the amount he took and intended to repay it?

HOLDING AND DECISION: (Lord Lawton, J.) Yes. Theft is defined as a dishonest appropriation of property belonging to another with the intention of permanently depriving the other of it. Whether the taking is dishonest relates to the person's state of mind, and whether an accused has a particular state of mind is a question to be determined by the jury. A taking made without evil intent does not appear to be within the concept of theft. Reversed.

▌ANALYSIS

Note that intent to repay is not a defense to embezzlement or false pretense charges. It is not clear whether this case changes that view or whether the court simply thought the trial judge invaded the province of the jury. It is also not clear if the decision was primarily a result of England's Theft Act of 1968, which redefined offenses in everyday language. It is possible that the concept of dishonesty is being given a more "everyday" meaning.

Quicknotes

THEFT The illegal taking of another's property with the intent to deprive the owner thereof. Theft is a popular term for larceny, but is generally a broader term that includes swindling and embezzlement.

■═■

People v. Reid

State (P) v. Convicted robber (D)

N.Y. Ct. App., 69 N.Y.2d 469, 508 N.E.2d 661 (1987).

NATURE OF CASE: Appeal from robbery convictions.

FACT SUMMARY: Reid (D) contended his claim of right, forced through violence, negated larcenous intent.

🏛 RULE OF LAW
A good-faith claim of right does not negate the intent to commit robbery through the use of force.

FACTS: Reid (D) used force to retrieve money owed to him. He was convicted of armed robbery and appealed, contending his good-faith claim of right to the money negated any criminal intent.

ISSUE: Does a good-faith claim of right negate the intent to commit robbery through the use of force?

HOLDING AND DECISION: (Simons, J.) No. The good-faith claim of right does not negate the intent to commit robbery through force. The legislature has implied that the claim of right defense is available only in enumerated situations and not in cases involving the use of force. Thus, the use of force renders defense unavailable. Affirmed.

▌ *ANALYSIS*

The court also indicated that policy considerations required this result. It was unwilling to expand permissible methods of self-help. Such unwarranted violence subverts the role of the judicial system in dispute resolution.

■═■

Quicknotes

ROBBERY The unlawful taking of property from the person of another through the use of force or fear.

■═■

Quick Reference Rules of Law

Inmates of Attica Correctional Facility v. Rockefeller

Prison inmates (P) v. Government officials (D)

477 F.2d 375 (2nd Cir. 1973).

NATURE OF CASE: Appeal from the dismissal of a civil suit that sought improper remedies.

FACT SUMMARY: Several inmates of New York's Attica Correctional Facility, along with the mother of a deceased former inmate, brought a civil suit against New York State officials and the local U.S. Attorney after the inmate uprising at the prison in 1971.

🏛 RULE OF LAW
Courts cannot compel prosecutors to investigate and initiate criminal prosecutions.

FACTS: The inmate uprising at New York State's Attica Correctional Facility in 1971 resulted in the deaths of 32 inmates and injuries to many others. Present and former inmates of the facility, along with the mother of an inmate who was killed during the uprising, sued various officials of New York State and the local U.S. Attorney after the incident. The complaint alleged that the state officials committed various crimes in the process of regaining control of the facility, and that the state officials were failing to prosecute the persons who committed those alleged crimes. The plaintiffs complained further that the local U.S. Attorney was also failing to investigate and prosecute the state officials. As remedies for their alleged injuries, Plaintiffs sought mandamus against both the U.S. Attorney and the state defendants to compel investigations. The defendants moved to dismiss on grounds that the complaint sought improper judicial relief, and the trial court granted the motions to dismiss. Plaintiffs appealed.

ISSUE: Can courts compel prosecutors to investigate and initiate criminal prosecutions?

HOLDING AND DECISION: (Mansfield, J.) No. Courts cannot compel prosecutors to investigate and initiate criminal prosecutions. Federal mandamus will lie only "to compel an officer or employee of the United States . . . to perform a duty owed to the plaintiff." Federal courts have never overturned a prosecutor's discretionary decision not to prosecute at the request of a private plaintiff. That reluctance stems partly from respect for separation of powers and partly from recognition that the decision whether to prosecute is far too complex for judicial resolution and oversight. Congress did not remove prosecutorial discretion in cases involving alleged civil-rights violations, despite the mandatory language in 42 U.S.C. 1987. Furthermore, these plaintiffs have identified no statute that imposes a mandatory duty on the state officials to perform the desire prosecutions. Affirmed.

▶ ANALYSIS

Largely for separation-of-powers considerations, respect for prosecutorial discretion is deeply embedded in American law. With respect to the state defendants in *Inmates of Attica Correctional Facility*, though, the trial court also could have dismissed the claims against those defendants because those defendants plainly were not "officer[s] or employee[s] of the United States," as the federal mandamus statute expressly required. Dismissal against the state defendants also would have been proper on the ground that having federal courts meddling in state officials' performance of discretionary duties would have violated the most basic principles of federalism.

Quicknotes

MANDAMUS A court order issued commanding a public or private entity, or an official thereof, to perform a duty required by law.

SEPARATION OF POWERS The system of checks and balances preventing one branch of government from infringing upon exercising the powers of another branch of government.

United States v. Armstrong

Federal government (P) v. Black defendant indicted for drug possession (D)

517 U.S. 456 (1996).

NATURE OF CASE: Appeal from affirmance of dismissal of indictment for drug and firearms possession.

FACT SUMMARY: After being indicted on drug and firearms charges, Armstrong (D) and other blacks moved for discovery on their claim that they were singled out for prosecution because of their race.

> 🏛 **RULE OF LAW**
> For a defendant to be entitled to discovery on a claim that he was singled out for prosecution on the basis of his race, he must make a threshold showing that the Government declined to prosecute similarly situated suspects of other races.

FACTS: In response to their indictment on "crack" cocaine and federal firearms charges, Armstrong (D) and other blacks filed a motion for discovery or for dismissal, alleging that they were selected for prosecution because of their race. On seven separate occasions, informants had bought a total of 124.3 grams of crack from Armstrong (D) and the others, and witnessed them carrying firearms during the sales. Federal agents searched the hotel room in which the sales were transacted, arrested Armstrong (D) and another in the room, and found more crack and a loaded gun. The agents later arrested others who were allegedly part of a related drug ring. The district court granted the motion over the Government's (P) argument, among others, that there was no evidence or allegation that it had failed to prosecute non-black defendants. When the Government (P) indicated it would not comply with the discovery order, the court dismissed the case. The court of appeals affirmed, holding that the proof requirements for a selective-prosecution claim do not compel a defendant to demonstrate that the Government (P) has failed to prosecute others who are similarly situated. The United States Supreme Court granted certiorari.

ISSUE: For a defendant to be entitled to discovery on a claim that he was singled out for prosecution on the basis of his race, must he make a threshold showing that the Government declined to prosecute similarly situated suspects of other races?

HOLDING AND DECISION: (Rehnquist, C.J.) Yes. For a defendant to be entitled to discovery on a claim that he was singled out for prosecution on the basis of his race, he must make a threshold showing that the Government declined to prosecute similarly situated suspects of other races. The Attorney General and United States Attorneys have broad discretion whether to prosecute, and, in the absence of clear evidence to the contrary,

courts presume that they have properly discharged their official duties. Under the equal protection component of the Fifth Amendment's Due Process Clause, the decision whether to prosecute may not be based on an arbitrary classification such as race or religion. To prove a selective-prosecution claim, the claimant must demonstrate that the prosecutorial policy had a discriminatory effect and was motivated by a discriminatory purpose. To establish a discriminatory effect in a race case, the claimant must show that similarly situated individuals of a different race were not prosecuted. Although such a rule has applied to state prosecutions, a similar rule applies where the power of a federal court is invoked to challenge an exercise of one of the core powers of the Executive Branch of the Federal Government, the power to prosecute. Discovery imposes many of the costs present when the Government must respond to a prima facie case of selective prosecution. Assuming that discovery is available on an appropriate showing in aid of a selective-prosecution claim, the justifications for a rigorous standard of proof for the elements of such a case thus require a correspondingly rigorous standard for discovery in aid of it. Thus, in order to establish entitlement to such discovery, a defendant must produce credible evidence that similarly situated defendants of other races could have been prosecuted, but were not. In this case, Armstrong (D) and the others (D) have not met this required threshold, because the evidence they rely on failed to show that non-blacks could have been prosecuted for the offenses for which Armstrong (D) and the others (D) were charged, but were not so prosecuted. Reversed.

DISSENT: (Stevens, J.) The scope of judicial review of particular exercises of federal prosecutorial discretion is not fully defined. However, there is no need for the rigid rule the majority enunciates. If a District Judge has reason to suspect that a federal prosecutor has singled out particular defendants for prosecution on the basis of their race, it is surely appropriate for the judge to determine whether there is a factual basis for such a concern. Here, the Court is correct that the defendants' showing was not strong enough to give them a right to discovery. Nonetheless, the judge did not abuse her discretion when she concluded that the factual showing was sufficiently disturbing to require a response from the prosecution, so the Court is wrong in its conclusion that no inquiry at all was permissible. The District Judge's order should have been evaluated in light of three circumstances that underscore the need for judicial vigilance over certain types of drug prosecutions involving crack cocaine. First, the penalties for possession

Continued on next page.

of small amounts of crack are very severe, and much more so than for powder cocaine. Second, the disparity between the treatment of crack cocaine and powder cocaine is matched by the disparity between the severity of the punishment imposed by federal law and that imposed by state law for the same conduct. Third, it is undisputed that the brunt of the elevated federal penalties falls heavily on blacks. The extraordinary severity of the imposed penalties and the troubling racial patterns of enforcement give rise to a special concern about the fairness of charging practices for crack offenses. Evidence tending to prove that black defendants charged with distribution of crack in a certain district are prosecuted in federal court, whereas members of other races charged with similar offenses are prosecuted in state court, warrants close scrutiny by the federal judges in that district. Accordingly, the District Judge acted well within her discretion to call for the development of facts that would demonstrate what standards, if any, governed the choice of forum where similarly situated offenders are prosecuted. Even if defendants failed to carry their burden of showing that there were individuals who were not black but who could have been prosecuted in federal court for the same offenses, it does not follow that the district court abused its discretion in ordering discovery. There can be no doubt that such individuals exist, and indeed the Government (P) never denied the same. In those circumstances, the district court should have been able to take judicial notice of this obvious fact and demand information from the Government's (P) files to support or refute defendants' evidence.

▶ *ANALYSIS*

The Court reserved the question of whether a defendant must satisfy the similarly situated requirement in a case involving direct admissions by prosecutors of discriminatory purpose. The Court also held that contrary to defendants' contention, Federal Rule of Criminal Procedure 16, which governs discovery in criminal cases, did not support the result reached by the court of appeals. The Court determined that Rule 16(a)(1)(C)—which, inter alia, requires the Government (P) to permit discovery of documents that are "material to the preparation of the ... defense" or "intended for use by the government as evidence in chief"—applies only to the preparation of the "defense" against the Government's (P) case in chief, not to the preparation of selective-prosecution claims.

Quicknotes

DISCRIMINATORY TREATMENT Unequal treatment of individuals without justification.

Brady v. United States

Admitted kidnapper (P) v. Federal government (D)

397 U.S. 742 (1970).

NATURE OF CASE: Appeal from a denial of post-conviction relief following the defendant's guilty plea.

FACT SUMMARY: A man pled guilty to a charge of kidnapping but later challenged his plea as not being based on a voluntary waiver of his constitutional rights.

⚖ RULE OF LAW
A guilty plea is not compelled and invalid under the Fifth Amendment if the defendant enters the plea to avoid the risk of greater penalties.

FACTS: Brady (P) was charged with kidnapping, and the charge could have supported the death penalty because the victim was harmed before being freed. Brady (P) eventually pled guilty to the charge to avoid the death penalty; the trial judge twice asked him whether the plea was voluntary and accepted the plea. Later, Brady (P) initiated post-conviction proceedings to challenge his plea, arguing that he did not voluntarily enter the plea because he entered it to avoid the death penalty. The trial court and intermediate appellate court both rejected Brady's (P) request for post-conviction relief. Brady (P) sought further review in the United States Supreme Court.

ISSUE: Is a guilty plea compelled and invalid under the Fifth Amendment if the defendant enters the plea to avoid the risk of greater penalties?

HOLDING AND DECISION: (White, J.) No. A guilty plea is not compelled and invalid under the Fifth Amendment if the defendant enters the plea to avoid the risk of greater penalties. A State clearly cannot induce a plea by physical harm or threats or physical harm, nor can it gain a plea by mental coercion. Brady's (P) claim fits neither of these categories: he claims that his plea was coerced solely because he wanted to avoid a harsher penalty. Both the defendant and the State benefit from a plea, and that mutuality of advantage makes the practice consistent with the Fifth Amendment. A plea induced by threats, misrepresentations, or bribes cannot stand, but Brady (P) has failed to make such a showing here. Affirmed.

▶ ANALYSIS

From the defendant's perspective, plea bargaining to avoid a harsher sentence must look like the very "mental coercion" that the Court says is impermissible. From the perspective of the Constitution, however, the "mutuality of advantage" in the practice relieves the coercive aspect of plea bargaining and ensures the practice's compliance with the Fifth Amendment by making a prosecutor's settlement offer more than just an overpowering threat.

■━■

Quicknotes

FIFTH AMENDMENT Provides that no person shall be compelled to serve as a witness against himself, or be subject to trial for the same offense twice, or be deprived of life, liberty, or property without due process of law.

■━■

Bordenkircher v. Hayes

State (P) v. Repeat felon (D)

434 U.S. 357 (1978).

NATURE OF CASE: Appeal of a conviction under a recidivist statute.

FACT SUMMARY: A prosecutor offered not to seek a conviction under a recidivist statute if Hayes (D) accepted a plea bargain.

🏛 RULE OF LAW
A prosecutor may use the threat of prosecution under a recidivist statute as a bargaining chip in plea negotiations.

FACTS: Hayes (D) was charged with forgery, a felony. He had twice before been convicted of felonies. Forgery carried a maximum term of ten years. The prosecutor offered to recommend five years if Hayes (D) pleaded guilty. Hayes (D) refused. The prosecutor then threatened to charge Hayes (D) under the state's three-felony recidivist statute, which carried a life term, if he did not accept. Hayes (D) rejected the offer. Hayes (D) was convicted of forgery and then sentenced under the recidivist statute to life imprisonment. The state court of appeals affirmed. The U.S. district court denied habeas corpus, but the Sixth Circuit reversed. The United States Supreme Court granted certiorari.

ISSUE: May a prosecutor use the threat of prosecution under a recidivist statute as a bargaining chip in plea negotiation?

HOLDING AND DECISION: (Stewart, J.) Yes. A prosecutor may use the threat of prosecution under a recidivist statute as a bargaining chip in plea negotiation. The Due Process Clause prevents a prosecutor from vindictive behavior against a defendant who has exercised his legal rights, such as having prevailed on appeal. Plea bargaining, however, is a different situation. There can be no element of punishment or retaliation in the give-and-take atmosphere of plea bargaining because the accused is free to accept or reject the prosecution's offer. Granted, acts such as those of the prosecutor here give the defendant difficult choices, but this is the inevitable result of a system that allows plea bargaining. Reversed.

DISSENT: (Blackmun, J.) The prosecution here was merely vindictive in filing the new indictment because the charge resulted solely from the defendant's choice to exercise his constitutional right to a trial. The opposite result might ultimately change nothing in this case—the prosecution would simply begin the process with its highest charge and then bargain from that point forward—but

it is better to make the prosecution accountable for its original charge.

DISSENT: (Powell, J.) The question must be asked whether the prosecutor would have charged a defendant under the recidivist statute before plea bargaining commenced. If the answer is no, as it is here, then prosecution thereunder must be seen as unconstitutionally vindictive.

▶ ANALYSIS

There is a good chance that Hayes (D) could have obtained habeas corpus had he sought it several years later. In 1983, the Court decided *Solom v. Helm*, 463 U.S. 277 (1983). That case involved a recidivist statute similar to the present one. It was held unconstitutional under the Eighth Amendment as calling for a punishment excessive to the crime.

■=■

Quicknotes

DUE PROCESS CLAUSE Clauses, found in the Fifth and Fourteenth Amendments to the United States Constitution, providing that no person shall be deprived of "life, liberty, or property, without due process of law."

HABEAS CORPUS A proceeding in which a defendant brings a writ to compel a judicial determination of whether he is lawfully being held in custody.

PLEA BARGAIN An agreement between a criminal defendant and a prosecutor, which is submitted to the court for approval, generally involving the defendant's pleading guilty to a lesser charge or count in exchange for a more lenient sentence.

■=■

Williams v. New York

Murderer (D) v. State (P)

337 U.S. 241 (1949).

NATURE OF CASE: Appeal from a murder conviction and a sentence of death.

FACT SUMMARY: A jury convicted the defendant of murder and recommended a sentence of life imprisonment, but the trial judge rejected the jury's recommendation and imposed a death sentence.

🏛 RULE OF LAW
Due process permits a sentencing judge to review evidence supplied by witnesses whom a convicted defendant has not had the opportunity to cross-examine or rebut.

FACTS: A jury convicted Williams (D) of first-degree murder and recommended a sentence of life imprisonment. After reviewing much information from witnesses whom Williams (D) had no opportunity to cross-examine or rebut, the trial judge imposed a death sentence. Williams (D) appealed, arguing that the Due Process Clause of the Fourteenth Amendment required that he have an opportunity to cross-examine witnesses and rebut the information relied on by the trial judge in imposing a sentence of death.

ISSUE: Does due process permit a sentencing judge to review evidence supplied by witnesses whom a convicted defendant has not had the opportunity to cross-examine or rebut?

HOLDING AND DECISION: (Black, J.) Yes. Due process permits a sentencing judge to review evidence supplied by witnesses whom a convicted defendant has not had the opportunity to cross-examine or rebut. This case differs from an initial determination of guilt, where stricter procedural safeguards are appropriate. Traditionally, more relaxed standards have been deemed appropriate at sentencing. For practical reasons, our society's preference for individualized sentencing requires a judge to review a broad range of materials—a range so broad that guilt-phase standards simply would overburden the proceeding and make it impossible to hold full-blown trials on issues collateral to guilt. Affirmed.

DISSENT: (Murphy, J.) Due process requires a fair hearing at all stages of a criminal proceeding. When a judge rejects a jury's recommendation of life imprisonment, and he does so based on what would normally be inadmissible evidence, the defendant has not received due process.

▶ ANALYSIS

In addition to deciding a due-process issue, *Williams* also highlights the dangers of discretionary sentencing. A trial judge must review expansive material about a defendant's background to craft a sentence that fits both the offense and the offender. At the same time, as Justice Murphy noted in dissent, fundamental fairness does require that a defendant should have an opportunity to rebut sentencing-phase allegations, certainly if they are as flagrantly prejudicial as the out-of-court information relied on by the sentencing judge in *Williams*. Today, a sentencing hearing provides a convicted defendant that opportunity for cross-examination and rebuttal of adverse sentencing-phase information.

Quicknotes

DUE PROCESS The constitutional mandate requiring the courts to protect and enforce individuals' rights and liberties consistent with prevailing principles of fairness and justice and prohibiting the federal and state governments from such activities that deprive its citizens of life, liberty, or property interest.

FOURTEENTH AMENDMENT DUE PROCESS CLAUSE Provides that protections mandated by the U.S. Constitution and observed by the federal government are equally applicable, and therefore must be observed by the States.

MURDER Unlawful killing of another person, either with deliberation and premeditation or by conduct demonstrating a reckless disregard for human life.

United States v. Deegan

Federal government (P) v. Convicted murderer (D)

605 F.3d 625 (8th Cir. 2010).

NATURE OF CASE: Appeal from lower court's decision to sentence defendant to ten years in prison.

FACT SUMMARY: Deegan (D), a Native American, gave birth to a baby boy and then intentionally abandoned the baby in her home for two weeks. Upon her return to the house, the baby was dead.

RULE OF LAW
Where a federal district court imposes a sentence within the applicable range of the advisory federal sentencing guidelines, appeals courts should accord the sentence with a presumption of reasonableness.

FACTS: Deegan (D), a Native American, gave birth to a baby boy in her home on the Fort Berth Indian Reservation. She then intentionally left the baby unattended in the home for two weeks. When she returned, the baby was dead. Deegan (D) attempted to discard the baby in a suitcase but it was later discovered. Because the incident occurred on an Indian Reservation, the federal Government (P) charged Deegan (D) in federal court with second-degree murder. Deegan (D) was found guilty and the lower court sentenced her to ten years in prison. The ten-year sentence was at the low end of the suggested range under the advisory federal sentencing guidelines. The lower court took into consideration Deegan's (D) long history of physical and sexual abuse at the hands of family members, including her father and the father of four of her children. The court also considered a report from a physician describing Deegan's (D) severe depression at the time of the incident. However, the court decided not to depart from the sentencing guidelines because of Deegan's (D) intentional steps to kill her newborn. Deegan (D) appealed, seeking a deviation from the sentencing guidelines based upon her history of physical and sexual abuse.

ISSUE: Where a federal district court imposes a sentence within the applicable range of the advisory federal sentencing guidelines, should appeals courts accord the sentence with a presumption of reasonableness?

HOLDING AND DECISION: (Collton, J.) Yes. Where a federal district court imposes a sentence within the applicable range of the advisory federal sentencing guidelines, appeals courts should accord the sentence with a presumption of reasonableness. The guidelines state that when a judge's sentence is within the suggested sentences for the typical type of case, the sentence is likely reasonable. Here, there were both aggravating and mitigating factors.

While the lower court duly recognized Deegan's (D) physical and sexual abuse, the lower court also recognized the need to impose a sentence that would reflect the seriousness of the crime. The dissent points to state cases that have applied three-year sentences. However, federal courts are not allowed, under the guidelines, to consider length of sentences in analogous state cases. Affirmed.

DISSENT: (Bright, J.) This is a clear sentencing error based upon Deegan's (D) life-long history of physical and sexual abuse at the hands of her father and the father of four of her children. Moreover, the killing of a child within 24 hours after its birth, known as neonaticide, is not the typical type of case federal courts deal with when deciding second-degree murder cases. This case is only in federal court because it occurred on an Indian Reservation. Analogous state sentences are only three years. Because of her history of abuse and because this case clearly is not a typical case, the lower court should have deviated from the guidelines and imposed a lesser sentence.

▶ ANALYSIS

While the federal sentencing guidelines are no longer mandatory, most courts use the suggested range when sentencing. The wrinkle here was that this incident would have been prosecuted in state court if it had not occurred on a federal Indian Reservation.

━■━■

Quicknotes

SECOND-DEGREE MURDER The unlawful killing of another person, without premeditation, and characterized by either an intent to kill or by a reckless disregard for human life.

━■━■

Common Latin Words and Phrases Encountered in the Law

A FORTIORI: Because one fact exists or has been proven, therefore a second fact that is related to the first fact must also exist.

A PRIORI: From the cause to the effect. A term of logic used to denote that when one generally accepted truth is shown to be a cause, another particular effect must necessarily follow.

AB INITIO: From the beginning; a condition which has existed throughout, as in a marriage which was void ab initio.

ACTUS REUS: The wrongful act; in criminal law, such action sufficient to trigger criminal liability.

AD VALOREM: According to value; an ad valorem tax is imposed upon an item located within the taxing jurisdiction calculated by the value of such item.

AMICUS CURIAE: Friend of the court. Its most common usage takes the form of an amicus curiae brief, filed by a person who is not a party to an action but is nonetheless allowed to offer an argument supporting his legal interests.

ARGUENDO: In arguing. A statement, possibly hypothetical, made for the purpose of argument, is one made arguendo.

BILL QUIA TIMET: A bill to quiet title (establish ownership) to real property.

BONA FIDE: True, honest, or genuine. May refer to a person's legal position based on good faith or lacking notice of fraud (such as a bona fide purchaser for value) or to the authenticity of a particular document (such as a bona fide last will and testament).

CAUSA MORTIS: With approaching death in mind. A gift causa mortis is a gift given by a party who feels certain that death is imminent.

CAVEAT EMPTOR: Let the buyer beware. This maxim is reflected in the rule of law that a buyer purchases at his own risk because it is his responsibility to examine, judge, test, and otherwise inspect what he is buying.

CERTIORARI: A writ of review. Petitions for review of a case by the United States Supreme Court are most often done by means of a writ of certiorari.

CONTRA: On the other hand. Opposite. Contrary to.

CORAM NOBIS: Before us; writs of error directed to the court that originally rendered the judgment.

CORAM VOBIS: Before you; writs of error directed by an appellate court to a lower court to correct a factual error.

CORPUS DELICTI: The body of the crime; the requisite elements of a crime amounting to objective proof that a crime has been committed.

CUM TESTAMENTO ANNEXO, ADMINISTRATOR (ADMINISTRATOR C.T.A.): With will annexed; an administrator c.t.a. settles an estate pursuant to a will in which he is not appointed.

DE BONIS NON, ADMINISTRATOR (ADMINISTRATOR D.B.N.): Of goods not administered; an administrator d.b.n. settles a partially settled estate.

DE FACTO: In fact; in reality; actually. Existing in fact but not officially approved or engendered.

DE JURE: By right; lawful. Describes a condition that is legitimate "as a matter of law," in contrast to the term "de facto," which connotes something existing in fact but not legally sanctioned or authorized. For example, de facto segregation refers to segregation brought about by housing patterns, etc., whereas de jure segregation refers to segregation created by law.

DE MINIMIS: Of minimal importance; insignificant; a trifle; not worth bothering about.

DE NOVO: Anew; a second time; afresh. A trial de novo is a new trial held at the appellate level as if the case originated there and the trial at a lower level had not taken place.

DICTA: Generally used as an abbreviated form of obiter dicta, a term describing those portions of a judicial opinion incidental or not necessary to resolution of the specific question before the court. Such nonessential statements and remarks are not considered to be binding precedent.

DUCES TECUM: Refers to a particular type of writ or subpoena requesting a party or organization to produce certain documents in their possession.

EN BANC: Full bench. Where a court sits with all justices present rather than the usual quorum.

EX PARTE: For one side or one party only. An ex parte proceeding is one undertaken for the benefit of only one party, without notice to, or an appearance by, an adverse party.

EX POST FACTO: After the fact. An ex post facto law is a law that retroactively changes the consequences of a prior act.

EX REL.: Abbreviated form of the term "ex relatione," meaning upon relation or information. When the state brings an action in which it has no interest against an individual at the instigation of one who has a private interest in the matter.

FORUM NON CONVENIENS: Inconvenient forum. Although a court may have jurisdiction over the case, the action should be tried in a more conveniently located court, one to which parties and witnesses may more easily travel, for example.

GUARDIAN AD LITEM: A guardian of an infant as to litigation, appointed to represent the infant and pursue his/her rights.

HABEAS CORPUS: You have the body. The modern writ of habeas corpus is a writ directing that a person (body) being detained (such as a prisoner) be brought before the court so that the legality of his detention can be judicially ascertained.

IN CAMERA: In private, in chambers. When a hearing is held before a judge in his chambers or when all spectators are excluded from the courtroom.

IN FORMA PAUPERIS: In the manner of a pauper. A party who proceeds in forma pauperis because of his poverty is one who is allowed to bring suit without liability for costs.

INFRA: Below, under. A word referring the reader to a later part of a book. (The opposite of supra.)

IN LOCO PARENTIS: In the place of a parent.

IN PARI DELICTO: Equally wrong; a court of equity will not grant requested relief to an applicant who is in pari delicto, or as much at fault in the transactions giving rise to the controversy as is the opponent of the applicant.

IN PARI MATERIA: On like subject matter or upon the same matter. Statutes relating to the same person or things are said to be in pari materia. It is a general rule of statutory construction that such statutes should be construed together, i.e., looked at as if they together constituted one law.

IN PERSONAM: Against the person. Jurisdiction over the person of an individual.

IN RE: In the matter of. Used to designate a proceeding involving an estate or other property.

IN REM: A term that signifies an action against the res, or thing. An action in rem is basically one that is taken directly against property, as distinguished from an action in personam, i.e., against the person.

INTER ALIA: Among other things. Used to show that the whole of a statement, pleading, list, statute, etc., has not been set forth in its entirety.

INTER PARTES: Between the parties. May refer to contracts, conveyances or other transactions having legal significance.

INTER VIVOS: Between the living. An inter vivos gift is a gift made by a living grantor, as distinguished from bequests contained in a will, which pass upon the death of the testator.

IPSO FACTO: By the mere fact itself.

JUS: Law or the entire body of law.

LEX LOCI: The law of the place; the notion that the rights of parties to a legal proceeding are governed by the law of the place where those rights arose.

MALUM IN SE: Evil or wrong in and of itself; inherently wrong. This term describes an act that is wrong by its very nature, as opposed to one which would not be wrong but for the fact that there is a specific legal prohibition against it (malum prohibitum).

MALUM PROHIBITUM: Wrong because prohibited, but not inherently evil. Used to describe something that is wrong because it is expressly forbidden by law but that is not in and of itself evil, e.g., speeding.

MANDAMUS: We command. A writ directing an official to take a certain action.

MENS REA: A guilty mind; a criminal intent. A term used to signify the mental state that accompanies a crime or other prohibited act. Some crimes require only a general mens rea (general intent to do the prohibited act), but others, like assault with intent to murder, require the existence of a specific mens rea.

MODUS OPERANDI: Method of operating; generally refers to the manner or style of a criminal in committing crimes, admissible in appropriate cases as evidence of the identity of a defendant.

NEXUS: A connection to.

NISI PRIUS: A court of first impression. A nisi prius court is one where issues of fact are tried before a judge or jury.

N.O.V. (NON OBSTANTE VEREDICTO): Notwithstanding the verdict. A judgment n.o.v. is a judgment given in favor of one party despite the fact that a verdict was returned in favor of the other party, the justification being that the verdict either had no reasonable support in fact or was contrary to law.

NUNC PRO TUNC: Now for then. This phrase refers to actions that may be taken and will then have full retroactive effect.

PENDENTE LITE: Pending the suit; pending litigation under way.

PER CAPITA: By head; beneficiaries of an estate, if they take in equal shares, take per capita.

PER CURIAM: By the court; signifies an opinion ostensibly written "by the whole court" and with no identified author.

PER SE: By itself, in itself; inherently.

PER STIRPES: By representation. Used primarily in the law of wills to describe the method of distribution where a person, generally because of death, is unable to take that which is left to him by the will of another, and therefore his heirs divide such property between them rather than take under the will individually.

PRIMA FACIE: On its face, at first sight. A prima facie case is one that is sufficient on its face, meaning that the evidence supporting it is adequate to establish the case until contradicted or overcome by other evidence.

PRO TANTO: For so much; as far as it goes. Often used in eminent domain cases when a property owner receives partial payment for his land without prejudice to his right to bring suit for the full amount he claims his land to be worth.

QUANTUM MERUIT: As much as he deserves. Refers to recovery based on the doctrine of unjust enrichment in those cases in which a party has rendered valuable services or furnished materials that were accepted and enjoyed by another under circumstances that would reasonably notify the recipient that the rendering party expected to be paid. In essence, the law implies a contract to pay the reasonable value of the services or materials furnished.

QUASI: Almost like; as if; nearly. This term is essentially used to signify that one subject or thing is almost analogous to another but that material differences between them do exist. For example, a quasi-criminal proceeding is one that is not strictly criminal but shares enough of the same characteristics to require some of the same safeguards (e.g., procedural due process must be followed in a parole hearing).

QUID PRO QUO: Something for something. In contract law, the consideration, something of value, passed between the parties to render the contract binding.

RES GESTAE: Things done; in evidence law, this principle justifies the admission of a statement that would otherwise be hearsay when it is made so closely to the event in question as to be said to be a part of it, or with such spontaneity as not to have the possibility of falsehood.

RES IPSA LOQUITUR: The thing speaks for itself. This doctrine gives rise to a rebuttable presumption of negligence when the instrumentality causing the injury was within the exclusive control of the defendant, and the injury was one that does not normally occur unless a person has been negligent.

RES JUDICATA: A matter adjudged. Doctrine which provides that once a court of competent jurisdiction has rendered a final judgment or decree on the merits, that judgment or decree is conclusive upon the parties to the case and prevents them from engaging in any other litigation on the points and issues determined therein.

RESPONDEAT SUPERIOR: Let the master reply. This doctrine holds the master liable for the wrongful acts of his servant (or the principal for his agent) in those cases in which the servant (or agent) was acting within the scope of his authority at the time of the injury.

STARE DECISIS: To stand by or adhere to that which has been decided. The common law doctrine of stare decisis attempts to give security and certainty to the law by following the policy that once a principle of law as applicable to a certain set of facts has been set forth in a decision, it forms a precedent which will subsequently be followed, even though a different decision might be made were it the first time the question had arisen. Of course, stare decisis is not an inviolable principle and is departed from in instances where there is good cause (e.g., considerations of public policy led the Supreme Court to disregard prior decisions sanctioning segregation).

SUPRA: Above. A word referring a reader to an earlier part of a book.

ULTRA VIRES: Beyond the power. This phrase is most commonly used to refer to actions taken by a corporation that are beyond the power or legal authority of the corporation.

Addendum of French Derivatives

IN PAIS: Not pursuant to legal proceedings.

CHATTEL: Tangible personal property.

CY PRES: Doctrine permitting courts to apply trust funds to purposes not expressed in the trust but necessary to carry out the settlor's intent.

PER AUTRE VIE: For another's life; during another's life. In property law, an estate may be granted that will terminate upon the death of someone other than the grantee.

PROFIT A PRENDRE: A license to remove minerals or other produce from land.

VOIR DIRE: Process of questioning jurors as to their predispositions about the case or parties to a proceeding in order to identify those jurors displaying bias or prejudice.

Casenote® Legal Briefs